CONTEMPORARY WRITING FROM THE CONTINENTS

CONTEMPORARY WRITING FROM THE CONTINENTS

OHIO UNIVERSITY PRESS

ATHENS, OHIO

LONDON

ANTHOLOGY EDITOR: DOUGLAS KNAPP

STAFF

Editor in Chief, Rainer Schulte
Associate Editors, Thomas J. Hoeksema, Roma A. King Jr.
Contributing Editor, Samuel Hazo
Copy Editor, Sandra Smith

This volume is a co-publication of Ohio University Press and
MUNDUS ARTIUM: A Journal of International Literature and the Arts.

Printed in the United States of America by
The University of Texas at Dallas.

ISBN 0-8214-0656-6
ISBN 0-8214-0657-4 pbk.

MUNDUS ARTIUM

A Journal of International Literature and the Arts

Volume XII and XIII, 1980 and 1981

CONTEMPORARY WRITING FROM THE CONTINENTS

A MUNDUS ARTIUM RETROSPECTIVE

INTRODUCTION

The writer's challenge is language, but language is also his curse. Through language he tries to build structures whose architecture reflects the dimension and intensity of his inner vision. He translates himself into language knowing quite well that total self-expression through words cannot be reached. In every expression and formulation lurks the recognition, permanently painful, that words approximate the shadow of the experience, not the experience itself. In his desire and frenzy for total self-expression, the writer struggles against words to mold them in the image of his creative intention. That involuntary flow of imaginative power nourishes confidence in the word as compromise, not as total artistic satisfaction.

The writer translates himself into the possibilities of his own language, rooted in the tradition of its literary, cultural and historical heritage. What becomes visible and defined within the boundaries of that language are the eruptions of the writer's imagination. Often imaginative outbursts demand that they be transmitted beyond the boundaries of a national language to stimulate diversity of perception and expression. In those cases, the writer speaks the language not only of his own linguistic geography but also of the entire human geography. Therefore, the inhabitants of the worlds that exist outside of one particular national language have the right to explore and experience these maps of human geography. The writer's self-expression translated into the words of his own language must now be translated into other languages, and the translator as an indispensable mediator comes into the picture.

To represent those living poets and writers who have continuously walked on the edge of the imagination to discover new vistas of human understanding has been the function of *Mundus Artium* during the last thirteen years. Writers from foreign countries, whether from the Eastern or Western hemisphere, were not selected because they had not been translated into English before, but because the power of their imagination required that they be translated into English to match and complement American poets and writers of similar stature.

No journal can or should exist without a clearly defined direction of taste. *Mundus Artium* is no exception. Writers were chosen because they interacted with the reality of their cultural and historical environments and elevated those realities to an aesthetic level of universal appeal and perception. Metaphorical transformation, conceptual paradox, incongruities, unexpected juxtapositions, rupture of the expected and unpredictable outbursts of the imagination inhale life into these works. Almost all of them are far removed from a photographic reproduction of reality where linear chronological considerations govern the writing process.

The reader who wants to get a feeling for the international literary activities of the 70s will find about 450 poets and writers in the back issues of *Mundus Artium*. Among them are well-established writers like Heinrich Böll, Vicente Aleixandre, Pablo Neruda, Richard Eberhart, and Denise Levertov, to name just a few. And then there are many poets and writers who had their first works published in the pages of *Mundus Artium*. The first issue of *Mundus Artium*, published in December of 1967, indicates its aesthetic orientation. Pablo Neruda, Gunter Grass, Giuseppe Ungaretti, Yves Bonnefoy, Ilse Aichinger, Homero Aridjis translated by such people as Ben Belitt, John Frederick Nims and Michael Hamburger were featured in this first issue.

Mundus Artium was not only the forum for established writers but also for young, unknown international writers who had their first manuscripts translated into English to be published in the journal. *Mundus Artium* also presented an incentive and orientation for prospective translators. Often, a translator would come in contact with a poet from another country through these initial translations in *Mundus Artium*. Experiencing a certain aesthetic affinity with the poet's work, the translator would then pursue the possibility of preparing an entire book collection of poems in translation for future publication. The well-known Spanish translator Donald Walsh first encountered the work of the Spanish poet Angel Gonzalez in the pages of *Mundus Artium*. He prepared an entire collection which was then published by Princeton University under the title of *Harsh World and Other Poems*. Many other book-length manuscripts of translations can be traced back to past issues of *Mundus Artium*.

What I saw to be the distinctive feature of *Mundus Artium* from its very beginning can be expressed by the phrase "avant-garde." This phrase has often been confused with being trendy and fashionable. However, I mean "avant-garde" with its original connotation: being at the forefront of imaginative and innovative literary developments. Writers who struck me as being solely interested in the gimmick or in the new just to be "novel" in their approach were never included in *Mundus Artium*. It became clear to me that in all ages, authentic writers and artists reflect the pulsating energy of their own present in the forms, colors and shapes of their works. That new forms have to come about is inevitable; and that new forms often are mistaken for empty gimmicks is also a known fact; but it is the substantive, imaginative backbone of a work that ultimately counts. Only history can speak the final word in this never-ending process of decision-making. Most of the writers presented in *Mundus Artium* caused a sense of inner conceptual excitement when they first came in to our editorial offices. These writers moved at the forefront of artistic innovation, out of a sense of inner necessity and conviction and not because they wanted to fit into the comfort of an already existing social structure that would give them immediate visibility and short-term satisfaction. These new, diverse voices needed to be heard not just within the confines of a national literature, but as a never-ending process of communication and artistic interaction from one country to another. The present anthology reflects the diversity of artistic voices that came to flourish during the 70s.

When I first started the journal, I knew that countries outside the United States, especially some European countries, had fostered journals and book publications through which contemporary American and English authors were made available through translation in these various countries. In the mid-sixties I could find no similar mechanism in the United States. American writers were beginning to influence the aesthetic orientation of European writers, and I felt that the exchange should not remain a one-way undertaking. I founded *Mundus Artium* to intensify the cross-fertilization between the United States and other countries.

During the 50s, the international orientation of literature had been promoted through the journal *Botteghe Oscure*, which, under the perceptive and refined editorship of Marguerite Caetani and centered in Rome, published many new and established writers from all over the world. These writers, however, were presented through the texts of their original languages rather than in translation. A French text could easily be followed by an English, German or Italian one. *Botteghe Oscure* had adopted a multilingual format; *Mundus Artium* became a bilingual journal in which all texts were transferred into English. Poetry was generally printed in bilingual format with the source language text on the left side and the corresponding translation on the right side. The bilingual format could not be maintained for languages that used a different alphabet.

To a certain extent, *Mundus Artium* pursued some of the same goals as *Botteghe Oscure*. When Wallace Fowlie reviewed *Mundus Artium* in the *New York Times Book Review* in 1973, he compared *Mundus Artium* to *Botteghe Oscure*, which was published from 1948 to 1960. He states: "*Mundus Artium* is making a notable contribution to the revival of literary translation in this country. . . . *Mundus Artium* provides a richness of poetry translation that is unequaled in the number of countries and tongues represented."

Mundus Artium was carried by a sense of discovery. The journal created ample space and place for the young, the innovative, the undiscovered and the ignored. These voices had to be presented in the best possible translation in English so that the power of their original source language works could be transmitted to the English-speaking reader. Thus, translation took on a very important role for *Mundus Artium*, especially because so many texts had been badly translated, resulting in an inadequate transplantation of the writer's aesthetic and artistic intent. An imaginative and innovative text written in another language needs a similarly energetic interpretive mind to produce a successful recreation of the original text into English. Therefore, most translators who submitted their translation manuscripts to *Mundus Artium* received very careful attention. Translations would be checked and reworked before they finally appeared in print. In all cases, we tried to match the intensity of translation with that of the original work.

The range of translators who have contributed to *Mundus Artium* is extensive. The list includes W.H. Auden, Kimon Friar, Ben Belitt, Gregory Rabassa, John Frederick Nims, W. S. Merwin, Margaret Sayers Peden, Paul Blackburn, H. E. Francis and many other prominent figures. In addition, from among the over 250 translators who have been published in *Mundus Artium*, a significant number of them have been younger writers and translators who published their first translations in *Mundus Artium*. Perhaps one of the major achievements of *Mundus Artium* can be seen in the reevaluation of the importance of the literary translator as a creative mediator between two languages. *Mundus Artium* has contributed greatly to giving the translator a crucial role within the literary and scholarly community. Perhaps the constant concern with translation generated through the activities of *Mundus Artium* led to the founding of the American Literary Translators Association, now in its third year of existence. Its official publication, the *Translation Review*, focuses entirely on profiling the translator's problems and achievements.

Mundus Artium also developed several specific features. This started in 1969, when a special selection of sixty pages was devoted to the poetry of Vicente Aleixandre. That selection remained the largest translation available in English when Aleixandre received the Nobel Prize in 1977. Aleixandre himself had arranged the sequence of these poems. In the following years, special issues were dedicated to Latin American Poetry, Latin American Fiction, Swedish poetry, Venezuelan poetry, Turkish writing, Central American writers, Serbo-Croatian writing, International Women Writers, African Writers, and Arabic literature. The Arabic issue (Volume X, Number 1), with its award-winning cover design, was a 200-page anthology of contemporary Arabic arts and letters that provided a first look at this fertile, but long-neglected area. In addition to the special selections and issues, *Mundus Artium* also presented several portraits of poets and writers who, because of their strong imaginative power, deserved a more extensive representation in the pages of the journal. In each case the selection of their works was preceded by an introduction to the aesthetic ramifications and intentions of their creations. The Spanish poet Angel Gonzalez, the German poet Karl Krolow and the American W. S. Merwin are among those who were presented in portrait form in past issues of the journal.

As the title of *Mundus Artium* (the World of the Arts) indicates, the journal was not supposed to be restricted to representing literary works. The subtitle "a journal of international literature and the arts" supports that intention. From the very first issue on, I tried to give space and a place to the young, unknown and undiscovered artists in the visual arts and music. The journal was obviously anchored in presenting as many international writers as possible through the art of translation next to American and English speaking authors. However, I thought that painters and sculptors alike were struggling with similar aesthetic problems and I wanted to see them featured next to the writers. Over 120 artists have been included in past issues of *Mundus Artium*.

To reproduce musical scores was beyond the printing possibilities of *Mundus Artium*. Therefore, new ideas and developments in the field of music had to be restricted to comments by composers and critics, among them Larry Austin, Morton Feldman. and Karlheinz Stockhausen. Perhaps one of the highlights in the visual arts was the series of photographs of the Marat/Sade production prepared by Max Waldman published in the second issue of *Mundus Artium*.

The interrelationship of literature and the other arts within the pages of *Mundus Artium* could be called eclectic. It never reached the level of intensity that I had originally planned for the journal. Many of the works reproduced in past issues should have been in color; color reproductions, however, were beyond our financial means. The color sequence in the Arabic issue presents a pleasant change in that editorial practice.

With respect to the future of *Mundus Artium*, certain changes will have to be made. Several journals of translation have begun publication during the last few years, and they can continue and expand some of the functions that were performed by *Mundus Artium* before.

What I sense is needed in the future could be described as closer interaction between literature and the other arts, both from a creative and a critical point of view. *Mundus Artium* could meet that need. The journal should become a meaningful forum where original works are featured next to imaginative essayistic writing. No journal of this kind currently exists in the English-speaking world. I believe that there is a great need for such a journal, especially since in the realm of scholarly writing, many scholars have removed themselves so far from the intention of an original text that they obscure rather than illuminate the reader's possible entrance into a verbal or non-verbal text. Thus, *Mundus Artium* could become a truly interdisciplinary journal in which critical and creative ideas begin a meaningful and stimulating dialogue. Today *Mundus Artium* is housed at The University of Texas at Dallas, where a new School of Arts and Humanities opened in 1975 to implement an interdisciplinary program in the Humanities. The future of *Mundus Artium* could find an anchor in the context of such a program and become its spokesman in order to revitalize interest in and study of the arts within the Humanities.

Rainer Schulte

CONTENTS

xi

xiii

Octavio Paz

tr. PAUL BLACKBURN

WIND FROM ALL COMPASS POINTS

The present is motionless
The mountains are of bone and of snow
They have been here since the beginning
The wind has just been born
                              Ageless
As the light and the dust
                              A windmill of sounds
The bazaar spins its colors
                    Bells   motors   radios
The stony trot of dark donkeys
Songs and complaints entangled
Among the beards of the merchants
The tall light chiseled with hammer-strokes
In the clearings of silence
                              Boys' cries
          Explode
Princes in tattered clothes
On the banks of the tortured river
Pray   pee   meditate
                    The present is motionless
The flood-gates of the year open
                              Day flashes out
          Agate
     The fallen bird
Between rue Montalambert and rue de Bac
Is a girl
          Held back
At the edge of a precipice of looks
If water is fire
               Flame
                    Dazzled
In the center of the spherical hour
          A sorrel filly

1

A marching battalion of sparks
                                        A real girl
Among wraithlike houses and people
Presence   a fountain of reality
I looked out through my own unrealities
I took her hand
                        Together we crossed
The four quadrants   the three times
Floating tribes of reflections
And we returned to the day of beginning
The present is motionless
                                        June 21st
Today is the beginning of summer
                                        Two or three birds
invent a garden
                        You read and eat a peach
On the red couch
                        Naked
Like the wine in the glass pitcher
                                A great flock of crows
Our brothers are dying in Santo Domingo
If we had the munitions
                        You people would not be here
                        We chew our nails down to the elbow
In the gardens of his summer fortress
Tipu Sultan planted the Jacobin tree
Then distributed glass shards among
The imprisoned English officials
And ordered them to cut off their foreskins
And eat them
                        The century
Has caught fire in our lands
                        With scorched hands
The cathedral and pyramid builders
Will raise their transparent houses
                        The present is motionless
The sun has fallen asleep between your breasts
The red covering is black and heaves

Not planet and not jewel
                              Fruit
You are named Date
                              Datia
Castle of Leave-If-You-Can
                              Scarlet stain
Upon the obdurate stone
Corridors
                    Terraces
                              Stairways
Dismantled nuptial chambers
Of the scorpion
                    Echoes   repetitions
The intricate and erotic guts of a watch
                                        Beyond time
                                        You cross
Taciturn patios under the pitiless afternoon
A cloak of needles on your untouched shoulders
If fire is water
                              You are a diaphanous drop
The real girl
                    Transparency of the world
The present is motionless
                                        The mountains
                              Quartered suns
                    Petrified storm earth-yellow
The wind whips
It hurts to see
The sky is another deeper abyss
                    Gorge of the Salang Pass
                    Black cloud over black rock
                    Fist of blood strikes
                                        Gates of stone
Only the water is human
In these precipitous solitudes
Only your eyes of human water
                                        Down there
In the cleft place
Desire covers you with both its black wings
Your eyes flash open and close
                              Phosphorescent animals
Down there

3

The hot canyon
The wave that lengthens and breaks
                        Your legs apart
The plunging whiteness
The foam of our bodies abandoned
                              The present is motionless
The hermit watered the saint's tomb
His beard was whiter than clouds
Facing the mulberry
                        On the flank of the rushing stream
You repeat my name
                        Dispersion of syllables
A kid with green eyes presented you
With a pomegranate
                  On the other bank of the Amu-Darya
Smoke rose from Russian cottages
The sound of an Usbek flute
Was another river, invisible, clearer
The boatman
                  On the barge was strangling chickens
The countryside is an open hand
                              Its lines
                  Marks of a broken alphabet
Cow skeletons on the prairie
Báctria
                  A smashed-up statue
I scraped a few names out of the dust
By these fallen syllables
Seeds of a charred pomegranate
I swear to be earth and wind
                              Whirling
Over your bones
                  The present is motionless
Night comes down with its trees
Night of electric insects and silken animals
Night of grasses that cover the dead
Confluence of waters which come from far off
Rustlings
                  Universes are strewn about
A world falls
                  A seed flares up
                  Each word beats, I

4

                  Hear you throb in the shadow
A riddle shaped like an hour-glass
                                  Woman asleep

Space   living spaces
Anima mundi
                  Maternal substance
Always torn from itself
Always falling into your empty womb
                                  Anima mundi
Mother of the nomadic tribes
                            Of suns and of men
The spaces turn
                                  The present is motionless

At the top of the world
Shiva and Parati caress
                  Each caress lasts a century
For the god and for the man
                            An identical time
An equivalent hurling headlong
                            Lahore
                                  Red river   black boats

A barefoot girl
                  Between two tamarinds
And her timeless gaze
                        An identical throb

Death and birth
A grove of poplars
Suspended between sky and earth
They are a quiver of light more than a tremble of leaves
                        Do they rise
                        Or fall?

The present is motionless
                            It rains on my childhood
It rains on the feverish garden
Flint flowers   trees of smoke
In a figleaf you sail on my brow
                        The rain does not touch you
You are a flame of water
                  The diaphanous drop of fire

                              5

Spilling upon my eyelids
I look out through my own unrealities
The same day is beginning

                                               Space wheels

The world wrenches up its roots
Our bodies
               Stretched out
                       Weigh no more than dawn

WHAT DOES POETRY MEAN?

OCTAVIO PAZ

tr. Elinor Randall

Poetry has been compared with mysticism and eroticism. The resemblances are incontestable, the differences no less so. The first and most decisive is meaning or, rather, object: that which the poet designates. The mystical experience—not excluding that of atheist sects such as Buddhism and primitive Jainism—implies the notion of a transcendental good. Essentially, poetic activity has for an object language. Whatever his beliefs and convictions, the poet specifies words more often than the objects they designate. I do not say that the poetic universe lacks significance or lives on the edge of meaning; I do say that in poetry the meaning is inseparable from the word— *is word*, while in ordinary discourse or the discourse of the mystic, meaning is that which words denote and which is beyond language. The poet's experience is above all a verbal one; or if you wish, all experience, in poetry, immediately acquires a verbal tonality. It is something common to every poet in every age, but since romanticism it has become what we call poetic *consciousness*, an attitude which tradition did not know. The ancient poets were no less sensitive to the value of words than are the moderns; on the other hand, they were indeed sensitive to their meaning. Góngora's hermeticism does not imply a criticism of meaning; that of Mallarmé or Joyce is, first and foremost, a criticism and at times a nullification of meaning.

7

Modern poetry is inseparable from the criticism of language which, in turn, is the most radical and virulent form of the criticism of reality. The place of the gods or of any other external entity or reality is now occupied by the word. The poem has no exterior object or reference; the reference of a word is another word. Thus, the problem of poetry's meaning becomes clear only when one observes that the meaning is not outside of the poem but within: not in what the words say, but in *what is said between them*.

You cannot read Góngora and Mallarmé, Donne and Rimbaud in the same way. Góngora's difficulties are external: grammatical, linguistic, mythological. Góngora is not obscure, he is complicated. His syntax is unusual, his historical and mythological allusions are veiled, the meaning of every phrase and even of every word is ambivalent. Once these asperities and sinuosities have been overcome, the meaning is clear. The same thing happens with Donne, a poet no less difficult than Góngora and more compact. Donne's difficulties are linguistic, and at the same time intellectual and theological. Once in possession of the key, the poem opens like a tabernacle. It is not a chance comparison; Donne's best poems contain a carnal, intellectual and religious paradox. In both of these poets the references are found outside of the poem—in nature, society, art, mythology or theology. The poet is talking about something outside of the poem—the eye of Polyphemus, the whiteness of Galatea, the horror of death, the presence of a girl. Rimbaud's attitude, in his central texts, is radically different. On the one hand his work is a criticism of the reality and the "values" which sustain or justify it: Christianity, morals, beauty. On the other it is an attempt to establish a new reality: a new fraternity, a new eroticism, a new man. All this will be the poetry's work—"the alchemy of the word." Mallarmé is no less rigorous but more so. His work, if one can apply the term "work" to a few signs on a few pages—vestiges of a voyage or an unparalleled shipwreck—is more than a criticism and more than a negation of reality: the reverse of being. The word is the reverse of reality: not nothingness but idea, the pure sign which no longer designates and which is neither being nor non-being. The "spiritual theater"—the Work or Word—is not only the duplicate of the universe, it is true reality. In both Rimbaud and Mallarmé the language is interiorized, ceases to designate, and is neither a symbol nor a question of the external realities, whether physical or supersensible objects. For Góngora a table is a "pine square" and for Donne the Christian Trinity is "bones to philosophy but milk to faith." The modern poet does not speak to the world but to the Word on which the world rests:

8

Elle est retrouvée!
Quoi? L'eternité.
C'est la mer allée
Avec le soleil.

The difficulty with modern poetry does not come from its complexity—Rimbaud is much simpler than either Góngora or Donne—
but it demands, as does mysticism and love, a total surrender (and a
no less total vigilance). If the word were not equivocal, I would say
that the difficulty is not intellectual but moral. It is a matter of an
experience implying a negation—even if provisional, as in philosophical
meditation—of the exterior world. To summarize, modern poetry is
an attempt to abolish all meanings, because modern poetry foresees
itself as the final meaning of life and of man. It is therefore at
once the destruction and creation of language. The destruction of words
and of meanings, the kingdom of silence; but it is equally "the word in
search of the Word." There is probably no lack of those who shrug their
shoulders at this "madness." Nevertheless, for more than a century
a few solitary souls, among the greatest and richest talents ever seen
by the eyes of man, have not hesitated in devoting their lives to this
mad undertaking.

FORM AND MEANING

The true ideas of a poem are not those occurring to the poet *before*
writing the poem; they are those that, voluntarily or not, are deduced
naturally from the work *later on*. Essence springs from form, not the
opposite. Or rather: each form secretes its own idea, its vision of the
world. Form expresses; and furthermore, in art only the forms have
meaning. Meaning is not what the poet wants to say but what the
poem actually does say. What we think we are saying is one thing;
what we are really saying is another.

João Cabral de Melo Neto

tr. ELOAH F. GIACOMELLI

THE SEASONS

A soft rain
fell on the towel;
it wet the clothes,
it filled the glasses;
it chilled the hearts
entwined on the trees
(against the cold that divides
like names).
The world full of rivers,
lakes, retreats
for our use.

In a deep sky
machines of clouds,
elephants of clouds
singing drift by.
Beneath the inert hands
the furniture perspires.
The domestic environment
wants to open the windows
to the dry leaves,
to dreams, to ghosts
dead-thirsty.

Men can
dream their gardens
of ghost matter.
Earth doesn't dream,
it blossoms: in the matter
sweet to the body: the flower,
a dream outside sleep
and outside night, like
the gestures in which you blossom
too (your irregular laughter,
the sun on your skin).

In the fruit on the table
I search for a verse
that will reveal autumn;
I search for the air
of the season; I imagine
an ash; I experiment
with tricks, with words
(facing the ripe fruit
on the brink of death,
motionless in the time
that it dreams of stopping).

João Cabral de Melo Neto

NOCTURNE

The sea blew bells
the bells were drying the flowers
the flowers were the heads of saints.

My memory full of words
my thoughts searching for ghosts
my nightmares late many nights.

At dawn my disengaged thoughts
sped like telegrams
and in the windows lit up all night
the portrait of the dead woman
made desperate efforts to escape.

W. S. MERWIN: A PORTRAIT

INTRODUCTION AND POEMS

Merwin stands in a long line of modern international poets. He belongs to a tradition that was started with the French poet Baudelaire over a hundred years ago. When Baudelaire wrote at the end of his long poem "The Voyage," "to plunge into the unknown to find something new," he is very close to Merwin's words "An hour comes/ to close a door behind me/ the whole of night opens before me." It is not the obvious that Merwin searches for in his poetry, not the object that can be reproduced with a photographic camera lens, not the landscape that is fixed in time and space. His mind opens up at the moment between light and darkness beyond the realm of logical comprehensibility, to portray an inscape that lives on silence and paradox.

Merwin achieves Rilke's lucidity, Stevens' philosophical perspective and Paz' rhythmic and conceptual intensity. His poems begin on the page and end on the page without having a definite point of beginning or a definite point of arrival. He needs no punctuation in the flow of the mind that detects the life-generating power behind each object: the eternal paradox born in moments of silence.

Merwin does not want to punctuate his poems; even though he breaks words into lines and lines into poems on the page, each poem carries beyond itself into the next. Once the reader has been taken into the flow of one poem, he resents his arrival at the last line; he wants more, and there is the first line of the next poem that began long before it started on the page. Merwin's poems never stop, they create energy for both the reader and the poet himself, an energy that finds release and form in the next poem. Today Merwin is only in his mid-forties, and yet it seems that his creative energy increases daily, judging by the rapid publication of several books of poems during the last few years.

No poet can start from a vacuum. He has to orient himself within the tradition he inherited from the past. Fortunately, Merwin has been exposed not only to the American literary tradition, but to the contemporary international literary scene. He has translated a book of poems by the French poet Jean Follain, he has transposed poems by Pablo Neruda, Nicanor Parra, Guillaume Apollinaire, García Lorca, Gottfried Benn and others. That he translates is not amazing: many other poets have done translations. But it is revealing which poets he has chosen to translate. Almost all of them share with his own poetry a conceptual intensity that reaches far beyond the instability of poetic fashion and makes them, in the true sense of the word, international in scope and meaning.

There is a vast silence in Merwin's poetry, and words lie only on the topmost surface. Voices from below beckon their submergence and the poet's ear is bent toward these voices. Still, this silence cannot remain silent; it has to find expression and form through words and the new meaning they create in the unique juxtaposition the poet has invented for them. Each time the poet touches a word, he must rely not on its fixed meaning but on the threads of its magnetic field that make new meaning possible. It must be a language comfortable in the realm of paradox, removed from the restricting barriers of visual representation and reproduction. Merwin speaks of "eyeless rocks," "unchopping a tree," "a cross is a door of the dead," "the blind voices are bleeding," and "April sinks through the sand of names." These are moments when his mind has captured fragments of silence, when the silence of his voices speaks in an attempt to populate the silence with the meaning of words. And then there are those moments when he desperately and nervously pushes us deeper and deeper into the zone of silent intensity: "dream after dream after dream walking away through it/ Invisible invisible invisible." Like isolated notes, simple and insistent, the words fall on the reader's mind, force him into the rhythm of his inner landscape where his words create new colors on the horizon. Once the rhythmic ritual has happened, he must fill the distances of the mind both in time and space. Natural to his vision, time and space lose their linear existence and become multiple in their simultaneous existence.

13

Merwin's inner landscape recreates the distant coldness of Benjamin Britten's *War Requiem*, isolated screams that change pitch but not key. They are always in a minor key, harsh in their tone and yet pleading in their movement toward an unknown distance ahead of the poet's eye, impenetrable kneeling at the gate of darkness: "the cold slope is standing in darkness," "before dark I would stop by the stream falling through black ice," "when the forests have been destroyed their darkness remains." The poet pushes forward into the darkness, where the roads are unlighted and words fall like feeble lights on the path that comes from nowhere and leads nowhere. But there is always a distance that must be conquered, the distance extending into space which is also the distance from the poet's mind to himself, from one man to another: "and once more celebrate our distance from men." And it is also the distance into silence, the silence between two notes that explodes with paradox and energy, the only certainty the poet has left in his life: "and the silence will set out/ tireless traveller/ like the beam of a lightless star." The poet yields to his dilemma. He must think on a level that excludes the possibility for beginning and end, and views his existence almost in Rilkean terms when he speaks about "Divinities": "There is no freedom such as theirs/ that have no beginning."

Then, after all, Merwin is not concerned with the beginning or the end, but with the inner time before it becomes either one: the life force, the intensity of the moment whose future is unpredictable and yet always there as the challenge to the present. "We are the echo of the future/on the door it says what to do to survive/ but we were not born to survive/ only to live." His poetry represents the fierce attempt at recreating or perhaps even at inventing the moment in the present that makes us not aware of what was there before and what might come thereafter, but involves us in the life of the present. To populate the inner distance with the energy of life through the invention of words is the poet's commitment and goal. The distance never ceases to exist since it always goes beyond itself into some other distance. "Beyond" is the key word that embraces Merwin's poetic vision. The paradox of words carries us beyond the meaning of words, the paradox invents new meaning between the words, and it is this sense of the paradox put into a rhythm of words that always flows without punctuation from one poem to the next. The struggle and the illumination of the inner distance celebrated through the color of words generate Merwin's poetic energy and make his poems universal, not just as an American poet but as an international poet. When he speaks, he speaks with the intensity of a blind man who sees deeper into himself, since light does not disturb his eyes.

14

W. S. Merwin

THE ARRIVAL

From many boats
ferries and borrowed canoes
white steamers and resurrected hulls
in which we were young together
to a shore older than waiting
and our feet bare on the wet shadowed sand
early in the evening of every verb
both of us at the foot of the mountain laughing

now will you lead me with the smell of almonds
up over the leafless mountain
in the blood red evening
now we pull up the keel through the rushes
on the beach
my feet miss the broken bottle
half buried in the sand
you did not notice it at last

now will you lead with your small hand
your child up the leafless mountain
past the green wooden doors thrown away
and abandoned shelters
into the meadows of loose horses
that I will ride in the dark to come

W. S. Merwin

THE TREE OF THE HEIRS

The tree of the heirs rises into a cloud
from which a few leaves fall
turning white

the whole sky is hiding in the cloud

slender elephant gray trunk
disappearing
all of its branches out of sight

the leaves lie where they fall
like white flames
you can see through

near the ground the huge roots spread out in folds
like the bones of a foot of a mountain
the gray wrinkled bark of the instep is worn and scuffed
the cloud is rustling
echoing
leaves rest on the wounds of the bark
like light reflected on water

there each of the heirs
comes and waits
for the other

each thinks that the other was coming
and wonders why the other
wanted to come here
can't understand agreeing
to come to the tree
thinks back to age after age of his life
and now sees the tree there
where it belonged
but forgets what anyone looked like
and the sounds of the birds
and goes on waiting alone
in the cool tender air
after the stroke of a bell in the autumn

W. S. Merwin

THE NEXT MOON

A month to the hour
since the last ear on earth
heard your voice

even then on the phone

I know the words about rest
and how you would say them
as though I myself had heard them
not long ago
but for a month I have heard nothing

and in the evening after the moon of deafness
I set foot in the proud waters
of iron and misfortune
it is a month to the hour
since you died
and it was only dusk
to the east in the garden

now it is a night street with another moon
seen for the first time but no longer new
and faces from the backs of mirrors

W. S. Merwin

THE SNOW

You with no fear of dying
how you dreaded winter
the cataract forming on the green wheated hill
ice on sundial and steps and calendar
it is snowing
after you were unborn it was my turn
to carry you in a world before me
trying to imagine you
I am your parent at the beginning of winter
you are my child
we are one body
one blood
one red line melting the snow
unbroken line in falling snow

W. S. Merwin

MIGRATION

Prayers of many summers come
to roost on a moment
until it sinks under them
and they resume their journey
flying by night
with the sound
of blood rushing in an ear

W. S. Merwin

WALLS

The mountains are there in every direction. Already we are high. They are higher in every direction. Sometimes the sun goes down behind one, sometimes behind another, depending on us. The mountains rise too steeply to .climb, in most places. As far as the mountains, in every direction, there are little courtyards, and tiled roofs, with trees rising out of some of the courtyards. Dogs bark. Balls fly into the air and drop. Voices of children flutter across the roofs. Roosters who never see each other, answer each other. Immortal storms break around the mountains. There are caves in the rocks. The clouds come down into the gardens at night. For hours at a time the streets are removed. They are folded up and the houses heal together over them. Then if you lay your ear to the heavy walls you may hear a heartbeat.

Meanwhile the streets are put away in the caves in the mountains. They lie there in the dark telling everything they know, without a word, and it is washed away, and they are returned, wet, and ready to go on watching. They are returned, a little washed away, otherwise the same, and to many the difference is not apparent. In the underground streams everything becomes transparent in the darkness. The only sound is that of running water, and only the streets can hear it. When the streets are returned, the houses stop breathing, which they can do for long periods at a time, without it being noticed.

The children who are born when the streets are away remember their own silences. Formerly, in order to rule in the country, a child of the blood royal had to be born at such a time, and so the royal midwife was accompanied by an assistant who remained with an ear to the wall throughout the entire delivery, praying for the streets not to return, not one, not even for a moment. Nowadays this is no longer considered important.

The caves do not listen to the streets, they merely wash away the stories. They know that the streets will not come to them forever to hear the sound of water, and that afterwards the houses will not heal, and both the streets and the walls will die their next death, which is of the body. Then the water, silent at last, will wear away nothing but faces long since transparent, leaving nothing but the eyes.

19

W. S. Merwin

THE DRIVE HOME

I was always afraid
of the time when I would arrive home
and be met by a special car
but this wasn't like that
they were so nice the young couple
and I was relieved not to be driving
so I could see the autumn leaves on the farms

I sat in the front to see better
they sat in the back
having a good time
and they laughed with their collars up
they said we could take turns driving
but when I looked
none of us was driving

then we all laughed
we wondered if anyone would notice
we talked of getting an inflatable
driver
to drive us for nothing through the autumn leaves

Cintio Vitier

tr. ENA HOLLIS

THE WORD

Then the words flowed
with the magic of things, or were spilt
in a dark jet like blood,
or like those hungry bonfires that bit
the hands that tried to trap them,
or crossed like birds or deer
in bright sunlight, between woods.

Now, when a word comes
—alone, enormous, unique, lost,
a messenger that has managed to cross
vast and naked distances—
it's important to receive it splendidly,
opening the doors, lighting the lamps,
waiting in silence until
unable to lie to us it has slept
and again merges with the things.

Cintio Vitier

EACH TIME I RETURN TO YOU

Each time I return to you,
quiet corner, poetry,
I think you ought to be a meadow
where the pastures are like animals.
There you recognize yourself spaciously
in the fierce solitude stretching to the beach
echoing against the grim cliffs,
and even beyond,
the mountain trembling like a star

where I ought to have died a thousand years ago
defending some indescribable cause.

But that's not you,
nor the corner where I was dreaming;
you are only the living street where I stand,
my body ageing with the throw of the dice,
this poor minute that'll never return,
streaked with anxiety and work.
And indeed, poetry, that other face,
the deepest mystery a man can know,
triviality and custom,
plain weariness of the bones
and of the world.

Translator: Sargon Boulus

Sameeh al-Qasim

FEAST

With blood in my eyes
and snakes in my suitcase
I wander through ruins
I prepare a full table
under the vaulted sky
Through the mail of massacre
I write invitations
with the bones of the dead
and sign them with scorpions
I invite to my feast
inhabitants of
a thousand graveyards!

Roberto Juarroz

tr. SERGIO MONDRAGÓN AND RAINER SCHULTE

One day I will find a word
to pierce your stomach with pregnancy,
to grow in your womb
like a hand, both open and closed.

I will find a word
to hold and turn your body
to embrace your body
to open your eyes like a god without clouds
to eat your saliva
to bend your knees.
Perhaps you will not hear it
or even understand it.
It will not be necessary.
It will roll through your insides like a wheel,
at last, from head to foot
woman mine and not mine,
and it will not stop even when you die.

Roberto Juarroz

Man,
the puppet of the night,
stabs the void with a dagger.

But one day,
the void returns the savage blow.

Then, only one thing remains:
a dagger in the void.

Roberto Juarroz

Death no longer faces mirrors.
He fears to destroy or shatter them.
And he is even more afraid
of destroying or shattering himself.

But
the mirror is still reflected by death,
as if he were simply
a mirror of mirrors,
one mirror faced by another,
with nothing in between.

Roberto Juarroz

I think that in this moment
perhaps no one in the universe thinks about me,
that only I think of myself,
and if I died now,
nobody, not even I, would think about me.

And here rises the abyss,
as when I fall asleep.
I am my own support and I remove it.
I help to wallpaper everything with absence.

Perhaps for that reason
to think about a person
means to save him.

Alejandra Pizarnik

tr. GEORGE McWHIRTER

A CONDITION (OF BEING)

You keep watch from this room
Where the awful shadow is your own.

There is no silence here
Only phrases you avoid hearing.

Signs on the walls
Narrate the beauty of distance.

(Be sure I don't die
Without seeing you again.)

Alejandra Pizarnik

VERTIGO OR THE CONTEMPLATION
OF SOMETHING THAT ENDS

This lilac sheds its blossoms.
From itself, it falls
And hides its old shadow.
I have to die of things
Like that.

Alejandra Pizarnik

CONTEMPLATION

The terrifying forms died, and no longer was there an inside or
an out. No one was listening to the place because the place didn't exist.
Only to listen, they're listening to the place. Night flashes inside
your mask. With fierce caws they pierce you. They hammer you with
jet black birds. Enemy colours merge in the tragedy.

Alejandra Pizarnik

A DREAM WHERE SILENCE IS MADE OF GOLD

The dog of winter bares its teeth in my smile. It happened on the bridge. I was nude and wearing a hat with flowers on it and I was dragging my corpse which was also nude and wearing a hat of dry leaves.

I have had many loves, I said, but the most beautiful was my love for mirrors.

Alejandra Pizarnik

For Octavio Paz

RESCUE

Always it's the lilac garden on the other side of the river. And if the soul asks if it remains far off, the reply will be: on the other side of the river, not this one, but that one.

Alejandra Pizarnik

AS WATER OVER A STONE

for whoever returns in search of his ancient search
the night shuts over him as water over a stone
as air over a bird
as two bodies close making love.

tr. Samuel Hazo

Adonis (Ali Ahmed Said)

THE PAST

Each day is a child
who dies behind a wall,
turning its face to the wall's
corners.
        Houses flee
before its ghost that rises
from the grave demanding
vengeance.
        Not from eternity
but from a bitter land
it comes, fleeing as if from bullets
through the town, the public
squares, the houses of the poor.

From the desert it comes,
and on its face is the hunger
of pigeons and parching flowers.

THE SLEEP OF HANDS

Today I offer my palms
to dead lands and muted
streets before death seams
my eyelids, sews me
in the skin of all the earth
and sleeps forever in my hands.

Adonis (*Ali Ahmed Said*)

ELEGY IN EXILE

Phoenix,
when the flames enfolded you,
what pen were you holding?
What feathers sprouted
when your old ones burned?
Buried in your own ashes,
what world did you confront,
what robe did you don,
what color did you choose?

Tell me.
Tell me what silence follows
the final silence
spun from the very fall of the sun?
What is it, phoenix?
Give me a word,
a sign.

Your banishment and mine
are one.
Your banishment and mine
and the banishment of heroes
are one.
Your banishment and mine
and the banishment of heroes
and the banishment of love and glory
are one.

What is it we love or fear
but shadows of ourselves?
When I recall your suffering,
my phoenix,
I forget my own.
No mother held you
when you left
until you burned for breath.
No father blessed your exile

in his heart
before you saw it born
in flame with each horizon.
I've left.
I've left my mother.
I've left my mother
on a mat of straw
to grieve my going.
Astray, I swallow dust.
I, who learned love
from my father's eyes,
have left my father's house
to be the prodigal.

I am a hunted bird.
I steal my bread.
All I see is desolation.
Pursued by falcons,
my small wings lose their feathers,
feather by feather.

"They say my song is strange
because it has no echo.
They say my song is strange
because I never dreamed
myself awake on silks.
They say I disbelieved the prophesies,
and it was true,
and it is still and always true."

My phoenix,
I learn with you
the banishment that murders me
in ruins and the sheerest voids.
I break from jail
to seek the man I keep becoming.
I leave the gate ajar,
the chain empty,
and the darkness of my cell
devours me like eyes in shadow.

Though banished,
I love all those who banished me,
who crowned my brow with chains

and waited to betray me.
I see my childhood
like an isolated Baalbek
with its longing pillars,
and I burn.
Horizon by horizon,
I am born to the chants of the sun.

My new wings grow
like yours, my phoenix.
Phoenix, we are born for death,
and death in life
deserves its springs and harvests,
its rivering Jesus,
its passion with the vineyard
and the mount.
But it is not all solitude
and echoes from the grave.

Phoenix, I remember one
who perished on a cross—
extinguished.
He burned in pools of cherry
like fire within fire—
extinguished.
Yet from the dark of the ashes
he glows.

His wings are numbered
with the flowers of our land,
with all the days of all the years,
with pebbles and the merest stones.

Like you, my phoenix,
he survived our hunger,
and his mercy feeds us.

Dying with his wings outspread,
he gathered all who buried
him in ashes
and became, like you,
the spring and fire of our agony.

Go now, my sweet bird,
show me the road I'll follow.

A DREAM FOR ANY MAN

I live in the face of a woman
who lives in a wave—
a surging wave
that finds a shore
lost like a harbor under shells.

I live in the face of a woman
who loses me
so she can be
the lighthouse waiting
in my mad and navigating blood.

Translator: Sargon Boulus

Sa'di Yusif

A STONE

it was rock
            i spoke to
a forsaken stone between
my house and the door
of familiar sky
a stone untouched by hands
a stone between the dew
and the familiar suns

for the prophet at play
    a stone
or the boy who gets tired
for the star growing dim
    a stone
and the fugitive in hiding
    a stone
for the country that hated me
    a stone

you who are assuaged
with dew and familiar suns
will the familiar sky remain
as you have found it?
a blue stone?
a blue-lipped stone?
a lip of stone?

31

Peter Huchel

NOVEMBER

tr. HENRY BEISSEL

November
Sleeps in the desolation
Of grubbed ground,
Boggy light and
Decay of reedy waters
Where the sickle flashes no more.

No sky rips open
Above the prisoners
On the river Chebar.

Small grey
Donkeys carry
The fog into town.
The stone-pines
Are sewing darkness.

Peter Huchel

VERONA

tr. HENRY BEISSEL

Between us fell the rain of forgetting.
In the well twilight wears away coins.
A cat on the wall,
She turns her head into the silence,
Recognizes us no longer.
The faint light of love
Falls on the stars of her pupils.

Clockwork clatters in the tower
And strikes the hour too late.
The earth gives us no time
Beyond death.
Sewn into the web of night
Voices sink away
Undiscoverably.

Two pigeons fly from the window ledge.
The bridge guards our vows.
This stone
In the water of the Etsch
Lives big in his stillness.
And at the hub of things
Grief.

tr. SAM GROLMES
AND YUMIKO TSUMURA

Ruichi Tamura

THE WITHERED LEAVES

and
they died   without shedding
green blood

before they return to the soil
they change to the color of soil
the color of silence that died
one death

why does everything
seem transparent   even though
we are endlessly walking
the border of night and day
in withered leaves

a man
whose star is fixed
does not look back

A DISTANT LAND

My distress is
a simple thing

            No special means are needed
            to raise an animal from a distant land

My poetry is
a simple thing

　　　　No special tears are needed
　　　　to read a letter from a distant land

My joy and sorrow are
very simple things

　　　　No special words are needed
　　　　to kill a man from a distant land

OCTOBER POEM

Crisis is my nature
There is a hurricane of feelings
under my smooth skin　　There is
a fresh corpse thrown up
on the desolate shore of October

　　　　October is my Empire　　My
　　　　hands manipulate things to be lost
　　　　eyes look at things to disappear
　　　　ears listen to the silence of things to die

Fear is my nature
The Time that murders every
thing flows in my rich blood　　There is
a new hunger trembling in
the cold sky of October

　　　　October is my Empire　　My
　　　　dead armies occupy all cities where rain falls
　　　　dead patrol planes circle over muddled souls
　　　　dead men sign their names for the dead

tr. Edith Shiffert
and Yuki Sawa

Ruichi Tamura

FOUR THOUSAND DAYS AND NIGHTS

In order for a single poem to come into existence,
you and I have to kill,
have to kill many things,
many loveable things, kill by shooting, kill by assassination,
    kill by poisoning.

Look!
Out of the sky of four thousand days and nights,
just because we wanted the trembling tongue of one small bird,
four thousand nights of silence and four thousand days of counterlight
you and I killed by shooting.

Listen!
Out of all the cities of falling rain, smelting furnaces,
midsummer harbors, and coal mines,
just because we needed the tears of a single hungry child
four thousand days of love and four thousand nights of compassion
you and I killed by assassination.

Remember!
Just because we wanted the fear of one vagrant dog,
who could see the things you and I couldn't see with our eyes
and could hear the things you and I couldn't hear with our ears,
four thousand nights of imagination and four thousand days of
    chilling recollection
you and I killed by poison.

In order for a single poem to come
you and I have to kill the beloved things.
This is the only way to bring back the dead to life.
You and I have to follow that way.

Lucebert

tr. LARRY TEN HARMSEL

HARVEST

night. the summer dies in the night
feathers shrivel in convulsion
strangle hills and clouds
lips in the villages whisper and clank

golden eyes have never gone that far
sleepers crouch in glittering woods
and silver nets bury the autumn sea

the soft games of rain
bring fruits of longing down
hands open the cross
a knife is kissed
and thirst drinks autumn flames

DOUBLE METAMORPHOSIS

because the world's flame expires
into barren clouds of worm-clotted blood
because the world's water steams
into lethean mirrors into garbage-loaded nets
I become a bird rising above the thirst of the stars

because a hand the hand of the beloved buried
in the earth of wretched sighs and biting tears
because an eye the eye of the beloved killed
with a shadow shy and cunning behind burnished doors
I become a star rising above the thirst of the birds

THE DUEL

JORGE LUIS BORGES

tr. NORMAN THOMAS DI GIOVANNI

Henry James—whose world was first revealed to me by one of my two characters, Clara Figueroa—would perhaps have been interested in this story. He might have devoted to it a hundred or so pages of tender irony, enriched by complex and painstakingly ambiguous dialogues. The addition at the end of some melodramatic touch would not have been at all unlikely, nor would the essence of the tale have been changed by a different setting—London or Boston. The actual events took place in Buenos Aires, and there I shall leave them, limiting myself to a bare summary of the affair, since its slow evolution and sophisticated background are quite alien to my particular literary habits. To set down this story is for me a modest and peripheral adventure. I should warn my reader ahead of time that its episodes are of less importance than its characters and the relationship between them.

Clara Glencairn de Figueroa was stately and tall and had fiery red hair. Less intellectual than understanding, she was not witty, though she did appreciate the wit of others—even of other women. Her mind was full of hospitality. Distinctions pleased her; perhaps that's why she traveled so much. She realized that her world was an all too arbitrary combination of rites and ceremonies, but these things amused her and she carried them out with dignity. Her family married

38

her off very young to a distinguished lawyer, Isidro Figueroa, who was to become the Argentine ambassador to Canada and who ended by resigning that post, stating that in a time of telephones and telegraph, embassies were anachronisms and amounted to a needless public burden. This decision earned him the disapproval of all his colleagues; Clara liked the Ottawa climate—after all, she was of Scottish ancestry —and the duties of an ambassador's wife did not displease her, but she never once dreamed of protesting. Figueroa died soon after. Clara, following several years of indecision and self-searching, took up the exercise of painting—stimulated, perhaps, by the example of her friend Marta Pizarro.

It is characteristic of Marta Pizarro that when speaking about her people referred to her as the sister of the brilliant Nélida Sara, who was married and divorced.

Before choosing palette and brush, Marta Pizarro had considered the alternative of writing. She could be quite clever in French, the language in which she had done most of her reading, while Spanish was to her—like Guaraní to ladies in the Province of Corrientes— little more than a household utensil. The literary supplements had placed within her reach pages of Lugones and of the Spaniard Ortega y Gasset; the style of these masters confirmed her suspicion that the language to which she had been born was less fit for expressing the mind or the passions than for verbal showing off. Of music, all she knew was what any person who attends a concert should know. Coming from the western province of San Luis, she began her career with faithful portraits of Juan Crisóstomo Lafinur and of Colonel Pascual Pringles, which were—as was to be expected—acquired by the Provincial Museum. From portraits of local worthies, she passed on to pictures of old houses in Buenos Aires, whose quiet patios she painted with quiet colors and not that stage-set showiness with which they are frequently endowed by others. Someone—surely not Clara Figueroa —remarked that her whole art drew its inspiration from the work of anonymous nineteenth-century Italian bricklayers. Between Clara Glencairn and Nélida Sara (who, according to gossip, had once had a fancy for Dr. Figueroa) there had always been a certain rivalry; perhaps the duel was between them and Marta was merely a tool.

As is well known, most things originate in other countries and only in time find their way into the Argentine. That now so unjustly forgotten school of painters who call themselves concrete or abstract, as if to show their utter scorn for logic and language, is but one of many examples. It was argued, as I recall, that just as music is expected to create its own world of sound, its sister art, painting, should be allowed to attempt a world of color and form without reference to any actual physical objects. The Dallas art critic Lee Kaplan wrote that their pictures, which outraged the bourgeoisie, followed the Biblical proscription, also shared by the Islamic world, that man shall make no images of living things. The iconoclasts, he argued, were going back to the true tradition of painting, which had been led astray by such heretics as Dürer and Rembrandt. Kaplan's enemies accused him of being influenced merely by broadloom rugs, kaleidoscopes, and men's neckwear.

All aesthetic revolutions put forth a temptation toward the irresponsible and the far too easy; Clara Glencairn chose to be an abstract painter. Having always been an admirer of Turner, she set as her goal the enrichment of abstract art with the diffused splendor of the Master. She worked under no pressure, painted over or destroyed a number of canvases, and in the winter of 1954 exhibited a series of temperas in a gallery on Suipacha Street whose specialty was paintings which a military metaphor then in vogue called the vanguard. Something paradoxical happened: on the whole, the reviews were favorable, but the sect's official organ condemned her anomalous forms, which, although they were not representational, suggested the tumult of a sunset, of a tangled forest, or of the sea, and did not limit themselves to dots and stripes. Perhaps the first person to smile was Clara Glencairn. She had tried her best to be modern and the moderns had rejected her. The act of painting, however, mattered more to her than its public success, and she went on working. Indifferent to this episode, art also went on.

The secret duel had already begun. Marta was not an artist alone; she was, as well, deeply committed to what may not unfairly be called the administrative side of art, and was assistant secretary of the organization known as the Giotto Circle. Sometime toward the middle of 1955, Marta managed to have Clara, who had already been accepted into the Circle, figure as a committee member among the Circle's new officers. The fact, in itself trivial, may be worth analyzing. Marta had lent support to her friend, but it is undeniable—although mysterious— that the person who confers a favor in some way stands above the one who receives it.

Around 1960, "two plastic artists of international stature"—may we be forgiven the jargon—were in the running for a first prize. One of the candidates, the elder, had dedicated solemn oils to the representation of awe-inspiring gauchos of a Scandinavian altitude; his rather young rival, a man in his early twenties, had won both praise and indignation through deliberate chaos. The members of the jury, all past fifty and fearing that the general public would impute outdated standards to them, tended to favor the latter painter, though deep down they rather disliked him. After arguing back and forth, at first politely and finally out of boredom, they could not reach an agreement. In the course of their third meeting, one of them remarked, "B. seems quite bad to me; really, I think he's even worse than Clara Figueroa."

"Would you give her your vote?" said another juror, with a trace of scorn.

"Yes," answered the first, at the brink of ill-temper.

That same evening, the prize was unanimously granted to Clara Glencairn. She was elegant, lovable, scandal had never touched her, and in her villa out in Pilar she gave parties to which the most lavish magazines sent photographers. The expected dinner in her honor was organized and offered by Marta. Clara thanked her with few and carefully chosen words, remarking that between the traditional and the new, or between order and adventure, no real opposition exists, and that what we now call tradition is made up of a centuries-old web of adventures. The banquet was attended by a large number of society people, by almost all the members of the jury, and by two or three painters.

All of us tend to think of our own circumstances in terms of a narrow range and to feel that other pastures are greener. The worship of the gaucho and the *Beatus ille* are but a wistfulness bred of city living; Clara Glencairn and Marta Pizarro, weary of the continual round of wealth and idleness, longed for the world of art, for people who had devoted their lives to the creation of things of beauty. My suspicion is that in heaven the Blessed are of the opinion that the advantages of that locale have been overrated by theologians who were never actually there. Perhaps even in hell the damned are not always satisfied.

A year or two later, in the city of Cartagena, there took place the First Congress of Inter-American Painting and Sculpture. Each country sent its representative. The topics of discussion—may we be forgiven the jargon—were of burning interest: Can the artist disregard the indigenous? Can he omit or slight flora and fauna? Can he be insensitive to problems of a social nature? Should he not join his voice to those suffering under the yoke of Saxon imperialism? Et cetera, et cetera. Before becoming ambassador to Canada, Dr. Figueroa had performed a diplomatic mission in Cartagena. Clara, a bit proud over the prize, would have liked returning there, this time as an artist. That hope was denied her; the government appointed Marta Pizarro. According to the impartial reports of correspondents from Buenos Aires, her participation (although not always persuasive) was on several occasions quite brilliant.

Life demands a passion. Both women found it in painting, or rather, in the relationship imposed on them by painting. Clara Glencairn painted against Marta and in a sense for Marta; each of them was her rival's judge and only public. In their pictures, which even then no one ever looked at, I think I observe—as was unavoidable—a mutual influence. Clara's sunset glows found their way into Marta Pizarro's patios and Marta's fondness for straight lines simplified the ornateness of Clara's final stage. It is important to remember that the two women were genuinely fond of each other and that in the course of their intimate duel they behaved toward one another with perfect loyalty.

It was during those years that Marta, who by then was no longer so young, rejected a marriage proposal. All that interested her was her battle.

On the second of February, 1964, Clara Glencairn died of a heart ailment. The columns of the newspapers devoted long obituaries to her of the kind that are still quite common in the Argentine, where a woman is regarded as a member of the species, not an individual. Outside of some hasty mention of her dabbling in painting and of her impeccable good taste, she was praised for her religious devotion, her kindness, her constant and almost anonymous philanthropy, her illustrious family tree—General Glencairn had fought in the Brazilian campaign—and her outstanding place in Society's highest circles. Marta realized that her life now lacked a meaning. She had never before felt so useless. Remembering her first endeavors, now so far in the past, she hung in the National Gallery a sober portrait of Clara after the manner of those English masters that the two women had so admired. Some judged it her finest work. She was never to paint again.

In that delicate duel, only suspected by a few close friends, there were neither defeats nor victories nor even an open encounter nor any visible circumstances other than those I have attempted respectfully to record. Only God (of whose aesthetic preferences we are unaware) can grant the final palm. The story that made its way in darkness ends in darkness.

FALSE LIMITS

VLADY KOCIANCICH

tr. NORMAN THOMAS DI GIOVANNI
IN COLLABORATION WITH THE AUTHOR

He would write a letter because to see his best friend and tell him face to face was impossible. He had often thought about speaking to him but never quite could; he imagined Enrique's face, the way his expression would change, his look of astonishment, his interruptions ("But it can't be—are you sure?"), which would force him to explain or perhaps excuse himself or at worst confess that it had only been a joke.

Up to now it had never occurred to him that friendship and love are, in certain cases, proofs of a helpless solitude. He could not face Enrique because Enrique would not understand. Someone not so close to him would have been better. He thought, if I had such a friend I'd tell him everything. But Enrique was so loyal, so good, that it was impossible to utter a word to him. Writing him might keep up the illusion of an understanding between them and at the same time give Enrique a chance to think over his reply, to weigh carefully each reason he would use to convince him he had been dreaming.

He didn't think the letter would be enough, but as an introduction it would at least spare him Enrique's looks of expectancy and bewilderment. He hesitated, and while hesitating—out of an impulse that ran contrary to his will—he was writing: "It's about my wife." He filled the letter with labored sentences, with excuses, with evasions, and with justifications. Suddenly he stopped and looked around. He was alone. He was peacefully surrounded by everyday things, as if nothing had really happened. He read: "It's about my wife. It's about Elisa. She's

43

not ill, nor is there another man mixed up in this. . . ." Denying, he could go on forever. Enrique would never find out the truth. Still roundabout in his approach, he gave one last trite explanation before getting down to the facts: "It's very hard to make certain things clear to outsiders, because to a married couple that's what others are—outsiders. How idiotic to think love unites. How sentimental. Two people living together stand as if on different planes, most of which are secret. I won't try explaining anything to you because I don't know myself what's happened, but here are the facts. . . ."

He stopped again. He had heard a noise behind him, the shuffle of slippers on the rug. Quickly he covered the letter with the first thing he could lay his hands on—a map of greater Buenos Aires—and began studying it: Adrogué, Lomas de Zamora, familiar routes. . . . He pronounced these names to himself, trying to escape Elisa and the silence, which was so obvious it was almost like another person in the room. But also, though he did not lift his eyes from the map, he listened hard for the faint sound of Elisa's approaching steps. Then, unable to bear it any longer, he called without turning around, "Elisa?"

"Yes?" Her voice was neutral, with the sweetness of utter indifference.

"Nothing—except that I'm going out."

"Oh."

"Do you want anything from town?" he asked, obedient to his old habit of adding a word or two when he felt guilty.

"No."

He got up hurriedly, relieved by her answer, which excused him from having to come back right away. He gathered up his papers, the letter among them, put everything into a leather briefcase, and, feeling both stupid and afraid, left for his office.

Of course, he did not mail the letter. He kept it in a pocket for several days, transferring it from one suit to another, but he never mailed it. At last Enrique rang him up, wondering why they had not been getting together for drinks. Elisa had spoken to him; she was surprised too. She said he was too old to break his habit of meeting Enrique either on Wednesday nights or Thursdays before seven. Elisa always teased him about his way of organizing his habits with the same thoroughness he applied to his work at the office. This time her remark sounded to him like mockery. The atmosphere of the house, the forced secrecy of horror, shattered Elisa's innocent words.

Up to that moment he had fought against all sorts of troubles and out of these battles he had emerged victorious; this had led him to believe that one of his rock bottom virtues was strength. Yes, he considered himself strong, able to face anything, even the worst situations, but how could he understand this madness which surrounded him now —in spite of the sensibleness of all his past acts and the smooth way his days had run—without any apparent cause?

A man like him does not become disturbed overnight; he waits to see what will happen and then takes the plunge into analysis. This had been his first impulse. At the very moment Elisa changed, he had thought, I must see an analyst.

He would call Enrique to find out if he knew a good one—not one of those clowns who organize LSD sessions, of course, but a sensible doctor, an understanding listener. As a listener, Enrique would have done well, but, preferring the impersonality of science, he never once spoke to him. He waited. And while postponing the moment of coming to grips with his problem, he tried to imagine a dialogue which might begin in this way:

"It's about my wife."

The analyst would not risk any conclusions, he would let him talk.

"I never noticed anything strange about her. She's a silent, quiet woman. But her character—Elisa herself—has nothing to do with what's happening to me. She's outside all this."

That was exactly why he could not talk to her. He stopped himself to ask if it had been always this way—Elisa distant from him, he trapped in his own silence, both of them avoiding the mention of anything unpleasant or dangerous. They'd had such a peaceful life.

"Elisa and I never had a quarrel—well, maybe once. Yes, now I remember, years ago we once had a fight, but I don't know what about. Yesterday, while we were having breakfast, I noticed that Elisa had no hands. Or maybe she did, maybe I just couldn't see them. No hands. She was sitting there as usual, but without hands."

He would stop to watch the doctor's reaction, but the doctor would display an impassive face so as not to lose his fee for subsequent visits. He would ask, very politely, "And what else?"

"I behaved as though nothing had happened. I tried to think—I still believe in this possibility—that it was only an hallucination, fatigue, overwork, my eyes."

That first day had been more uncomfortable than anything else. He denied the change in her with all his strength and with less courage than would have been required to take it lightly, at the same time piling explanation on explanation—his fatigue, his vision.

This visit to the doctor was so real that he decided not to see him.

He told himself that what he wanted was an answer, not theories. Elisa without hands was a terrifying sight but still bearable, since she had not lost them in an accident (there were no traces of blood or of torn flesh). It was like the lingering remnants of a nightmare, and one easily grows used to nightmares, so long as they don't make much sense. At some point later on, weakened by fear and sorrow, he wondered why he had not immediately run out of the house instead of trying to grow gradually accustomed to the horror.

This attitude of well-mannered acceptance lasted till the moment Elisa's eyes disappeared. She had lifted her empty face to him for its morning kiss, and he stepped back instinctively for the door. Moving clumsily in his fear, he got into his car, the keys clinking together in his trembling hand, and started the motor. Then a neighbor, a face he did not bother to identify, was approaching him, wanting to be helped with his car, which had gone dead or had sunk into a soft shoulder or something of the kind. As at the outer limits of a nightmare, he was held back by this series of efforts he was forced to make against his will and by his neighbor's small talk, all the while feeling Elisa's empty stare at the back of his head. But he did not see a doctor, nor did he mail the letter to Enrique. He only thought about escaping. It might have been a sensible decision not to return home. But he could not leave. That would have meant confronting Elisa and explaining why he was leaving her. And where would he go? He put forward these and other excuses so as not to have to admit the inexplicable feeling tying him to his home and his wife. All he did was shut himself up in his work. There was no detail into which he did not enter, no meeting he did not attend. His colleagues seemed not to mind, but were somewhat taken aback when he began meddling in the affairs of others. Now he was coming home very late; he would stay on at the office or at a bar, hoping on his return to find Elisa asleep.

Not wanting to wake her, he avoided turning on the lights. He would then grope for the bed and lie with his back to her, in one corner, like an angry child.

For a long time, for nearly a month, he let himself go on living in his nightmare, leaving home early each morning and coming back late at night. Not so late as to arouse Elisa's suspicions, however, but late enough to find her already asleep. With a glance at her side of the bed he could vaguely make out her head, a large spot of golden hair on the pillow. He would then be tempted to put his arms around her, not out of love but out of desperation, driven by a need to do something—anything. But he huddled in fear on his side of the bed and pulled the sheets over his head.

During the day, in a rush of endless tasks, he tried to forget his wife's gradual disappearance; but Elisa, handless, eyeless, like a broken doll, often broke into the conversation when he was lunching with other people, and made his blood run cold. He began to take little notice of his behavior. He was no longer able to cover up his fear before others and would stop a moment before any door and pray not to have Elisa open it for him.

He endured his nights stoically, sure there was no way of avoiding them, and, out of desperation, always managed to sleep. He had not had a single sleepless night, but in his dreams he found himself with Elisa. Once, he had cried out in his sleep and she stirred. He held his breath, rigid on his side of the bed. He heard her softly saying, "Are you all right? What is it?"

Close to tears in his fright, he begged her to go on sleeping, assuring her that he was perfectly all right. She turned her back to him without another word. They never talked again.

Now it was no more a matter of seeing an analyst or waiting for Enrique's advice. He had passed the limits of one nightmare and was entering into another, as if a last door had been closed on him. Motionless at the edge of the bed, knowing that if he stirred or got up she would come after him, he imagined the color of her hair in the dark. It was the only thing about her he still remembered.

He began to weep silently, while striking up an imaginary dialogue with his wife.

"Elisa, what's happening to us?"

He saw himself and Elisa in a trap, two figures drawn by the same hand, making up part of who knew what bewildering picture.

He began to regret the long-past time when they were both open and things were clear and they loved each other. With the certainty that nothing could now save him from his present horror, admitting for the first time that no tomorrow would come, all at once he understood everything. Violently, desperately frightened, he turned toward Elisa's incomplete body to take her in his arms, to try to hold together what little was left of her, feeling that this is what he should have done that first time. But there on the pillow lay nothing but a lock of golden hair, and in a matter of moments it too disappeared.

"These are the facts, Enrique," he wrote. "Elisa's gone. I can hear her. If I were to touch her, I could feel her skin; sometimes, when I brush against her, I can hear her breath. If she didn't exist, if she were really dead, I don't think it would matter to me. But living with her this way is unbearable and living without her is impossible. I have not gone back to work. I'm telling you all this without pain or fear because I have no other fate than to remain here. I care for nothing in this world but Elisa."

"Raúl."

It was his wife's voice calling him after such a long time. He got up from the desk, turned, and saw her. Elisa once again, Elisa tall, whole, beautiful, watching him with a grave look in her eyes, while he dared not speak for fear of breaking the spell of this new dream. He was trembling and had to support himself against the desk.

It took him an eternity to come back to life. It meant just that— to be living again in this small, simple world of manageable troubles, troubles shared with others. He would never be alone again.

When he came to his senses, to the almost unbearable happiness of being himself again, he heard Elisa explaining to him, perhaps for the fifth time, "I'm sorry, Raúl, but I'm leaving. I'm in love with another man."

Translator: Eloah F. Giacomelli

TIGRELA

LYGIA FAGUNDES TELLES

I ran into Romana in a cafe. She was half drunk, but deep below her obvious drunkenness I sensed that dense silt surging fast whenever she stood lost in thought. Then her mouth would sag, heavy, and her eyes, fleeting, would change from hunter into prey. She clasped my hands twice, I need you, she said, but right away she no longer did, and her fear turned into indifference, almost disdain, a mean line swelling her lips. She was again an adolescent when she laughed, without any mysteries, the best in our class. Without any dangers. She used to be extremely beautiful, and she still was, but now her decadent beauty was sad even in joy. She told me that she was separated from her third husband and that she lived with a small tiger in a penthouse.

With a tiger, Romana? She laughed. Once, a friend who had been traveling in Asia brought Tigrela back with him in a small basket, she was so tiny he had to nurse her with a bottle. She has grown into a large cat, one of those with golden eyes and tawny stripes on their ginger coat. Two thirds tiger and one third woman, she has become humanized and now—At first she was always mimicking me, it was funny, then I too began to mimic her, and we ended up by becoming so involved with each other that now I don't know if it was from her that I learned how to look at myself in the mirror with narrowed eyes. Or if it was from me that she learned how to stretch out on the floor and lean her head on her arm to listen to music. She is so well-proportioned, so clean, said Romana, dropping an ice-cube into the glass. Her coat is this color, she added, stirring the whiskey. With her fingertips she picked up a blade of ice that lay melting in the bottom of the days she used to bite into popsicles. She sure liked whiskey this Tigrela, but she held her liquor well, she was restrained, only once did she get really stoned. And Romana smiled at the thought of the animal frolicking about, tumbling over the furniture until she leaped onto the chandelier and then started to swing, to and fro, and Romana made a feeble imitation of a pendulum swinging. She and half of the chandelier finally landed on the bolster and then the two of us danced a tango together. It was a riot. Then she became depressed and in her depression she gets excited, she almost wrecked the garden, she tore my housecoat, she broke things. Then she wanted to throw herself from the balcony, just like people, exactly. Exactly, Romana repeated, groping about my wrist for my watch. She resorted to a man walking past our table, the time, do you have the time? When told that it was just before midnight, she lowered her eyes, brooding. She remained silent. I waited. When she spoke again, she struck me as an excited gambler, dissembling under an artificial speech: I had a steel grille placed on top of the balustrade, of course, if she wants to, she can easily climb this grille. But I know that she only tries to kill herself when she's drunk and then it will be enough to shut the door that opens into the balcony. She's always been so lucid, she went on, lowering her voice, and her face darkened. What's the matter, Romana? I asked, and touched her hand. It was ice-cold. She gazed at me, her eyes crafty. She was thinking of something else when she told me that at sunset, the sun, hitting the top of the building slantwise, projected the shadow of the grille onto the middle of the carpet in the living-room, and if Tigrela was lying asleep on the bolster, it was beautiful to see the net of shadows descending like a snare upon her coat.

She sank her forefinger in the glass, moving the ice around in the whiskey. On this finger she wore a square emerald, like a queen would. Really extraordinary, isn't it? The limited space of an apartment has restricted the growth of an Asiatic tiger, thanks to the judicious magic of adaptation; she became a mere overgrown cat, as if she had sensed that she had to confine herself to being nothing more than an oversized cat. Nobody except me knows that she has grown, nobody except me has noticed that she's taking up more space now, lately there has hardly been room for the two of us, one of us would really have to . . . She interrupted herself to light a cigarillo, the flame wavering in her unsteady hand. She sleeps with me, but when she's not on speaking terms with me, she sleeps on the bolster, her back turned to me, rigid like a sphinx.

She must have created problems, what about the neighbors? I asked. Romana stiffened the finger that was stirring the ice. There aren't any, one apartment only on each floor of a highrise, completely white, Mediterranean style. You should see how Tigrela and the apartment match so perfectly well. I've traveled in Persia, you heard about it, didn't you? That's where I got the fabrics and the rugs, she loves this velvety comfort, she's so sensitive to textures, to smells. When she wakes up restive, I light an incense stick, the scent relaxes her. I turn on the record-player. Then, after much stretching of limbs, she falls asleep, I have a suspicion that like the dragons, she also sees better with her eyes closed. I had some trouble convincing Aninha that she's just an oversized cat, Aninha's the maid. But now everything is fine, the two of them keep their distance, but they respect each other, that's what really counts, respect. She has accepted Aninha, who is old and ugly, but she almost attacked the previous maid, a young woman. While this young woman remained with me, Tigrela would hardly leave the garden, she kept herself hidden behind the leaves, her eyes two slits, her claws dug in the earth.

The claws, I started, and then didn't know what else to say. The emerald dropped sideways like a defenceless head and it hit against the glass, the finger much too thin for the ring. The sound of the stone against the glass aroused Romana, momentarily apathetic. She raised her head, and her eyes roamed over the tables, all of them filled. Quite noisy, isn't it? I suggested that we leave but instead of the bill, she asked for another whiskey. Don't worry, I'm used to it, she said, and took a deep breath. She held herself upright, Tigrela loves jewelry and Bach, yes, Bach, she insists on the same pieces, especially The Passion According to Saint Matthew. One evening, as I was getting ready to go out for dinner, she came up to me to have a look, she hates me going out, but that evening she was cheerful, she approved of my dress, she prefers the classic styles and this one was a full-length, straw-colored silk dress, with long sleeves and a low waist line. How do you like it, Tigrela? I asked and she drew nearer, placed her paws on my neck, licked my chin lightly so as not to spoil my make-up and then with her teeth she started to pull at my amber necklace. Would you like to have it? I asked, and she growled softly but firmly. I removed the necklace and put it around her neck. She looked at herself in the mirror, her eyes moist with pleasure. Then she licked my hand and walked away, the necklace hanging from her neck, the largest beads grazing the floor. When she's relaxed, her eyes turn into a clear yellow, the color of amber.

Does Aninha sleep in the apartment? I asked, and Romana started as if suddenly realizing that Aninha came in early in the morning and left in the evening, leaving the two of them by themselves. I looked hard at her and she laughed, I know, you think I must be crazy, but from the outside nobody can understand it, it's complicated. And so simple, but you'd have to step inside to understand it. I put on my jacket, but had it really turned cooler? Do you remember our graduation party, Romana? I asked. I still have some photographs, the shoes you had bought for the dance were too tight and so you ended up by dancing barefoot; during the waltz I watched you from afar, you were whirling away in a light dress, your hair hanging down; I thought it beautiful this idea of yours of dancing barefoot. She was looking at me attentively but she wasn't listening at all. We're vegetarians, I've always been a vegetarian, you know. I didn't. Tigrela eats nothing but cereals and fresh vegetables and milk with honey, absolutely no meat at home, meat causes bad breath. And thoughts, she added, and clasped my hand, I need you. I leaned over to listen, but the waiter stretched his arm to pick up the ashtray and she was once more frivolous, interested in the ashtray being cleaned. Have you ever tried milk blended with watercress and molasses? The recipe is a cinch, blend everything in a blender and then strain it, she said, and stretched her hand out, do you have the time, sir? Do yo have an engagement? I asked, and she said, no, she didn't. No, no, she repeated, and I had the feeling that she turned pale as her lips parted to formulate some obscure computation. She caught a dwindling ice-cube on the tip of her tongue and crunched it in her teeth. It hasn't happened yet, but it will, she said with some difficulty because the ice froze her tongue. I waited. A gulp of whiskey seemed to give her some warmth. Any night now, when I get home, the doorman might rush towards me saying, you know, madam, from one of those balconies . . . but then he might say nothing and I'll have to go up and behave normally so that she won't notice, and wait for another day. At times we size each other up and I don't know the outcome, I've taught her much, and I've learned as much from her, Romana said with a gesture she left unfinished. Have I mentioned that it's Aninha who clips her fingernails? She would give her her paw without the least resistance but she wouldn't allow her to brush her teeth, her gums are ultra-sensitive. I've bought her a natural bristle toothbrush, the brushing is done very gently with up and down strokes and the toothpaste is mint flavored. Dental floss is not necessary because she doesn't eat anything stringy, but if one day she were to she'd know where to find the floss.

I ordered a sandwich; Romana ordered some carrots, raw and well-washed. And salt, she said, and pointed to the empty glass. While the waiter poured the whiskey we didn't talk. When he went away, I broke into laughter. Is it true, Romana, all this you've been telling me? She didn't reply, she was tallying memories and amidst them, there was one stifling her: she gasped, loosening the knot of her scarf. A blue bruise on her neck became exposed; I turned away to the wall. In the mirror I saw her retie her scarf and then sniff at the whiskey. She smiled. Tigrela could tell an adulterated whiskey, something I never could. One night, with a kick she sent a bottle flying away, why did you do it, Tigrela? She didn't reply. When I examined the broken pieces, I recognized the brand, it was one that once had given me a hell of a hangover. Would you believe that she knows more about my life than Yasbeck ever did? And there has never been anybody more jealous than Yasbeck, he even hired a detective to watch me. She feigns indifference but her pupils dilate and overflow like some black ink spilling over the eyes, have I mentioned those eyes of hers? It's in them that I see her emotions, her jealousy. Then she grows sullen. She refuses the blanket, the cushion, and goes to the garden, the apartment is in the middle of a garden designed especially for her, a mini-jungle. There she remains all day long, all night long, sulking behind the leaves, I can call her until I'm blue in the face, but she won't come to me, her muzzle wet with dew, or could it be tears?

I was staring at the small circle of water the glass had left on the table. But Romana, wouldn't it be more humane to send her to a zoo? Let her become an animal again, I think it's cruel to force your kind of cage on her when she might be happier in some other kind. You've enslaved her, and you've ended up enslaved as well, it was inevitable. Won't you at least give her the freedom of choice? Annoyed, Romana sank a carrot into the salt. She licked it. Freedom is comfort, my darling, Tigrela also knows it is so. She has been provided with all comforts, just as I had been until Yasbeck ditched me.

And now you want to ditch her, I said. At one of the tables a man started to sing an excerpt from an opera at the top of his voice, but it was soon drowned in laughter. Romana was talking so fast now that I had to interrupt her, slow down, I can't follow you at all. She did, but a moment later she was racing away again like mad as if she were running out of time. Our worst fight was because of him, Yasbeck, you know how it is, this turmoil of an old love that suddenly turns up again. Sometimes he phones me and then we sleep together, she realizes perfectly well what's going on, she overheard our conversation, when I got home she was awake waiting for me, standing like a statue at the door, of course I dissembled as much as I could, but she's cunning and kept sniffing at me until she detected the male smell in me, then she grew wild. I think that nowadays I'd like to have a unicorn, you know, that tawny horse with the pink horn on his forehead, I saw one in a tapestry, so deeply in love with the princess who was holding up a mirror so that he could look at himself, but where's the waiter? Waiter, would you please tell me the time? And bring me some more ice. She spent two days without eating, tigerish, Romana went on. She was speaking slowly now, her voice thick, one word after the other, the numbers of her computation filling the empty slots. Two days without eating at all, dragging her necklace and her haughtiness around the apartment. I was puzzled, Yasbeck had said he'd call me and he didn't, he sent a note instead, what's the matter with your telephone? it's dead. When I examined it, I saw that the cord had been completely ground, there were teeth marks all over the extension cord. I didn't say anything, but I felt her watching me from behind those slits of hers that can cut through glass or wall. I guess it was that very same day that she realized what I had been thinking, we distrusted each other, but even so, do you understand me? She was so passionate . . .

Was? I asked. She spread her hands on the table, and faced me. Why are you looking at me like this? What else could I do? She must have waked up at 11, the hour she usually does, she loves night. Instead of milk, I filled her bowl with whiskey and turned off the lights; when lost in despair, she sees better in the dark, and today she was lost in despair because she overheard me, she thinks I'm with him now. The door to the balcony is wide open, it has been so for the past several nights and nothing has happened, but one never knows, she's so unpredictable, she added, her voice fading away. She wiped the salt from her fingers with a paper napkin. I'm off now. I always get home trembling because I never know if the doorman will come to me saying that a naked young woman with an amber necklace around her neck has thrown herself from one of the balconies.

KARL KROLOW: A PORTRAIT
INTRODUCTION AND POEMS

Karl Krolow, now in his fifties, is established as Germany's most important poet since World War II. Selections of his poetry are available in three English book-length translations: *Poems Against Death*, translated by Herman Salinger, *Invisible Hands* and *Foreign Bodies*, both translated by Michael Bullock. These three books do not cover Krolow's vast poetic production; a great number of poems still remain untranslated.

There are no prescribed ways to enter a poet's universe. However, a walk through the pages of Krolow's poems should include the following poems: "Strand" (Beach), "Manchmal" (Sometimes), "Die Neugier" (Curiosity), "Schattenspiel" (Shadow Show), "Kindertheater" (Children's Theatre), "Sonntag" (Sunday), "Zeitlos" (Timeless), "Krankes Wetter" (Sick Weather), "Kindheit" (Childhood) and "Liebesgedichte" (Love Poems). These poems represent Krolow, his particular way of looking at the world; they speak of things that are almost too delicate to be put into words and they push words to the border where meaning becomes transparent not through the word but between words. Nothing is obvious in this kind of poetry. Krolow follows a long line of familiar ancestors: Baudelaire, Mallarmé, Rilke and Valéry. They are difficult and subtle poets; they reject that which is obvious and they try to say that which cannot be said. The result is the poem at the limit of light and darkness; it says what cannot be said.

54

Krolow's major concern is the language of the poem as reflection of the creative process. Often the creative process becomes the subject of the poem. Whatever the poet touches with the eyes of his imagination, he is incapable of explaining the final transformatory act that makes the poem as art possible.

At what particular moment the poem takes off remains a mystery to the poet as well as his reader. Both know intuitively that it has happened, but the actual process cannot be explained. This idea intrigues Krolow and he often talks about it in his essays and lectures.

Krolow's poetry does not embrace big themes. If a consistency of thematic development can be detected within the pages of his poetry, it is the persistence with which his mind wanders from one state of isolation to the next. His poems resemble the vast isolation that dominates Tanguy's paintings, words dropped into echoless space, close and yet so distant, resplendent with mysterious terror. Above all, Krolow is an artist of words. He handles them with the ear of a musician listening to the inherent possibilities of each word, discovering new aspects and testing the solidity of one word in relation to another. The strength of his poetic expression lies in the never-failing innovation of creating tension between two words.

His is a poetry of clashing words and metaphors: tension between the logical and illogical, between the visible and invisible, between the archaic and the new. He invents: "ashes of the voice;" "broken water of days;" "the shadow of your certainty;" "carriers of water which collect thirst in their buckets;" "eyes of dead seamen/ look out for a blue/ that no longer exists;" "the blue syllables of water." These are moments of surprise for the reader who is participating in the act of a poetic transformation. Whether the transformation takes place on a metaphorical level or in the dialectical juxtaposition of opposites no longer matters. The reader has the feeling that he is neither word nor object, but a being between words and objects soaring upward to attain a higher level of perception and insight. Krolow once remarked that "inspiration lies in the detail." It explains a specific aspect of his poetic creation. When he gives simple titles like "Willow," "Wind," "Beach," "Every Morning," "The Afternoon" to his poems, he has established a certain visual frame, but now his mind must dissect these objects so that they project the intricate pattern of his imagination. They are familiar objects, but Krolow says the familiar in unfamiliar ways and establishes a new tension between himself and the objects that surround him. No moment, even the most trivial one, exists without mystery. All of Krolow's poetic endeavors are "a voyage into the inner life of moments."

These poems cannot be judged in terms of a traditional meaning. Their point of reference is not an external object or reality, but something inside the poem: the reference of one word to another. Thus, the meaning of these poems is not what the word says but what is said between words. The reader must lose all preconceived notions of meaning so that his mind can undertake the subtle voyage from one word to the next. The experience is never the same, since one word invents the following in an endless process of unexpected associations.

Transformation is the poem's meaning. Krolow once said that poetry becomes richer in proportion to its moments of surprises and ambiguities. Both elements imply the notion of a continuous change and explain why Krolow places such a high value on the power of metaphors. Stylistically, they perform the change and invent the new. The poetic moment creates an estrangement from established familiar objects, it builds a world of insecure, flexible boundaries and Krolow the poet makes us see things not with the comfort of an understanding mind, but with the uncertainty of a questioning mind. Whatever his mind touches, dissolves.

Playfully, he turns the familiar into the unfamiliar, surprises himself with his own surprises and leads the reader from one metaphorical invention to the next higher level of conceptual insight. In these moments, Baudelaire, Mallarmé and Guillén are his spiritual brothers.

Karl Krolow

TOO LATE

Not until now does the thought strike me,
incidentally for example, perhaps even tomorrow,
I shall grow curious (like a cat),
I shall perceive that—in starts,—
not until now do I have the feeling
everywhere, presumably as early as yesterday,
behind me (possibly)
I shall find a connection,
it seems to me as if I,
if I grow curious (like a cat),
suddenly feel—
that it really is.

Karl Krolow

BEHAVIOR IN FAIR WEATHER

A beautiful day one should
leave just as beautiful as it feels
if one has any feeling for
the right sky above the housetops
and in easily grasped language
can create an agreement
between perpendicular blue,
boredom, metabolic variations
and eyes that make one understand
that at the precise moment
various things are possible,
while it is growing hot too quickly
and phenomena are standing still
in the light that, acid-like,
is stinging the eyes.

Karl Krolow

FOREVER

To lose time forever.
Snow begins to fall
around me forever
without a way to return home.
It's as simple as
in summer letting oneself
fall into the grass forever
and then watching what happens
to a thought-free landscape
that lets itself be destroyed
forever and which a person
finally gets tired of when he
has said Spring for a long enough time.

Karl Krolow

SMALL CHANGE

A door in my head,
left open by someone.
Everything floats in the air.
It is easy to go on
in a dream about a dream.
A little change
and everything is different—
one long look. One must
put a period
after whatever was,
such as violence, which
forces another body
to move under pressure.
One can find no name for it—
to have enough and say good-bye.
Only behavior will still show
what is at stake.

Karl Krolow

SUMMER. FORMS.

Forms,
formed in the air by the heat.
Let us go past.
With one's body one writes
the history of the summer.
Parts of the landscape
are sewn to one another
with coarse stitches.
Objects are
carried away
by motionless waters.
Oval fruits, thickening
in shadow.
With controlled hand one contours
over an amputated tree.
Evenings a cigarette will
once more light up
a portion of your face.

Karl Krolow

THE SKIN INTO WHICH ONE IS PUT

The mechanical toy of my childhood,
Fantasy, having matured,
earlier a means of not being seen.
The lamp and wardrobe tell me
that I inhabit without owning myself.
One gets used to the skin
into which one is put.
Reality—a series of pictures,
guided by choice.
In between: sleep, lying next to each other,
the approach of death.
She wore some kind of dress
through which her
legs and thighs showed.
Forget everything. The approach
of any kind of destruction.
What shall we do with this life?

Karl Krolow

CLOSENESS

tr. MICHAEL BULLOCK

Blind to the cluster
of straight lines in the plane
as long as we
look from too close,
too close a surface
with objects that insist
upon themselves, without reduction
of magnitude, without curving
into the distance, nothing but
an absolutely successful
road, a
row of gardens with
completely unalterable
plants, no field of vision
beyond.
Blind
to the flat surface of signs
in which bodies become spatial,
only these carnations
arbitrarily arranged
in the cylindrical bottle,
apples too, unprojective
and exaggerated in the foreground —
a still-life that
kills perspectives.

Karl Krolow

SHADOWS IN THE AIR

Shadows in the air: ghosts
Out of blue uniforms like great butterflies.

Dreams are clad with suspicion:
Prehistoric fauns
That grew sober on the presence
Of the airy events.

Shadows from above: rather uncertain like
Monday's thoughts; and Sunday was
Full of birds' feathers, a light-coloured girl's glove.

The gentle water sky: once there bathed in it
closed eyes, many leaves.
But now
Cold is here, the smell
Of loneliness. No goldfish now
Swims in the glass of noon.

Air full of shadows! And the marble
Of past flesh shivers.
A black banner
— Sleep without dream —
Unrolls and flows slowly over shoulders.

Karl Krolow

SICK WEATHER

The air is a blackened grave,
traces of the Atlantic in it.
Eyes of dead seamen
look out for a blue
that no longer exists.

These are bad times
for crystals.

No sound now
in shattered shells.

The confusion is great
in the sky. The sounds
of dying come from rooms
that the wind robbed through their windows.

Cods' heads are bleeding
all over the land.

Karl Krolow

CHILDHOOD

Candlelight in a bottle:
Childhood.

The heart of the darkness glowed
as charcoal.

At the mouth of the river
the ships called one another
by name
till the night was over.

A dream appeared
as the figurehead of a galleon
on the ceiling.

Leaves, green veil of gauze.
I was a water-dove
that had lost its way
and was wailing over the Weser,
that gray, flapping flounder.

Susan Musgrave

AFTER THE BATTLE

Unaware that anything was wrong
I crawled out from under you
after the battle
and stood
remote and changed
in the place beside you
that should have been your own.

Yours was the only corpse, I noticed.
Some small animal
circled cautiously behind your eyes.
Your mouth had no edges,
no place for hanging on.
It was, instead, a place for lizards.

Your body is the sanctuary
for all the wildlife
that isn't me. A remnant of your hand
encloses all.
I am some bad flower
sent deliberately to spoil your grave.
I grow best in blood.

Lying here,
you accuse me in the darkness
without even turning
certain beauty to design.
You want everything to reappear
out of a past I can't explain.

I am not at fault
because you fell in a place of stone.
The blood will dry,
the stone will still be cold.
Your body will be
the singular thing
containing all.
That is—
            nothing to remain,
            nothing to destroy.

Judith Minty

WOMEN POETS

I

It is rumored that we speak now
with a single voice, we
women poets, that we have lost
the ring of individuality,
that the protest
has molded us into one
hard, metallic soprano
whose ear is pressed
to her own lips.

If this is true, then
do all our tits turn hard
on the same day of the month
and does all our bleeding
flow into one Amazon River?
And this bulky child
that we carry in our bellies,
when we birth him, will he then
be only one homogeneous poem?

If we would believe
the critics, if we have destroyed
our separate selves in the struggle
and now wear identical cloaks,
then we must find salvation, sisters,
before we join hands
form a circle, and in the soil
between our toes, cultivate
the petals of one perfect penis.

II

And if those snorting stallions
and bearded goats of poets
neigh and whinny at our songs, let them

roar their fragile words. We
will twist our lips into a Giaconda smile
and nod as fear
sparks behind their wild eyes.

We know how they court the Muse,
promise her laurel and honey as we
sit quiet with hands
folded delicately on our aprons
and watch her throw crumbs.
We see how their hooves
trample the clearing near her altar.

She is a seductress, that woman,
bent and wrinkled, yet still
she draws their seminal fluid.
But it is to us she comes
at night, laughing and weeping, to us
that she finally speaks.
She is our mother, our grandmother.
She is one of us.

III

Rumors grow often in gardens. They blister
among the flowers. If we are careless
and turn our faces to the mirror,
the rose may be drained of its color.
We must bend our backs and weed
out those black roots row on row.

For our voice is not single. It is full
of descants and grace notes. Our melody
rises from the earth's ovens. It flies
like a brown wren through trees and leaps
with waves along the shoreline. It is
all colors that hiss and crackle in hearth fires.

We are not one, but everywoman. Kora or Kali,
devouring or benevolent, Circe or the Virgin,

we know our power. And our poems, finally,
they breathe without us. Hear them now
as they ring like a thousand bells
from the fingers of our children.

Judith Minty

CONJOINED

The onion in my cupboard, a monster, actually
two joined under one transparent skin:
each half-round, then flat and deformed
where it pressed and grew against the other.

An accident, like the two-headed calf rooted
in one body, fighting to suck at its mother's teats;
or like those other freaks, Chang and Eng, twins
joined at the chest by skin and muscle, doomed
to live, even love, together for sixty years.

Do you feel the skin that binds us
together as we move, heavy in this house?
To sever the muscle could free one,
but might kill the other. Ah, but men
don't slice onions in the kitchen, seldom see
what is invisible. We cannot escape each other.

Translator JOHN FREDERICK NIMS

Homero Aridjis

EPITAPH FOR A POET

Before the mists descended on your body
long before hesitations clotted in the eyes of your mask
before the death of your first sons and the lower depths
before a confusion of sadness and destitution
and the savage cry in the frankness of a man
before having murmured of desolation on the bridges
and the falsity of a cupola through the window that had no glass

almost when your lakes were suns
and the children were words in the air
and the days were the shadow of what was easy

when eternity was not the exact death we were looking for
nor the dust more likely than memory
nor sorrow our cruelty for being divine

then when all could have been said with impunity
and laughter like a flower of petals falling

then when you owed nothing but the death of a poem
you were your own and not mine and I had not lost you

Translator MARGARET S. PEDEN

THE PURSUED

HORACIO QUIROGA

One night when I was at Lugones' home, the rain so increased in intensity that we rose to look at it from the windows. The wild pampa wind whistled through the wires and whipped the rain in convulsive gusts that distorted the reddish light from the street lamps. This afternoon, after six days of rain, the heavens had cleared to the south leaving a limpid cold blue sky. And then, behold, the rain returned to promise us another week of bad weather.

Lugones had a stove, which was extremely comforting to my winter debility. We sat down once again and continued our pleasant chat concerning the insane. Several days before, Lugones had visited an insane asylum, and the bizarre behavior of the inmates, added to behavior I myself had once observed, afforded more than enough material for a comfortable vis-à-vis between two sane men.

Given the circumstance of the weather, then, we were rather surprised when the bell at the street door rang. Moments later Lucas Díaz Vélez entered.

This individual has had quite an ominous influence over a period of my life, and that was the night I met him. As is customary, Lugones introduced us by our last names only, so that for some time I didn't know his given name.

Díaz was much slimmer then than he is now. His black clothes— the color of dark *mate* tea—his sharp face and large black eyes gave him a none too common appearance. The eyes especially, of surprising steadiness and extreme brilliance, demanded one's attention. In those days he parted his straight hair in the middle, and perfectly smoothed down it looked like a shining helmet.

Vélez spoke very little at first. He crossed his legs, responding only when strictly necessary. At a moment when I had turned towards Lugones, I happened to see that Vélez was observing me. Doubtless in another I would have found this examination following an introduction very natural, but his unwavering attention shocked me.

Soon our conversation came to a standstill. Our situation was not very pleasant, especially for Vélez, since he must have assumed that we were not practicing this terrible muteness before he arrived. He himself broke the silence. He spoke to Lugones of some honey cakes a friend had sent him from Salta, a sample of which he should have brought that night. They seemed to be of a particularly pleasing variety, and as Lugones showed sufficient interest in tasting them, Díaz Vélez promised to send him the means to do so.

Once the ice was broken, after about ten minutes we returned to our subject of madmen. Although seeming not to lose a single word of what he heard, Díaz held himself apart from the lively subject; perhaps it was not his predilection. As a result, when Lugones left the room for a moment, I was astonished by his unexpected interest. In one minute he told me a number of anecdotes—his expression animated and his mouth precise with conviction. He certainly had much more love for these things than I had supposed, and his last story, related with great vivacity, made me see that he understood the mad with a subtlety not common in this world.

The story was about a boy from the provinces who after emerging from the debilitating weakness of typhoid found the streets peopled with enemies. He underwent two months of persecution, committing as a result all kinds of foolish acts. As he was a boy of certain intelligence, he commented on his own case so cleverly that listening to him it was impossible to know what to think. It sounded exactly like a farce; and this was the general impression of those who heard him discuss his own case so roguishly—always with the vanity characteristic of the mad.

In this fashion he spent three months displaying his psychological astuteness until one day his mind was cleansed in the clear water of sanity and his ideas became more temperate.

"He is well now," Vélez concluded, "but several rather symptomatic acts have remained with him. A week ago, for example, I ran into him in a pharmacy; he was leaning against the counter, waiting for what I don't know. We started chatting. Suddenly an individual came in without seeing him, and as there was no clerk he rapped with his fingers on the counter. My friend abruptly turned on the intruder with truly animal quickness, staring into his eyes. Anyone would have turned like that, but not with that rapidity of a man who is always on his guard. Although he is no longer pursued, he must have kept, unawares, an underlying fear that explodes at the least hint of sudden surprise. After staring for a moment, not moving a muscle, he blinked and averted his disinterested eyes. It is as though he had guarded a dark memory of something terrible that happened to him in another time, something he wants never again to catch him unprepared. Imagine then the effect on him of someone's grabbing his arm on the street. I think it would never leave him."

"Undoubtedly the symptom is typical," I confirmed. "And did the psychological talk come to an end also?"

A strange thing: Díaz became very serious and gave me a cold, hostile look.

"May I know why you ask me that?"

"Because we were speaking precisely *of* that!" I replied, surprised. But obviously the man had seen how ridiculous he had been, because immediately he apologized profusely.

"Forgive me. I don't know what happened to me. I've felt this way at times . . . unexpectedly lost my head. Crazy things," he added, laughing, and playing with a ruler.

"Completely crazy," I joked.

"And *so* crazy! It's only by chance that I have an ounce of sense left. And now I remember, although I asked your pardon—and I ask it again—that I haven't answered your question. My friend does not talk about psychology any more. And now that he is eminently sane, he does not feel perverse in denouncing his own madness as he did before, forcing that terrible two-edged sword one calls reason, you see? It's very clear."

"Not very," I allowed myself to doubt.

"Possibly," he laughed, conclusively. "Another really crazy thing." He winked at me and moved away from the table, smiling and shaking his head like someone who is withholding many things he could tell.

Lugones returned and we dropped the subject—already exhausted. During the remainder of the visit Díaz spoke very little, although it was clear that his own lack of sociability was making him very nervous. Finally, he left. Perhaps he tried to overcome any bad impression he may have made by his extremely friendly farewell, offering his name and the hospitality of his house along with the prolonged clasp of affectionate hands. Lugones went down with him, since the now dark stairway was so precipitous that no one was ever tempted to try it alone.

"What the devil kind of person is he?" I asked when Lugones returned. He shrugged his shoulders.

"A terrible individual. I don't know how he came to speak ten words to you tonight. He often sits a whole hour without speaking a word, and you can imagine how pleased I am when he's like that.

On the other hand, he comes very seldom. And he's very intelligent in his good moments. You must have noticed that, since I heard you talking."

"Yes, he was telling me about a strange case."

"What case?"

"About a friend who is pursued. He knows as much about madness as the devil himself."

"I guess so since he himself is pursued."

Scarcely had I heard what he said than a flash of explanatory logic illuminated the darkness I had felt in the other. Undoubtedly. . . ! I remembered above all his irritable air when I asked him if he didn't discuss psychology any more. . . The good madman had thought I had guessed his secret and was insinuating myself into his consciousness. . . .

"Of course!" I laughed. "Now I understand! But your Díaz Vélez is fiendishly subtle!" And I told him about the snare he had thrown out to me to amuse himself at my expense: the fiction of a pursued friend, and his comments. But I had scarcely begun when Lugones interrupted.

"There is no friend; that actually happened. Except that his friend is he himself. He told you the complete truth; he had typhoid, was very ill, and is cured to this degree, and now you see that his very sanity is questionable. It's also very possible that the business of the store encounter is true, but that it happened to him. He's an interesting individual, eh?"

"And then some!" I responded, as I toyed with the ashtray.

It was late when I left. The weather had finally settled, and although one could not see the sky above, one sensed the ceiling had lifted. It was no longer raining. A strong, dry wind rippled the water on the sidewalks and forced one to lean into it at street corners. I reached Santa Fe Street and waited a while for the streetcar, shaking the water from my feet. Bored, I decided to walk; I quickened my pace, dug my hands into my pockets, and then thought in some detail about Díaz Vélez.

The thing I remembered best about him was the look with which he had first observed me. It couldn't be called intelligent, reserving intelligence to be included among those qualities—habitual in persons of certain stature—to be *exchanged* to a greater or lesser degree among persons of similar culture. In such looks there is always an interchange of souls: one delves into the depths of the person he has just met, and at the same time yields part of his own soul to the stranger.

Díaz didn't look at me that way; he looked only *at* me. He wasn't thinking what I was or what I might be, nor was there in his look the least spark of psychological curiosity. He was simply observing me, as one would unblinkingly observe the equivocal attitude of some feline.

After what Lugones had told me, I was no longer astonished by the objectivity of the madman's stare. After his examination, satisfied surely, he had made fun of me, shaking the scarecrow of his own madness in my face. But his desire to denounce himself, without revealing himself, had less the object of making fun of me than of entertaining himself. I was simply a pretext for his argument, and above all a point of confrontation; the more I admired the devilish perversity of the madman he was describing to me, the more he must have been furtively rubbing his hands. The only thing that kept him from being completely happy was that I didn't say: "But isn't your friend afraid they'll find him out when he denounces himself that way?" It hadn't occurred to me, because the friend didn't interest me especially. But now that I knew who the pursued one was, I promised myself to provide him with the wild happiness he desired. This is what I was thinking as I walked along.

Nevertheless, two weeks passed without my seeing him. I knew through Lugones that he had been at Lugones' house to bring him the confections, a good gift for him.

"He also brought some for you. Since he didn't know where you live—I don't think you gave him your address—he left them at my house. You must come by and get them."

"Some day. Is he still at the same address?"

"Díaz Vélez?"

"Yes."

"Yes, I suppose so; he didn't say a word about leaving."

The next rainy night I went to Lugones' house, sure of finding Díaz Vélez. Even though I realized, better than anyone, that the logic of thinking I would meet him *precisely* on a rainy night was worthy only of a dog or a madman, the probability of absurd coincidence always rules in such cases where reason no longer operates.

Lugones laughed at my insistence on seeing Díaz Vélez.

"Be careful! The pursued always begin by adoring their future victims. He remembered you very well."

"That doesn't matter. When I see him it's going to be *my* turn to amuse myself."

I left very late that night.

But I didn't find Díaz Vélez. Not until one noon, just as I was starting to cross the street, I saw him on Artes Street. He was walking north, looking into all the shop windows, not missing a one, like a person preoccupied. When I caught a glimpse of him I had one foot off the sidewalk. I tried to stop, but I couldn't and I stepped into the street, almost stumbling. I turned around and looked at the curb, although I was quite sure there was nothing there. One of the Plaza carriages driven by a Negro in a shiny jacket passed so close to me that the hub of the rear wheel left grease on my trousers. I stood still, staring at the horse's hooves, until an automobile forced me to jump out of the way.

All this lasted about ten seconds, as Díaz continued moving away, and I was forced to hurry. When I felt sure of overtaking him, all my hesitation left and was replaced by a great feeling of self-satisfaction. I felt myself in perfect equilibrium. All my nerves were tingling and resilient. I opened and closed my hands, flexing my fingers, happy. Four or five times a minute I put my hand to my watch, forgetting that it was broken.

Díaz Vélez continued walking and soon I was two steps behind him. One step more and I *could* touch him. But seeing him this way, not even remotely aware of my presence in spite of his delirium about persecution and psychology, I adjusted my step exactly to his. Pursued! Very well. . . ! I noted in detail his head, his elbows, his clenched hands—held a little away from his body—the tranverse wrinkles of his trousers at the back of the knee, the heels of his shoes, appearing and disappearing. I had the dizzying sensation that once before, millions of years before, I had done this: met Díaz Vélez in the street, followed him, caught up with him, and having done so, continued to follow behind him—*behind him*. I glowed with the satisfaction of a dozen lifetimes. Why touch him? Suddenly it occurred to me that he might turn around, and instantly anguish clutched at my throat. I thought that with my larynx throttled like this I wouldn't be able to cry out, and my only fear, my terrifyingly unique fear, was that I would not be able to cry out if he turned around; as if the goal of my existence were suddenly to throw myself upon him, to pry open his jaws and shout unrestrainedly into his open mouth—counting every molar as I yelled.

I had such a moment of anguish that I forgot that it was *he* I was seeing: Díaz Vélez's arms, Díaz Vélez's legs, Díaz Vélez's hair, Díaz Vélez's hatband, the woof of Díaz Vélez's hatband, the warp of the warp of Díaz Vélez, Díaz Vélez, Díaz Vélez. . .

The realization that in spite of my terror I hadn't missed one moment of him, Díaz Vélez, assured me completely.

A moment later I was possessed by the mad temptation to touch him without his noticing it, and immediately, filled with the greatest happiness one's own original creative act can hold, softly, exquisitely, I touched his jacket, just on the lower edge—no more, no less. I touched it and plunged my closed fist into my pocket.

I am sure that more than ten people saw me. I was aware of three: one of them, walking in the opposite direction along the sidewalk across the street, kept turning around with amused surprise. He was carrying a valise in his hand that pointed towards me every time he turned.

Another was a streetcar inspector who was standing on the curb, his legs spread wide apart. From his expression I understood that he had been watching us even before I did it. He did not manifest the least surprise or change his stance or move his head, but he certainly did follow us with his eyes. I assumed he was an elderly employee who had learned to see only what suited him.

The third person was a heavy individual with magnificent bearing, a Catalan-style beard, and eyeglasses with gold frames. He must have been a businessman in Spain. He was just passing us, and he saw me do it. I was sure he had stopped. Sure enough, when we reached the corner, I turned around and I saw him, standing still, staring at me with a rich honorable bourgeois look, frowning, with his head thrown back slightly. This individual enchanted me. Two steps later, I turned my head and laughed in his face. I saw that he frowned even more and drew himself up with dignity as if he doubted whether he could be the one intended. I made a vague, nonsensical gesture that disorganized him completely.

I followed Díaz Vélez, once again attentive only to him. Now we had crossed Cuyo, Corrientes, Lavalle, Tucuman and Viamonte (the affair of the jacket and the three looks had occurred between the latter two). Three minutes later we had reached Charcas and there Díaz stopped. He looked towards Suipacha, detected a silhouette behind him and suddenly turned around. I remember this detail perfectly: for a half second he gazed at one of the buttons on my jacket, a rapid glance, preoccupied and vague at the same time, like someone who suddenly focuses on one object, just at the point of remembering something else. Almost immediately he looked into my eyes.

"Oh, how are you!" he clasped my hand, shaking it rapidly. "I haven't had the pleasure of seeing you since that night at Lugones'. Were you coming down Artes?"

"Yes. I turned in at Viamonte and was hurrying to catch up with you. I've been hoping to see you."

"And I, you. Haven't you been back by Lugones'?"

"Yes, and thank you for the honey cakes, delicious."

76

We stood silent, looking at each other.

"How are you getting along?" I burst out, smiling, expressing in the question more affection than real desire to know how he was.

"Very well," he replied in a similar tone. And we smiled at each other again.

As soon as we had begun to talk I had lost the disturbing flashes of gaiety of a few moments before. I was calm again; and, certainly, filled with tenderness for Díaz Vélez. I think I had never looked at anyone with more affection than I did at him on that occasion.

"Were you waiting for the streetcar?"

"Yes," he nodded, looking at the time. As he lowered his head to look at his watch, I saw fleetingly that the tip of his nose touched the edge of his upper lip. Warm affection for Díaz swelled from my heart.

"Wouldn't you like to have some coffee? There's a marvelous sun . . . That is, if you've already eaten and are in no hurry. . . "

"Yes, no, no hurry," he answered distractedly, looking down the tracks into the distance.

We turned back. He didn't seem entirely delighted at the prospect of accompanying me. I wished he were happier and more subtle —especially more subtle. Nevertheless, my effusive tenderness for him so animated my voice that after three blocks Díaz began to change. Until then he had done nothing but pull at his right moustache with his left hand, nothing but not looking at me. From then on he began to gesticulate with both hands. By the time we reached Corrientes Street—I don't know what damned thing I had said to him—he smiled almost imperceptibly, focusing alternately on the moving toes of my shoes, and gave me a fleeting glance from the corner of his eye.

"Hum . . . now it begins," I thought. And my ideas, in perfect order until that moment, began to shift and crash into each other dizzily. I made an effort to pull myself together, and I suddenly remembered a lead cat sitting on a chair that I had seen when I was five years old. Why that cat? I whistled, and quickly stopped. Then I blew my nose and laughed secretly behind my handkerchief. As I had lowered my head, and the handkerchief was large, only my eyes could be seen. And then I peeked at Díaz Vélez, so sure he wouldn't see me that I had the overwhelming temptation to spit hastily into my hand three times and laugh out loud, just to do something crazy.

By now we were in *La Brasileña*. We sat down across from one another at a tiny little table, our knees almost touching. In the half-dark, the Nile-green color of the cafe gave such a strong impression of damp and sparkling freshness that one felt obliged to examine the walls to see if they were wet.

77

Díaz shifted in his chair towards the waiter, who was leaning against the counter with his towel over his crossed arms, and settled into a comfortable position.

We sat for a while without speaking, but the flies of excitement were constantly buzzing through my brain. Although I felt serious, a convulsive smile kept rising to my lips. When we had sat down I had bitten my lips trying to adopt a normal expression but this overwhelming tic kept breaking through. My ideas rushed headlong in an unending procession, piling onto one another with undreamed-of velocity; each idea represented an uncontrollable impulse to create ridiculous and, especially, unexpected situations; I had a mad desire to undertake each one, then stop suddenly and begin another; to poke my forked fingers in Díaz Vélez's eyes; to pull my hair and yell just for the hell of it; and all just to do something absurd—especially to Díaz Vélez. Two or three times I glanced at him and then dropped my eyes. My face must have been crimson because I could feel it burning.

All this occurred during the time it took the waiter to come with his little machine, serve the coffee and go away, first glancing absentmindedly into the street. Díaz was still out of sorts, which made me think that when I had stopped him on Charcas Street he had been thinking about something quite different from accompanying a madman like me. . .

That was it! I had just stumbled onto the reason for my uneasiness. Díaz Vélez, a damned and pursued madman, knew perfectly well that he was responsible for my recent behavior. "I'm sure that my friend," he must have said to himself, "will have the puerile notion of wanting to frighten me when next we see each other. If he happens to find me, he'll pretend to have sudden impulses, psychological manifestations, a persecution complex; he'll follow me down the street making faces, he will then take me somewhere to buy me a cup of coffee . . ."

"You are com-plete-ly wrong," I told him, putting my elbows on the table and resting my chin in my hands. I looked at him, smiling no doubt, but never taking my eyes off him.

Díaz seemed to be surprised that I had come out with this unexpected remark.

"What do you mean?"

"Nothing. Just this: you are com-plete-ly wrong!"

"But what the devil do you mean? It's possible that I'm wrong, I guess. . . Undoubtedly, it's very probable that I'm wrong!"

"It's not a question of whether you guess, or whether there's any doubt: what I'm saying is this—and I'm going to repeat it carefully so you'll be sure to understand—You-are-com-plete-ly-wrong!"

78

This time Díaz, jovially attentive, looked at me and then burst out laughing and glanced away.

"All right, let's agree on it!"

"You do well to agree, because that's the way it is," I persisted, my chin still in my hands.

"I think so, too," he laughed again.

But I was very sure the damned fellow knew exactly what I meant. The more I stared at him, the more dizzyingly the ideas were careening about in my head.

"Dí-az Vé-lez," I articulated slowly, not for an instant removing my eyes from his. Díaz, understanding that I wasn't addressing him, continued to look straight ahead.

"Dí-az Vé-lez," I repeated with the same incurious vagueness, as if a third, invisible, person sitting with us had intervened.

Díaz, pensive, seemed not to have heard. And suddenly he turned with a look of frankness; his hands were trembling slightly.

"Look," he said with a decided smile. "It would be good if we terminated this interview for today. You're acting badly and I'll end up doing the same. But first it would be helpful if we spoke to each other frankly, because if we don't we will *never* understand each other. To be brief: you and Lugones and everyone think I'm pursued, is that right or not?"

He continued to stare at me, still with the smile of a sincere friend who wants to eliminate forever any misunderstandings. I had expected many things, anything but this boldness. With these words Díaz placed all his cards on the table, and we sat face to face, observing each other's every gesture. He knew that *I knew* he wanted to play with me again, as he had the first night at Lugones', but nevertheless, he dared incite me.

Suddenly I became calm; it was no longer a matter of letting the flies of excitement race surreptitiously through my own brain and wait to see what would happen, but to still the swarm in my own mind in order to listen attentively to the buzzing in another's.

"Perhaps," I responded vaguely when he had completed his question.

"*You* thought I was pursued, didn't you?"

"I thought so."

"And that a certain story I told you at Lugones' about a mad friend of mine was to amuse myself at your expense?"

"Yes."

"Forgive me for continuing. Lugones told you something about me?"

"He did."

"That I was pursued?"

"Yes."

"And you believe, more than you did before, that I am, don't you?"

"Exactly."

Both of us burst out laughing, each looking away at the same instant. Díaz lifted his cup to his lips, but in the middle of the gesture noticed that it was empty, and set it down. His eyes were even more brilliant than usual, with dark circles beneath them—not like those of a man, but large and purplish like a woman's.

"All right, all right," he shook his head cordially. "It's difficult *not* to believe it, it's possible, just as possible as what I'm going to tell you. Listen carefully: I may or I may not be pursued; but what is certain is that your eagerness that I see that *you* are too will have this result: in your desire to study me, you will make me truly pursued, and then I will occupy myself in making faces at *you* when you're not looking, as you did to me for six blocks only a half hour ago . . . which certainly is true. And there is another possible consequence: we understand each other very well; you know that I—an *intelligent* and truly pursued person—am capable of feigning a miraculous normality; and I know that you—in the larval stage of persecution—are capable of simulating perfect fear. Do you agree?"

"Yes, it's possible there's something in that."

"Something? No, everything!"

We laughed again, each immediately looking away. I put my elbows on the table and my chin in my hands, as I had a while before.

"And if I truly believe that you are following me?"

I saw those two brilliant eyes fixed on mine.

In the exchange of our glances there was nothing but the perverse question that had betrayed him, the brief suspension of his shrewdness. Did he mean to ask me that? No; but his madness was so far advanced that he could not resist the temptation. He smiled as he asked his subtle question, but the madman, the real madman, had escaped and was peering at me from behind his eyes.

I shrugged my shoulders carelessly, and like someone who casually places his hand on the table when he is going to shift his position, I surreptitiously picked up the sugar bowl. But the moment I did it, I felt ashamed and put it down. Díaz watched it all without flickering an eyelid.

"Just the same, you were afraid," he smiled.

"No," I replied happily, drawing my chair a little closer. "It was

80

an act, one that any good friend might put on—any friend with whom one has an *understanding*."

I knew that *he* wasn't putting on an act, and that behind the intelligent eyes directing the subtle games still crouched the mad assassin, like a dark beast seeking shelter that sends out decoy cubs on reconnaissance. Little by little the beast was withdrawing, and sanity began to shine in his eyes. Once again he became master of himself, he ran his hand over his shining hair, and laughing for the last time he stood up.

It was already two o'clock. We walked towards Charcas talking about various things, in mutual tacit agreement to limit the conversation to ordinary things—the sort of brief, casual dialogue a married couple maintains on the streetcar.

As is always true in these circumstances, once we stopped neither of us spoke for a moment, and, also as always, the first thing we said had nothing to do with our farewell.

"This asphalt is in bad shape," I ventured, pointing with my chin.

"Yes, it never is any good," he replied in a similar tone. "When shall we see each other again?"

"Soon. Won't you be going by Lugones'?"

"Who knows. . . Tell me, where the devil do you live? I don't remember."

I gave him the address.

"Do you want to come by?"

"Some day . . . "

As we shook hands, we couldn't help exchanging a look, and we burst out laughing together for the hundredth time in two hours.

"Goodbye, be seeing you."

After a few feet, I walked very deliberately for a few paces and looked over my shoulder. Díaz had turned around, too. We exchanged a last salute, he with his left hand and I with my right, and then we both walked a little faster.

The madman, the damned madman! I could still see his look in the cafe. I'd seen it clearly. I'd seen the brutish and suspicious madman behind the actor who was arguing with me! So he'd seen me following him in the glass of the shop-windows! Once again I felt a deep need to provoke him, to make him see clearly that *he* was beginning now, he was losing confidence in me, that any day he was going to want to do to me what I was doing to him. . .

I was alone in my room. It was late and the house was sleeping; in the entire house there was not a sound to be heard. My sensation of isolation was so strong that unconsciously I raised my eyes and looked around. The incandescent gaslight coldly and peacefully illuminated the walls. I looked at the cone and ascertained that it was not burning with the usual small popping. Everything was deathly still.

It is well known that one has only to repeat a word aloud six or seven times for it to lose all meaning and for it to be converted into a new and absolutely incomprehensible utterance. That is what happened to me. I was alone, alone, alone. . . What does *alone* mean? And as I looked up I saw a man standing in the doorway looking at me.

I stopped breathing for an instant. I was familiar with the sensation and I knew that immediately the hair would rise at the back of my neck. I lowered my eyes, continuing my letter, but out of the corner of my eye I saw that the man had appeared again. I knew very well that it was nothing. But I couldn't help myself, and suddenly, I looked. That I looked meant I was lost.

And all of this was Díaz's work; he had got me overexcited about his stupid persecutions and now I was paying for it.

I pretended not to notice and continued writing, but the man was still there. From that instant, the lighted silence and the empty space behind me surged with the annihilating anguish of a man who is alone in an empty house, but doesn't feel alone. And it wasn't only this, *things* were standing behind me. I continued my letter, but the eyes were still in the doorway and the things were almost touching me. Gradually the profound terror I was trying to contain made my hair stand on end, and rising to my feet as naturally as one is capable in such circumstances I went to the door and opened it wide. But I know what it cost me to do it slowly.

I didn't pretend to return to my writing. Díaz Vélez! There was no other reason why my nerves should be like this. But I was completely certain, too, that an eye for an eye, and a tooth for a tooth, he was going to pay for all this evening's pleasures.

The door to the street was still open and I listened to the bustle of people leaving the theatre. "He could have attended one of them," I thought. "And since he has to take the Charcas streetcar, it's possible he passed by here. . . And if it's his idea to annoy me with his ridiculous games, pretending he already feels himself pursued and knowing that I'm beginning to believe he is. . . "

Someone knocked at the door.

He! I leaped back into my room and extinguished the lamp in a flash. I stood very still, holding my breath. My skin tingled painfully as I awaited a second knock.

He knocked again. And then after a while I heard his steps advancing across the patio. They stopped at my door and the intruder stood motionless before its darkness. Of course there was no one there. Then suddenly he called me. Damn him! He knew that I had heard him, that I had turned out the light when I heard, and that I was standing, not moving, by the table! He knew *precisely* what I was thinking, and that I was waiting, waiting, as in a nightmare, to hear my name called once again!

He called me a second time. Then, after a long pause:

"Horatio!"

Damnation! What did my name have to do with all this? What right did he have to call me Horatio, he who in spite of his tormenting wickedness would not come in because he was afraid! "He knows that this is what I am thinking at this instant, he is convinced of it, but the madness is upon him, and he won't come in!"

And he didn't. He stood an instant more before he moved away from the threshold and returned to the entrance hall. Rapidly, I left the table, tiptoed to the door and stuck out my head. "He knows I'm going to do this." Nevertheless, he continued at a tranquil pace and disappeared.

Considering what had just happened, I appreciated the superhuman effort the pursued one made in not turning around, knowing that behind his back I was devouring him with my eyes.

One week later I received this letter:

My dear X.

Because of a bad cold, I haven't been out for four days. If you are not afraid of the contagion, you would give me great pleasure by coming to chat with me for a while.

Yours very truly.
Lucas Díaz Vélez

P.S. If you see Lugones, tell him I have been sent something that will interest him very much.

I received the letter at two o'clock in the afternoon. As it was cold and I was planning to go for a walk, I hurried over to Lugones'.

"What are you doing here at this time of day?" he asked me. I didn't see him very frequently in the afternoon in those days.

"Nothing. Díaz Vélez sends you his regards."

"So it's still you and Díaz Vélez," he laughed.

"Yes, still. I just received a letter from him. It seems he hasn't been out of the house for four days."

It was evident to both of us that this was the beginning of the end, and in five minutes' speculation on the matter we had invented a million absurd things that could have happened to Díaz. But since I hadn't told Lugones about my hectic day with Díaz, his interest was soon exhausted and I left.

For the same reason, Lugones understood very little about my visit. It was unthinkable that I had gone to his house expressly to tell him that Díaz was offering him more honey cakes; and since I had left almost immediately, the man must have been thinking everything except what was really at the heart of the matter.

At eight o'clock I knocked at Vélez's door. I gave my name to the servant, and a few moments later an elderly lady obviously from the provinces appeared; her hair was smooth and she was wearing a black dressing gown with an interminable row of covered buttons.

"Do you want to see Lucas?" she asked, looking at me suspiciously.

"Yes, Ma'am."

"He is somewhat ill; I don't know whether he will be able to receive you."

I objected that nonetheless I had received a note from him. The old lady looked at me again.

"Please be good enough to wait a moment."

She returned and led me to my friend. Díaz was sitting up in bed with a jacket over his nightshirt. He introduced us to each other.

"My aunt. . . "

When she withdrew, I said, "I thought you lived alone."

"I used to, but she's been living here with me for the last two months. Bring up a chair."

The moment I saw him I was sure that what Lugones and I had conjectured was true: he absolutely did not have a cold.

"Bronchitis. . . ?"

"Yes, something like that. . . "

I took a quick look around. The room was like any other room with whitewashed walls. He too had incandescent gas. I looked with curiosity at the cone, but his whistled, whereas mine popped. As for the rest, a beautiful silence throughout the house.

When I looked back at him, he was watching me. It must have been at least five seconds that he had been watching me. Our glances locked, and a shiver sent its tentacles to the marrow of my bones. But he was completely mad now! The pursued one was living just behind Díaz's eyes. The only thing, absolutely the only thing in his eyes, was a murderous fixation.

"He's going to attack me," I agonized to myself. But the obstinacy suddenly disappeared and after a quick glance at the ceiling Díaz recovered his habitual expression. He looked at me, smiling, and then dropped his eyes.

"Why didn't you answer me the other evening in your room?"

"I don't know."

"Do you think I didn't come in because I was afraid?"

"Something like that."

"But do you think I'm not really ill?"

"No. . . Why?"

He raised his arm and let it fall lazily on the quilt.

"I was looking at you a little bit ago. . . "

"Let's forget it, shall we!"

"The madman had escaped from me, hadn't he?"

"Forget it, Díaz, forget it!"

I had a knot in my throat. His every word had the effect on me of one more push towards an imminent abyss.

If he continues, he'll explode! He won't be able to hold it back! And then I clearly realized that Lugones and I had been right. Díaz had taken to his bed because he was afraid! I looked at him and shuddered violently. There it was again! The assassin was once more staring through eyes now fixed on me. But as before, after a glance at the ceiling, the light of normalcy returned to them.

"One thing is certain, it's fiendishly quiet here," I said to myself.

A moment passed.

"Do you like the silence?"

"Absolutely."

"It's funereal. Suddenly you get the sensation that there are things concentrating too much on you. Let me give you an example."

"What do you mean?"

His eyes were shining with perverse intelligence as they had at other times.

"Well, suppose that you, like me, have been alone, in bed, for four days, and that you—I mean, I—haven't thought about you. Suppose you hear a voice clearly, not yours, not mine, a clear voice, anywhere behind the wardrobe, in the ceiling—here in this ceiling, for example —calling you, insult. . . "

He stopped: he was staring at the ceiling, his face completely altered by hatred, and then he shouted: "There are! There are!"

Shaken to my soul I instantly recalled his former glances; he heard the voice that insulted him from the ceiling, but I was the one who pursued him. No doubt he still possessed discernment enough not to link the two things together.

His face had been suffused with color. Now, by contrast, Díaz had become frightfully pale. Finally, with an effort, he turned away from the ceiling and lay quietly for a moment, his expression vague and his breathing agitated.

I could not remain there any longer. I glanced at the night table and saw the half-open drawer.

"As soon as I stand up," I thought with anguish, "he's going to shoot me dead." But in spite of everything, I rose and approached him to say goodbye. Díaz, with a sudden start, turned towards me. In the time it took me to reach his side, his breathing stopped and his fascinated eyes took on the expression of a cornered animal watching the sights of a shotgun drawing near.

"I hope you feel better, Díaz. . . "

I did not dare hold out my hand; but reason is as violent as madness and it is extremely painful to lose it. Díaz came to his senses and extended *his* hand.

"Come tomorrow, I'm not well today."

"I'm afraid I. . . "

"No, no, come. Come!" he concluded with imperious anguish.

I left without seeing anyone, feeling, as I found myself free and remembering with horror that extremely intelligent man battling with the ceiling, that I was cured forever of psychological games.

The following day, at eight o'clock in the evening, a boy delivered this note to me:

Sir:

Lucas insists on seeing you. If it wouldn't be a bother I would appreciate your stopping by here today.

Hoping to hear from you,
Desolinda S. de Roldán

I had had a disturbing day. I couldn't think about Díaz that I didn't see him shouting again during that horrible loss of conscious reason. His nerves were strung so tight that a sudden blast from a train whistle would have shattered them.

I went, nevertheless, but as I walked along I found I was painfully shaken by the least noise. So when I turned the corner and saw a group in front of Díaz Vélez's door, my legs grew weak—not from any concrete fear, but from coincidences, from things foreseen, from cataclysms of logic.

I heard a murmur of fear.

"He's coming, he's coming!" And everyone scattered into the middle of the street. "There it is, he's mad," I said to myself, grieved by what might have happened. I ran, and in a moment I stood before the door.

Díaz lived on Arenales Street between Bulnes and Vidt. The

house had an extensive interior patio overflowing with plants. As there was no light in the patio, as contrasted with the entryway, the patio beyond lay in deep shadow.

"What's going on?" I asked. Several persons replied.

"The boy who lives here is crazy."

"He's wandering around the patio. . . "

"He's naked. . . "

"He keeps running out. . . "

I was anxious to know about his aunt.

"There she is."

I turned, and there against the window was the poor lady, sobbing. When she saw me she redoubled her weeping.

"Lucas. . . ! He's gone mad!"

"When?"

"Just a while ago. . . He came running out of his room . . . shortly after I had sent you. . . "

I felt someone was speaking to me.

"Listen, listen!"

From the black depths of the patio we heard a pitiful cry.

"He yells like that every few minutes. . . "

"Here he comes, here he comes!" everyone shouted, fleeing. I didn't have time or strength to run away. I felt a muffled, precipitous rush, and Díaz Vélez, livid, completely nude, his eyes bulging out of his head, rushed into the entrance hall, carried me along in front of him, made a ridiculous grimace in the doorway, and ran back into the patio.

"Get out of there, he'll kill you," they yelled at me. "He shot at a chair today."

Everyone had clustered around the door again, peering into the shadows.

"Listen. . . again."

Now it was a cry of agony that emerged from the depths. "Water. . . ! Water. . . !"

"He's asked for water two times."

The two officers who had just arrived had decided to post themselves on either side of the entrance hall at the rear, and seize Díaz the next time he rushed into the hall. The wait was even more agonizing this time. But soon the cry was repeated, and following it, the scattering of the crowd.

"Here he comes!"

Díaz rushed out, violently hurled an empty vase into the street, and an instant later was subdued. He defended himself fiercely, but

87

when he saw it was hopeless to resist, he stopped struggling, astonished and panting, and looked from person to person with surprise. He did not recognize me, nor did I delay there any longer.

The following morning I went to have lunch with Lugones and told him the whole story. This time we were very serious.

"What a shame; he was very intelligent."

"Too intelligent," I confirmed, remembering.

All this was June, 1903.

"Let's do something," Lugones said to me. "Why don't we go to Misiones? That will give us something to do."

We went and four months later we returned, Lugones with a full beard and I with a ruined stomach.

Díaz was in an Institution. Since the crisis, which had lasted two days, there had been no further incidents. When I went to visit him he received me effusively.

"I thought I'd never see you again. Have you been away?"

"Yes, for a while. Getting along all right?"

"Just fine. I hope to be completely well before the end of the year." I couldn't help looking at him.

"Yes," he smiled. "Although I feel fine, I think it's prudent to wait a few months. But deep down, since that night, nothing has happened."

"Do you remember. . . ?"

"No, but they told me about it. I must have been quite a sight, naked."

We entertained ourselves a while longer.

"Look," he said seriously, "I'm going to ask you a favor: come see me often. You don't know how these gentlemen bore me with their innocent questions and their snares. All they succeed in doing is making me bitter, eliciting ideas from me that I don't like to remember. I'm sure that in the company of someone a little more intelligent I will be wholly cured."

I solemnly promised him to do it, and for two months I returned frequently, never denouncing the least fault, sometimes even touching on our old relationship.

One day I found an intern with him. Díaz winked lightly and gravely introduced me to his guardian. The three of us chatted like judicious friends. Nevertheless, I noted in Díaz Vélez—with some pleasure, I admit—a certain fiendish irony in everything he was saying to his doctor. He adroitly directed the conversation to the patients, and soon placed his own case before us.

"But you are different," objected the doctor. "You're cured."

"Not really, if you consider that I still have to be here."

"A simple precaution . . . you understand that yourself."

"But what's the reason for it? Don't you think it will be impossible, absolutely impossible, ever to know when I'm sane—with no need for 'precaution,' as you say. I can't be, I believe, more sane than I am now."

"Not as far as I can see," the doctor laughed happily.

Díaz gave me another imperceptible wink.

"It seems to me that one cannot have any greater conscious sanity than this—permit me: You both know, as I do, that I have been pursued, that one night I had a crisis, that I have been here six months, and that *any* amount of time is short for an absolute guarantee that the thing won't return. Fine. This 'precaution' would be sensible if I didn't see all this clearly and discuss it intelligently. . . I know that at this moment you are recalling cases of lucid madness and are comparing me to that madman in La Plata. The one who in bad moments quite naturally made fun of a broom he thought was his wife, but when completely himself, and laughing, still kept his eyes on the broom, so that no one would touch it. . . I know, too, that this objective perspicacity in following the doctor's opinion while recounting a similar case to one's own is itself madness . . . and the very astuteness of the analysis only confirms it. . . But . . . even so—in what manner, in what other way, may a sane man defend himself?"

"There is no other way, absolutely none," the intern who was being interrogated burst out laughing. Díaz glanced at me out of the corner of his eye and shrugged his shoulders, smiling.

I had a strong desire to know what the doctor thought about this super-lucidity. At a different time I would have valued such lucidity even at the cost of disordering my own nerves. I glanced at the doctor, but the man didn't seem to have felt its influence. A moment later we left.

"Do you think. . . " I asked him.

"Hum! I think so . . . " he replied, looking sideways at the patio. Abruptly, he turned his head.

"Look, look!" he told me, pressing my arm.

Díaz, pale, his eyes dilated with terror and hatred, was cautiously approaching the door, as he had surely done every time I came— *looking at me!*

"Ah! You hoodlum!" he yelled at me, raising his fist. "I've been watching you come for two months now!"

Tomas Tranströmer

THE SCATTERED CONGREGATION

1

We got ready and showed our home.
The visitors thought: You live well.
The slum must be inside you.

2

Inside the church, pillars and vaulting
white as plaster, like the cast
around the broken arm of faith.

3

Inside the church there's a begging bowl
that slowly lifts from the floor
and floats along the pews.

4

But the church bells have gone underground.
They're hanging in the drainage pipes.
Whenever we take a step, they ring.

5

Nicodemus the sleepwalker is on his way
to the Address. Who's got the Address?
Don't know. But that's where we're going.

Isabel Fraire

NOON

In order to see
    one is infinitely revealed
and in this revelation
    the image is lost

the mirror-face before the mirror

       *   *   *

we have separated day into two halves of an orange
one part for no one and the other for no one
and we are in the center, motionless,
    cleansed by the sun

       *   *   *

no one is shadow
    no one is mirror
        the sun's dust scatters
           attracted to everything

       *   *   *

in the center of day
    I am transformed into nothing
objects stir before my eyes
        filled with their own presence
purified by light
        full of themselves

       *   *   *

above the trees
    the air—full of light

in the shadows each thing in its place
blade after blade of grass
ridge after ridge of bark

91

Claude Esteban

Glance

that the morning invades
to injure.

Whiteness too close
to the eyes.
                    Open tongs.

To erect
the dismantlement of all power
in the heart.

Claude Esteban

No one yet against the sky
with his black spade.

The earth pitted
with screams.
                    Unchanged.

Only the tree walked against the sky
enduring.

Claude Esteban

With each stone

in the cold glare
of the day

the earth reveals, naked, each disaster.

All was dark. The turf
of the days

rotted long against the vast

immobile wall.

                    Order
born of order. The sun
gave dead objects
their shape.

The assault, later. The long gap.

Translator Jože Lazar

Niko Grafenauer

SILENCE

The word silence has settled into silence like a stone.
The world wavers in the brown fog, quietly the roads have closed.
Time arises in the thoughts of the living like a wall.
Spring will come full of serpent's spittle and traces of moisture.

A late rain colors the landscape with a grey weight.
Everything silent pierces me quietly like a sword.
The earth on which I stand rises toward me like a woman.
Thin light outlines objects in the dead eye.

I run around inside a mousetrap, dust curls like a sneer.
There is no shelter to swallow me like a black blaze.
Steep immobility on the horizon eclipses the world.
The word silence has settled into silence like a stone.

Translator YVONNE L. SANDSTROEM

Lars Gustafsson

LINES FOR THE COUNT OF VENOSA

We leave Robinson here

He was nothing but a character in an adventure story
That everyone has read before.

In November 1971 it was windy (as usual)
A terrible storm, the planes couldn't land

I sat until late at night
With some people in Gothenburg

And understood that they didn't understand me (as usual),
Fetching up in Lund the next afternoon

I almost said Holy Lund,
For the wind suddenly stopped blowing.

Professor Ehrenswärd was sitting
Behind a very small desk

During our conversation he sucked a milk carton
As if it were a mother's nipple

And he told me about the world of the future,
About the sailing ships, the hordes of cyclists

Going out to the fields at dawn,
The charcoal kilns, the little inns

Along the rained-out roads, the sects
The trains of flagellants, seafarers on the long voyage

To America, the madrigal singing and the reed flutes
In the wide sweep of gardens in April,

The earth proletarians behind their plows,
And high up, floating slowly

On the moonlit side of the clouds, the voyagers
In their hot-air balloons.

Yes

Beauty is the only thing that lasts.

And I thought of the stones, the stones pure and simple,

Because they live so slowly
That they don't even discover our existence.

(Certain quartzes, Caillois tells us,
Contain some trapped water
Older than all the seas in our world
And it swishes around in the stone's darkness
Like a very small, very clean sea.)

Yes

Beauty is the only thing that lasts

No bloody matter how you misuse your life
You'll still find the way home to yourself

Although of course it isn't the home
You left, far away

Mahler & Bruckner wrote enormous slow symphonies
To convince us that death isn't so bad after all,

Like the Swedes in the nineteen seventies
They lived in a technologically advanced monarchy

Which no longer believed in itself
Where the postal system already functioned irregularly

Mahler & Bruckner is a congenial firm,
The immensely slow adagio which closes

Mahler's Ninth Symphony ought to get an award
Just like penicillin or polio vaccine.

Together with Mahler & Bruckner,
Both of them wearing soulful little eyeglass frames

Stubbornly swaddled in their lap robes against the evening chill
I went by jeep to an unusually nice place,

The monastery of St. Catherine in the Sinai desert,
An unreal place between red mountains

With admittedly minor parking problems.

Together we viewed the Codex Sinaiticus,
The first handwritten manuscript in a Slavic tongue,

Demonstrating that Bishop Cyrillus of Ohrid
Wasn't so stupid after all

As those Byzantine louts had always claimed

And then the guide insisted on showing us the ossuary
Mahler with Guide Bleu, & Bruckner with a cigar

Were amazed that the bones of bishops are always kept together
While all other bones are sorted according to kind

As in wholesaler Whitman:

"Wrists and wrist-joints, hand, palm, knuckles, thumb, fore-
        finger, finger-joints, finger-nails"

Neatly as in a spare parts warehouse
Every damn finger joint there was in St. Catherine's

Nicely sorted and logged by those Bedouins
Who were slaves in the monastery during the early Middle Ages

It's just like at home in the Cathedral of St. Stephen
Mahler said, as we came out, putting on his sunglasses,

(You don't fool with the light in the Sinai with impunity)

(A kind of immense primeval light over naked mountains
And a man riding becomes immense,
In his dark cloak, a single man
Can fill a square mile with solemn presence)

It's because the bishops have to *pull themselves together*
First on the Last Day, Bruckner said,

They must get on their legs quickly to take command,
Mahler suggested, like some kind of reserve lieutenants,

"I beat and pound for the dead," said Mahler,
"I blow through my embouchures my loudest and gayest for them"

Yes

The wind stopped blowing over Holy Lund
And the guardrails on the turnpike were down for long stretches

As if a bad child had been playing with them
An express train took me to Karlstad

Where an old Lap woman and a swell football player
Were going to read from their memoirs and I from mine

(When the last decade was still young
Jack Kerouac went first class across the Atlantic
In the dining room, the second day, he met
A little psychiatrist in gold-frame glasses and silver tie
Who wanted to unravel his neuroses
"Neuroses," Kerouac said, "inhibitions!"
"OK, now we'll see who's inhibited, you or me,
I'll count to three and then we'll drop our pants!")

The acoustics reminded me of the Sture Bath
And the next day the press considered that people from Värmland
Generally are better writers
And that Gustafsson, above all, is unnecessarily *learned*

And in the midst of confusion I saw, in the second row,

The beautiful young Donna Maria d'Avalos
With her red-gold hair, her wonderful lips

Her hairnet worked with pearls, oh ye gods!

97

Afterward I found her in the bar of the City Hotel
Talking to a communist professor

Who was detailing the latest dollar crisis
And squabbling with a liberal councilman

At the next table. This gave me a chance.

Donna Maria, I said,
And she presented me with her prettiest smile.

And your husband, the Count. . .
(I bit my tongue because I remembered a thing or two.)

The Count, oh yes, the Count, she answered impassively:

Yes he writes the most beautiful masses and madrigals. . .

Yes

Beauty is the only thing that lasts

Mahler & Bruckner. Delicatessen.

A very small sea, completely dark
Trapped in age-old quartz.
Water that's never been in touch with water.
Wet before any dew had fallen
Over the sterile desert mountains of our planet.

I came home one night around nine.
New snow had fallen. Already by the fence

My dog nipped my trouser cuffs, jumping about
In the snow. It's nice to feel loved.

Translators JOHN GETSI AND LUCIA GETSI

Serge Meurant

in nameless signs
you seek
the weight
of bitter genesis

pure resonance

Serge Meurant

Sometimes form explodes
with the violence of typhoons:
in its centre a calm eye

sometimes night lays there
the terrible egg, without seam
which vibrates tenderly
in my voice

an impalpable wound
of hard light
worms
into the groove of breathing

always I am pierced
bored through
by the wind of mourning

Reynaldo Pérez Só

FROM *TO DIE OF ANOTHER DREAM*

Do you think of the months of rain?

will there be a time
when one can laugh
with no remorse?

I loved
and what's left?

    *   *   *

I know I'm the cause
                of some trouble

they find nothing
but this being that keeps quiet
and knows nothing
            like the wind.

    *   *   *

I don't care about myself
because I'm not
an important fact

like my father
or
like my mother
they were different
or the piece of land
behind the house

that was more important

    *   *   *

I ought to believe
in god
that's why I'm scared
of racing on this side of the river

at times I hear the whisper
of his coarse voice
and the fire whistling
for the dawn

or
I feel small
and walk

he is in front of me
looking at me

　　　*　*　*

this is a chair
only a chair
in it
my father sat
my brothers
all
my best friends

now
it's alone
with nobody

a chair

　　　*　*　*

we who dream
feel the handsomest dream

we die early
because we are not dreams
or birds
and air weighs nothing

yet with all that
we come back each night

to die of another dream.

      *   *   *

an image of rain
falls
and suddenly the birds
soar

from the grass
they cause no wind
I hear music.

(the birds fly)

in the open
field
I look

alone

and the very image
of the rain
carries me off.

Ida Vitale

ANSWER OF THE DERVISH

Perhaps
wisdom consists
of retreating
when something vibrates with our rhythm
(for the horrid spider
falls upon its victim)
to perceive
        the distant reality
reflected like a star.

Thus
     the situation
blossoms before our eyes
            —or loses
one by one
        its petals—
as a strange species
seen for the first time.
Under our sad verdict,
          futile darnings
which repair nothing,
the insignificant sketch of our gesture,
a dubious amulet
against
the migration of certainties.

Luis Suardíaz

QUESTIONS AND ANSWERS

I

Immersed in the very instant of acting,
we would not know how to gestate the slow-moving future.
Man exists for the tomorrow that is not his.

The past is inside us, although it lessens us;
it takes a direction contrary to our powers.
It has formed us. It's a mirror in which we are unable
to see ourselves as we are, as we were. A mirror filled with smoke.
And that was our life.

II

We know that eventually our powers will fail
in this chaotic universe that no one created, that will never
be finished.
Meanwhile, we return, from time to time, to our *work*,
that other world. One book of ours will stir up the dust
that we will not even be. That's glory, immortality. . .

Who knows what his true work is. Man is mortal.
His glory is knowing he is immortal, in the man to come,
kindling a great blaze with his heart, so that
                    nothing's lacking
for his extraordinary successor, that unknown one.

III

And the shudder of living?
And the constant pain that brims in the eyes of an ox
or a threatened dog?
But that's another question. Let's eat breakfast,
                    shave. And keep moving
for tomorrow's another day.

R. D. Gregory

LULLABY

night:
city empty
darkness thinned by a tincture of light
delicate
as the eye of a hummingbird
lying there on your palm
stray lights in the buildings vanish
the eye holds their light for an instant
city a black leather jacket
tossed on the dining room table
near the white jug that holds dried stalks
of cattail, maidenhair, chicory . . .
the room now filled, like an hourglass
with darkness, the darkness
of empty sockets
but the mind refuses to rest
is frantic inside the skull
the tips
of its delicate wings
on the cool thick surface

Yannis Goumas

ON THE TIP OF THE TONGUE

the other side of the voice
seeks the word at its source
traveling deep in this desire—

dying a slow death
because of its strong will
to live

Translators ANN MCBRIDE
AND MARY MCBRIDE

Juan Sánchez Peláez

FROM *THE FLEEING AND THE PERMANENT*

They ignore me
the fleeing and the permanent
Two bodies join and dawn is the leopard
My broken grief
Leaps to the face of the jester;
If you come in or go out
The echo disturbs
A dense halo;
If you think,
the storm calls out in several directions;
If you look,
The morning star trembles;
If I live,
I live in memory.
My legs empty into an alley without light
I speak to the one I was, already on my
way back.
I alone stroke myself
with the opposite side
of fiery branches.
Through you, my absent one,
I hear the sea at five
paces from my heart,
And the flesh is my heart
whom my long ago resembles.
If you come in or go out,
The trust of love returns to love.
Tell me
If I wrest a rainbow
from the years;
Tell me if maturity is vain fruit;
The woman shakes a sack in the rarefied air
Goes down to the sand and runs in the ocean;

At daybreak,
For you,
my absent one,
The chrysalis in rose form
A rose of pure water is darkness.

Translator ROBIN FULTON

Göran Sonnevi

GROUND

Almost nothing—

Wariness.
Its resonance.

Also questions are possible.

Göran Sonnevi

CLEARNESS

As in a clear water
the stone sinks
deeper and deeper

I can ask here
what water?
what stone?
and here is the dissolving, the vanishing.

There remain
clarity, sinking, depth.

THERE'S A MAN IN THE HABIT OF STRIKING ME ON THE HEAD WITH AN UMBRELLA

FERNANDO SORRENTINO

tr. NORMAN THOMAS DI GIOVANNI
AND PATRICIA DAVIDSON CRAN

There's a man in the habit of striking me on the head with an umbrella. It is exactly five years to the day since he began striking me on the head with his umbrella. At first I couldn't stand it; now I've grown accustomed to it.

I don't know his name. I know he's an ordinary man, with a plain suit, graying at the temples, and a vague face. I met him one sultry morning five years ago. I was sitting peacefully on a bench in Palermo Park, reading the newspaper in the shade of a tree. All of a sudden I felt something touch my head. It was this same man who now, as I write, automatically and impassively keeps striking me blows with his umbrella.

That first time I turned around full of indignation (I become terribly annoyed when I'm bothered while reading the paper); he went right on, calmly hitting me. I asked him if he were mad. He seemed not to hear me. I then threatened to call a policeman. Completely unruffled, he went on with what he was doing. After a few moments of hesitation—and seeing he was not about to back down— I stood up and gave him a terrific punch in the face. No doubt he is a weak man; I know that despite the force generated by my rage I do not hit all that hard. Still, breathing a tiny moan, the man fell to the ground. At once, making what seemed to be a great effort, he got up and again began hitting me over the head with the umbrella. His nose was bleeding, and I don't know why but at that moment I felt sorry for him, and my conscience troubled me for having struck him that way. Because, after all, the man was not hitting me very hard; he was really striking me quite soft and completely painless blows. Of course, such blows are terribly annoying. Everyone knows that when a fly settles on a person's forehead a person feels no pain; he feels annoyed. Well, that umbrella was a huge fly which, at regular intervals, kept settling on my head. Or, to be more precise, a fly the size of a bat.

At any rate, I could not stand that bat. Convinced that I was in the presence of a lunatic, I tried to get away. But the man followed me, in silence, without once letting up his blows. At this juncture, I began running (I may as well point out right here that there are few people as fast as I am). He set out after me, trying without luck to get in a whack or two. The man was gasping, gasping, gasping, and panting so hard I thought if I kept him running like that my tormentor might sink dead on the spot.

For that reason I slowed to a walk. I looked at him. His face displayed neither gratitude nor reproach. He just kept hitting me over the head with his umbrella. I thought of making my way to the police station and saying, "Officer, this man is hitting me over the head with an umbrella." It would be a case without precedent. The policeman would stare at me suspiciously, he would ask for my papers, he would begin questioning me with embarrassing questions, he would probably end up placing me under arrest.

I thought it better to go home. I got onto the Number 67 bus. Not once letting up with his umbrella, the man got on behind me. I took the first seat. He stationed himself beside me, holding on to the strap with his left hand while with his right he kept swinging at me with his umbrella, implacable. The passengers began to exchange shy smiles. The driver was watching us in his mirror. Little by little, a fit of laughter, a growing convulsion, seized all the other riders. I was on fire with shame. My persecutor, completely unaffected by the uproar, went on striking me.

I got off—we got off—at the Puente Pacífico. We continued on down Santa Fe Avenue. Everyone foolishly turned around to stare at us. I felt like saying to them, "What are you staring at, you idiots? Haven't you ever seen anyone whacking a man on the head with an umbrella before?" But it also occurred to me that they probably hadn't.

Five or six kids began to follow us, shouting like a pack of wild Indians.

But I had a plan. Arriving home, I tried slamming the door in his face. I didn't manage it. With a firm hand—anticipating me—he grabbed the handle, there was a momentary struggle, and he entered with me.

From that time on, he has continued striking me on the head with the umbrella. As far as I know, he has never slept or had a bite to eat. All he does is hit me. He accompanies me in all my acts—even the most intimate ones. I remember, in the beginning, that the blows kept me from sleeping; I now believe it would be impossible to sleep without them.

Nevertheless, our relations have not always been good. Countless times, in all possible tones, I have asked him for an explanation. It's never been any use; in his quiet way he has gone on whacking me over the head with the umbrella. On several occasions, I have dealt him punches, kicks, and—God help me!—even umbrella blows. He took these things meekly, as though they were all in a day's work. And this is exactly what is scariest about him: his quiet determination, his absence of hatred. In short, his inner conviction of carrying out a secret and superior mission.

Despite his apparent lack of physiological needs, I know when I strike him he feels the pain, I know he's weak, I know he's mortal. I also know a single shot would free me of him. What I don't know is whether when we're both dead he will go on striking me on the head with his umbrella. Neither do I know whether the shot ought to be aimed at him or at me. In any case, this reasoning is pointless. I know full well I wouldn't dare kill either him or myself.

On the other hand, it has recently occurred to me that I could not live without his blows. More and more frequently now I have a horrible premonition. I am distressed—deeply distressed—to think that perhaps when I most need him, this man will go away and I will no longer feel those soft blows of his umbrella which help me sleep so soundly.

110

Harry Martinson

CREATION NIGHT

We met on the stone bridge,
the birches stood watch for us,
the river gleaming like an eel wound toward the sea.
We twisted together in order to create God,
there was a rustling in the grain,
and a wave shot out of the rye.

Harry Martinson

OLD FARMHOUSE

The frail blossoms of the goat chevril
are the last curtains this house will ever have.
The roof back broken has dropped into the walls.
The path is just grass where no one arrives.
But the juniper bush and the stone have moved closer.
In a hundred years they will marry.

Harry Martinson

MARCH EVENING

Nearly dark, winterspring, thawing.
Boys have put a candle inside a snowball house.
For the man rattling by in the evening train
it is a red memory surrounded by gray time,
calling, calling out the twiggy woods just coming awake.
And that man never got home to his house,
his life is still back there in the candle.

Translator YVONNE L. SANDSTROEM

Harry Martinson

THE BUTTERFLY

Born to be a butterfly
my cool flame flutters
on the heavy velvet of the grass.
The children chase me. The sun goes down behind the tufts of grass,
                    the mallows,
saving me to night.
The moon rises; it's far, I'm not afraid,
I listen to its beams.
My eyes get membranes for protection.
My wings are stuck together with dew.
I sit on the nettle.

Lucia Ungaro de Fox

NECROPOLIS AND PERSPECTIVES

The wilderness levels
and the folds of your cerebrum
endlessly cross the extensions of Chan Chan.
More and more, in the mud shrines
the geometrical patterns of duck
and fish
splinter off in the rubble.
And so in your dreams the well-loved
symbols keep falling away.
I see you there, seated,
weighing failure and death
like a latter-day augur of ruins
and punishment.
But plagues are bloodier now,
and your wish, too feeble
to shore up your faltering prayers.
We talk on and on, while the wind
hacks at your dearest
convictions of living and working, like something possessed.
I watch the slant stain
of your lack-love approaching
in the miserable curve of the waves.
I think: here, as always where the dead in their tumuli
die out of memory, the disinfected morgue of yourself
cuts out a stupefied trail,
casual, wandering, lost;
and you search for yourself
in every poor devil
that comes to you nameless and shapeless.
Pathologist of modern contagion,
what odd fate has buried you alive
in this pre-Columbian silence of echoes,
wasted away, but surviving?

Carol Adler

it is the pure shape
the stone prism
water
clarified by wood

the pure shape of meeting
the small separations and the change
the leaving behind and
the falling apart

the pure shape of pain
a child's wonder
when he first discovers the dawn
that makes division permanent

terror is a short-lived nightmare
until it is real

and then there is an equalization

there are different degrees of terror
different bits of glass in the eye's cathedral

too little to reach
and tall enough to want
that

is the paradox

the space between bars is
intentional it

holds up other columns

Feriha Aktan

Come, when you can,
Drag the winds after you,
Borrow the stars for your brain,
Come, just
When you can.

I know the hooker that sleeps
In you;
Yet, dowse some storm from the clouds;
Just be here,
Near the dawn.

Flowers blush red, they say, in the spring,
I heard,
Bad dreams are nibbled;
Still,
Come,
Tell me about it,
As you can.
Bring a kind of laughter
To my brain.

Robert Bringhurst

PORTRAIT IN BLOOD

Dance draws the blood to focus
through the muscle of the dancer, through
the watcher's eye, dance draws
the nerve to focus and the mind through the nerve
to the eye, to the blood
of the dancer, the watcher,
the dance of the dancers
echoing beyond them, echo into song, as of
song into singing. . .

    the dance that is sculpture
    of the form of man in time,
    the dance that is portraiture
    in motion, in time,

    the dance that is joy
    of the body in motion,
    rhythm written in the body
    and the body in motion,

    the dance that is motion
    made order, the dance
    that is order made motion
    in space and in time,

    the dance that is order
    in time, creating place, creating
    order in the interface
    of motion, space and time

The dance draws time
and space to focus, which is place, and place is
order gone beyond the place
of order. Order echoes, order
eddies back, or boomerangs,
entering into the ear, the eye,
the nerve, the blood, the red bone, drawing
the body into dance, the mind into the dance,

dance into other dance, echo into new
re-echo, gesture into gesture, as of
song into song, creating
echoes between them,
intertwining tempo, texture,
posture, intermixture
of melody, of deep and shallow
shoalwater currents, waves,
combers, breakers, tides, tides running
full, hurtling, climbing, swirling, tides that mash the moorings
under the stage, topple the seats, scatter the dancers, drive
the mind into the dead end of the tooth, the torn nail

      listen at the stillness,
      listen for the sound

of the grace that will be thunder
that will run the grace aground and under
it all the accidental
order of unordered
space and time,
the opportunity to dance
from time to time,
sometimes with patience and with pleasure
and sometimes with adventure
and sometimes in terror, going
faster and faster. . .

      the dance that is sculpture
      of the form of man in time,
      the dance that is portraiture
      in motion, in time,

      the dance that is joy
      of the body in motion,
      rhythm written in the body
      and the body in motion,

      the dance that is motion
      made order, the dance
      that is order made motion
      in space and in time,

the dance that is order
in time, creating place, creating
order in the interface
of motion, space and time.

Translator: Lilvia Duggan

Pedro Lastra

NOSTRADAMUS

The future is not what will come
(of that we know more than he himself believes)
the future is the absence
that you and I will be
the absence that we are already
this emptiness
that right now,
stubbornly,
inhabits us.

BRIEF ACCOUNT

and then they begin to enter your night
and they glare at you
and your dream is now their aquarium
an unlikely medium for such a terrestrial being
and there is no time nor space for other portents.

Translator NICOMEDES SUAREZ

Carmen Naranjo

LISTEN

Listen:
they say it began as a clear point
that grew into lightning,
raping space.
It flashed through the darkness
and slowly began to collapse
like a withering flower's
tangled plumage.
They say that a fisherman
cast a net of luminous knots
and in the hollow funnels of the sea
wings were born to fly above the vertigo.
They say that the roads sang
with the harmony of purring waves
and knives of fire
were in every stroke of the wings.
They say that it rained, always rained
cold mornings, cracked walls concealing roses,
seeds, stars.
And they say that the earth arrived,
and with the earth, the sea.
I bring centuries on my back,
voiceless songs still heard in the mountains,
impulses my modesty conceals,
fears that scandalize
my civilized gestures.
I come from a yesterday of centuries
like the earth and the sea,
my appetites are white-haired and withered,
and before the entire mystery of my beginnings,
I can only sleepwalk
with rigid steps.
Listen:
something takes place before you,
a new birth,
that fills me with tenderness
like dusk growing in the earth and the sea.

IN THE HEART OF THE HEART OF ANOTHER COUNTRY

ETEL ADNAN

PLACE

So I have sailed the seas and come . . .
                    to B . . .
a town by the sea, in Lebanon. It is seventeen years later. My absence
has been an exile from an exile. I'm of those people who are
always doing what somebody else is doing . . . but a few weeks
earlier. A fish in a warm sea. No house for shelter, but a bed, from
house to house, and clothes crumpled on a single shelf. I am
searching for love.

MY HOUSE

I should say my side of the bed. Half a bed makes a big house at
night. My dreams have the power to extend space and make me live
in the greatest mansions. During the day it doesn't matter. There are
many streets, a few remaining sidewalks, and, yes, the cafe
"Express", in which I move, hunted by memories.

POLITICS

Oh, it's too much, too much. Once I dreamed of becoming the new
Ibn Khaldoun of America or the de Tocqueville of the Arabs. Now I
work for a newspaper and cover the most menial things. So I don't
understand how it is that there are kings without kingdoms and
Palestinians without a Palestine. As for the different scandals, they do
not matter to me. Why should I care that some thieves steal from
other thieves. Should I?

PEOPLE

The Lebanese go on two feet, like the Chinese for example; sometimes,
on four, to pick up a dime under the table. Their country is small, their
desires too, and their love affairs. Only their cars are big. Detroit made
Chevies and Buicks. All the unsold Buicks of America are on our roads.
So, in this country, you only see the heads of the people. Their
bodies are carefully washed and stored away. As for the women,
there aren't any. They all consider themselves as being the other half
of their men. With one exception.

120

EDUCATION

Everybody speaks Arabic, French, English, Armenian, Greek and
Kurdish. Sometimes one language at a time, sometimes all of them
together. And even the children are financiers.

PEOPLE

This is the cruellest place. A man in a motor boat hit a swimmer and
sped away. The skull was broken. A large space of blood covered
the sea. Painters rushed to the scene to make a painting for sale. A
girl was killed by her brother because she smiled to her lover. A
house in the city was set on fire because they wanted the tenants
out. A rebellion has started, the rebellion of the rich
against the poor. Yes, to make sure that the latter do not multiply,
and rather be dead, the sooner the better.

PLACE

My place is at the center of things. I am writing from within the
nucleus of an atom. Blood beating under my ears. Some dry heat
radiating from my nerves. A pressure trying to push my eyes
ahead of me; they want to travel on their own. My place: highways,
trains, cars. One road after another, from ocean shore to ocean shore.
From Beirut to the Red Sea. From Aden to Algiers. From Oregon to
La Paz. I keep going, prisoner of a body, and my brain is just a radio
station emitting messages to outer space. Angels, astronauts all dressed
in white, I would like some strange being to take me somewhere where
no disease blurs my perception. I will grow wings and fly.

EDUCATION

They teach the children to obey: it is a castration. They teach the
children the names of cities that have disappeared: they make them love
death. There should be only one school, the one where you learn the
future . . . without even any students. Located in the guts of the
species. Where you would say:
"If you could step out of your mind and walk in the fields, what would
you do?
"Nothing."
"What do you mean? If you could step out of your mind and walk in
the fields, where would you go?"
"Nowhere."
"What do you mean?"
"I myself would like to know."

Luis García Morales

ALWAYS

Hear the violent blow
perpetual qualities of the tiger
in four sharp-edged idioms
I am yours within your passion
defenseless
a sequence of blows
and the moans reveal spaces
between unknown syllables
mother syllables
and the foam that grows on the lips
of a subdued language where I
search for fire
useful food spoiled food
of delirium and fear
and I find only the vanishing trace
of an animal without shape
severed by your blows
and the timeless echo of your wandering

Peter Paul Fersch

tr. DERK WYNAND

WINTERSCAPE

Beneath the blue lid of ice
the eye of a landscape shines on the horizon.

Air hangs in the sky like a frozen scream
and taciturn snow heaps up the voice of wilderness.

Breath shatters
on stones of air
like glass in deep-frozen silence.

For a moment
spilled blood of the white-haired sun
glows on the neck of brown twilight.

Grey fish of evening swim in the eye of night
and arms and thighs of the shadows freeze solid.

The nighthawk quietly circles the moon
which bleeds nightly on the horizon.

HIDDEN BEHIND FLOWERS

Hidden behind flowers,
I await the ambush of light.

Visual event:
with tropical aesthetics, the sun blooms
above the unconscious landscape.

Green metaphors burn out
in the heat of strange eyes.

Alfredo Silva Estrada

OVER THE LIMIT

We'll have to see why we love the limit
The question
must be seen stuck like a spike through the limit

the skinny shadow

we are seeing the skinny homeless shadow
the shadow of the spike
the shadow of the spike beyond the limit

the shadow of the spike is cast
next to the projection of our shadow
our shadowy homeless quarters
our wandering through the limit

And we love something passing by
something stopping briefly in the shadow
we are fond of the darkness of a lump of earth
the darkness of our earth
the dead in us
and every memory tied up
and sunk
in a landslide

*　　*　　*

Our footprints of earth over earth
our wandering through the limit
the dead in us wandering over the limit

the burial of god in our viscera
the burial of god each first time
the burial of god stopping at the limit
god wandering in us
wandering beyond the limit
with footprints of earth over earth

*　　*　　*

The earth slips

something pierces the limit
something silences the limit

the tacit fire in its dusty hell

in its multiple limit exploded
in a landslide
where the footsteps no longer echo

* * *

We travel over an absence of echoes
we are remote
and perceive the spike of leaving
in the turning wave
we move in the dizziness of flesh
we move in the exile of flesh

where footsteps no longer echo
in something that happens quickly
in something that echoes purely
a gazing floods over

* * *

Something that becomes a limit
a violent glittering becomes a rubbing:
immersion in the limit
a shared construction

* * *

We are born by the lone abandonment
of dead faces that blot out
all the buzzing clatter of the stars

A surprising hunger eats up our arteries
beyond that limit the eclipses revoke

* * *

Not to be here
in this wind that caves in
to the negating poison

Torn out fitfully by depossession
recovering the earth with our body
we come out into an unmoving depossession
or again we shoot for the promise of the limit

J. Penzi

CYCLONE

there is a long passage through the wind
and tireless birds circle your heart
i wanted to know nothing of these things
to see no images
hear no foaming memories
or glass silence breaking over your mouth
a valley of starless waters
grey against the rain
twisted and turning
a cold flame
devoured by stones

THE VOICE

the morning stained my blood
my voice trembling yet immobile
trapped by color
desired to rest under a light
soft as your fingertips
i smeared myself with white clay
and sat among sad stones
waiting for the darkness
to heal the wounds of the horizon
of your shoulder
waiting for the moon
to pass above you like a pale vessel
returning memory
to fire

James P. White

BOWLBOUND

In a bowl
one feels himself
confined.

The smooth roundness
coolly presses, and
curves inward
from above.

If he speaks,
there is resounding, a
slipping of syllables
off polished walls.

His edge is a
continuous lip
open to sky.

If he moves,
there is the binding
curvature and marble
hardness when he falls.

So in his bowl
he contemplates,
and chooses waiting
over cracking out
alive.

THE KILLING STATION

H. E. FRANCIS

They have made the legal punishment for crime so great that most criminals or intended criminals, those who have grudges or fears or angers which they wish to express, choose the station. Indeed, the station has so cut down on national crime that families are the first to recommend the choice. Entry is purely voluntary.

Station 51—there are three hundred over the nation—is a four-square-mile area in the middle of the potato fields of Eastern Long Island. With his victim(s) the offender or to-be offender need only press the entry button and a narrow metal door slides open on a small square the size of an elevator. This door closes on darkness and a light reveals a passage to a similar door fifteen feet beyond and opening on a similar area.

The far door opens on barren flats white as alkali, apparently endless; actually it is a mile to the next square wall enclosed within it like a Chinese box. The offender is sometimes momentarily blinded by the brightness and stops, soon to discover that the alkali is hot and burns his soles unless he keeps moving. If he turns back and attempts to climb the wall, he comes upon millions of infinitesimal, nearly invisible needles which cause him to scream and the myriad pinpricks to bleed. Everywhere there are human bones. The white is accumulated lime sifted in fine layers over the dead in

128

periodic sprays in a complex system imbedded in the ground. Sometimes, from whatever passion, the to-be offender kills his opponent at once and only then becomes aware of his surroundings; sometimes the murder is not perpetrated and the two are driven to pursue their course together. They do not backtrack because, as they soon learn, the stone is less hot as they move ahead across the flats. Their movement is therefore usually more rapid as they approach the next wall.

The second wall is permanently cool and damp, so the offender often clings to it, following the wall either left or right to find a way through, but the entrance is on the opposite side of the square from which they entered the first wall and they must find their way around to it.

The discovery is simple: steps lead up three-quarters of the way in the wall to a shaft down which the offender must slide into the next square. A faint trickle of water pours from the sides. Here he may drink. The water moistens the slide. If he chooses, he may drink and step back down and remain in the first quadrangle permanently. Nearly all, especially when they grow hungry, slide down the shaft into the second quadrangle.

The terrain is damp. Visibility is good for a hundred yards or so, but there a fog similar to that off the ocean makes a white wall which looks impenetrable. It is impossible for the criminal to return to quadrangle one through the slide because it is overgrown with a dense slippery green algae and the wall itself is sheer barnacles against which flesh may be scraped beyond recognition. The ground is almost at the freezing point, and he moves toward the warmth which creates the fog.

Inside the fog he may wander for hours or days or weeks, dependent on his constitution, careful to dodge the pointed stakes which protrude from the ground. These become more dense as he moves ahead: with the vague warmth they are his only evidence of progress. If he is with another, he must touch him or talk constantly or may lose him for days and weeks or forever. At this stage one has been known to feed on the other. If he moves toward the source of an aroma, crawling at last through thickly planted stakes toward the greater warmth, there is an abrupt clear space under a heavy fog, higher here, and under this a third wall is visible.

This new wall is heavily charged and the least touch will throw the body down, but the ground is still too cold to lie on and the offender must keep moving unless he is too weak or dies. He must follow the wall—right or left does not matter—until he finds a rubber seat (there is one on either lateral), and when he sits in it, automatically it revolves. When it stops, if he does not rise it ejects him. A thick transparent substance walls off the opening; he cannot return.

This is the stretch of flat yellow sand and a sun so bright that at once the vision is impaired. Periodic winds rile up the sand and smite the eyes, seal mouth and nose and ears and pores, and numb the head and mind. But because the area is small, the next wall is already visible from the revolving chair. The criminal may almost reach the wall and be driven back. This action may occur many times. Against the wall lie deep piles of bones, which he must scale before he can top the wall and reach the final one.

The last is an area of infinite stillness—six feet square, six feet high. The walls are dark, with the normal temperature of the body, and on each of four sides is a round tunnel large enough for a body to crawl through on its stomach. When he crawls in, the light becomes overpowering. The floor of this area, and the walls, are mirrors. The sun blazes against them. In the quadrangle, whichever way he faces there is someone else: himself. But in no time the sun burns his remaining vision away. If another accompanies him, sound keeps them together, and touch, though neither can move far. One may eat of the other's flesh or parts of his own. Eventually he cannot move and dies.

After each death the sprinkler system pours an acid over the flesh and only bones remain. Periodically the bones are collected to be ground for fertilizer and human manufactures, but the team of men, the collectors, are put to death to keep secret the functioning of the killing stations.

The engineer is the most valued person alive—his achievement miraculous. He meets with subofficials as a voice only or in disguise. He has had petitions from many countries to set up a comparable network of killing stations. All over the world nations are begging for his help. They promise him anything. They will ask no questions. Everywhere mystery will be restored.

Translator H. E. FRANCIS

KAFKA 72

DANIEL MOYANO

Juan roved about in circles of power, where the Savior was supposed to be, and before evident signs that things were not going well —at least they had not gone well in his forty years of existence—he had the courage to say, "Some things are not going very well."

The man beside him heard him; but since the man wore no uniform and his face was normal, Juan relaxed.

"You mustn't relax," the man said, "because I'm a guardian, and I heard what you said."

His voice was kind, soft, and violent.

Juan swallowed and, feeling the fear begin to flow up his legs, noted how the man's eyes glowed with some mad secret.

"You were about to change the order," the man assured him.

"I was just passing by," Juan said, feeling how futile words were, "and I thought I'd say something. I think I said—I said it to myself— some things weren't going very well."

"But I heard and those weren't exactly your words. I believe I heard—and I'm never wrong—*everything* goes badly, not *some* things, as you say now. So you're trying to change the order—I mean, you've put all the others in danger."

"I meant to say that many people have problems, that one can't always say what he feels, that there are many people in jail because they said what they thought—that's what I tried to say, not because I thought it, but because it happens, or both things at the same time."

"That's the best definition of subversion I've ever heard in my

131

life. You're afraid, aren't you? And exactly what do you think of me?"

Juan, though his fear weakened him, said, "You're repulsive."

"Then," said the guardian, "you'd better start running, although you know it's useless. But not running would be shameful, because that would mean you deny your own freedom."

Juan began to run slowly, proving his persecutor was right, and consoled himself by thinking that if he hadn't fled, the guardian would have seized him somehow. Both fled, running through the dirty streets of the indifferent city. The persecutor for one instant thought this was the ideal flight—not only for capturing his victim but for preserving the order. He never looked at his victim. This routine part of the action gave him no special pleasure.

In the heart of the city, the guardian came up beside Juan.

"It strikes me that it's better not to run. Almost everybody runs in these cases; that's how they lose. And although we want you alive, don't think you'd be faster than bullets. Even in this crowd I could tell the back of your head."

Despite these words, the city looked cheerful now. A group of girls came out of a studio. In the show windows, the colorful objects, despite the winter, brought home the springtime joy of the sea.

The guardian, who was sweating a little because of his fat, took out some papers and said, "You could be filling out these questionnaires with your views and personal data. You'll save yourself a long wait in the jail office."

Juan, without answering and without taking the papers the man handed him, saw the glow in his eye, which was intolerable, and began to run—to the gradual indifference of the people who were not changing the order as he was.

Again the pursuer came up beside him.

"I understand your desire to flee like this, but I can't run. I'm a family man and the strain could do me a lot of harm. Besides, I'm about to retire. I'll run up to the corner just to please you, but then I'll have to stop."

At the corner Juan saw that his pursuer did stop—and made signs, trying to tell him he would wait there. Not seeing his face made Juan almost calm.

When Juan got to the suburb where he lived, the pursuer had disappeared. At the door of his house, his own family barred his way. "If you've fallen into disgrace, it would be better to give yourself up. They're looking for you," they told him. He stood still for an instant, but even his stillness was a flight.

From that moment, and the more he walked along the many

132

streets looking for that congruent self to flee from, he felt he was somebody else and was afraid of himself. His skin was as cold and rough no doubt as the skin of all the prisoners who long since filled the prisons of the south.

Fatigue halted him near the place where his pursuer had halted. People passing looked at him sometimes as at a beggar, sometimes a man whom they are going to justify, and always a stranger who captures the attention by bearing banners and halos without knowing he wears them. They looked at him as if saying *Stupid* or *Poor man!* but discreetly, without hurting him too much. He had sat down on a mailbox, his hands over his head. The girls from the studio went by. A few raised their arms to wave. Others smiled with understanding. Somebody told him to get off the mailbox to avoid attracting so much attention.

He sat on the curb and could not avoid the thought that things were not going very well. *But the important thing is not to trust anyone but accept what happens, not to trust your own thoughts, not to be led astray or be too attentive, and to reject every impulse which doesn't help save me,* he thought. And, far off, the pursuer heard every one of his thoughts.

While he was thinking all that, some of the girls from the studio still went on smiling and in a strange way still his pursuer kept asking him to fill out the questionnaires. Even the girls' smiles warned him of the futility and the needed brevity of his thoughts. A voice which—miraculously—he could trust said, "I saw everything. You don't have to tell me a thing. I heard all you said. Half the city heard you. I tried to warn your family, but they already knew. Besides, they complained because this will bring them trouble. In any case, I brought you this bottle so you can get drunk enough to stand all this."

"Are you sure the bottle has nothing to do with my detention?"

"I can assure you it doesn't. But I was with your future jailer—he says he's expecting you."

"I knew I couldn't trust anybody."

"Why do you say that? It would be easy to blame me for everything you did today. Or do you intend to complicate things for the rest of us? Why do you say that?"

"Because you can't trust anybody now. You can't even trust yourself in times like these," Juan said, bowing his head.

Translator *Sandra Smith*

REHEARSAL; OR, TWO SONS

ANGELIKA MECHTEL

A son, the midwife says, and I hear her give the date and time of birth, note down length, weight and sex.

He swallowed some amniotic fluid. He's blue in the face. He's screaming. For a moment I register the cry of the newborn child and the data the midwife is listing. I think of the old woman in the house out back—she had a son too. He's forty now. His mother died yesterday, without her son. I wonder: What did she want from her son when she brought him into the world? What do you want from this child that you just pushed out of you, that you should take up and perhaps lick off, like a cat does her kittens? This is a little crazy.

Or: How will it be when your bundle here is forty, when you are old and perhaps even think you are being poisoned? When you believe it all the last weeks of your life?

Sometimes your friend came to visit. You wouldn't accept anything edible from anyone else anymore, but you let her shop for you.

When she went to the little general store across the street, she was waited on first. She could only buy pre-packaged things, sealed milk and meat spreads in cellophane—anonymously prepared wares. There was surely no one who hated you in those food packaging plants.

Your friend could pretend better than you. For the last ten years of your life you had played the role of the eccentric old lady, but your character was no longer in demand. Finally you believed it yourself, and your persecution complex wasn't even your last big number. This fear of actually being poisoned! While your son is travelling somewhere. Absorbed by business, concerned with getting positions someone else loses. He knows how to do that. He was a good student; he has never lost, only won more; knowledge, and little personality; marketable.

And only one obsession. Like you. He sits at his desk, a heavy piece of furniture, oak, in the middle of his construction business, making money on the building boom, on rising prices and cheap foreign labor. Behind him is a wood-panelled wall and his management, in front of him his contracts.

As you raised him, so has he become.

I come out of the anesthesia, hear the midwife announcing my son. Date, time, weight, length fifty-two centimeters. See a nurse take him to the newborn station, think: it's still a bundle of needs, hunger and sleep, this miniature edition of a man; think of the possibilities of raising him.

Think: you want to make a peaceable man of him.

You raised him right where he belonged. For him the world began among machines, construction sites and board rooms.

My son's going to get up in the world, you said.

When he was thirty, he had his obsession, his construction business, a wife and children, his order and his old mother in the house out behind the business. There she sat every day at the window looking over the courtyard past the front building to the street. Saw that the housekeeper was pregnant, was sweeping the courtyard. Later saw the child running along beside the housekeeper, who was going into the main building with a pail and scrubrag to clean the hall of the construction and real-estate firm.

The old woman got along well with the other people in the building. Now and then her friend came, who had not married and had no son. She had always worked. What could she tell her friend about her son? At thirty he had reached his goal and his obsession. Sat at his desk and cut fat white erasers into paper-thin slices with a razor blade.

He thought of marzipan and his secretary, a pretty young girl. She had to buy him supplies of fat. white. plush erasers at wholesale. Otherwise he was a man an advertising agency could have drawn up. A whiskey, pipe and underwear man, an electronics and robot man, a sport car and cologne man, efficient, clever and vital, confident, in top shape and capable.

A man as you imagine him, in four-color print and Cinemascope.

A man who is trained and ready, behind a desk or in a foxhole. One who is universally useful. especially when things become serious.

A catastrophe.

Your son, the midwife says, and the nurse holds him up in front of me. Seven pounds and fifty-two centimeters. We both came through the birth with no complications. He was just a little blue in the face. He had swallowed amniotic fluid.

Your son, the midwife said. Does she mean the one imitating the men shot in westerns, the one with the holster on his hip, the one standing there with his legs spread apart, pelvis forward, always ready to slay the enemy? A notch in his Colt—a corpse.

Nurtured up from his diapers by his mother, he'll become a man, schooled between nursery and kitchen, between racetrack and hobby-horse.

Your son.

Or do you want more?

You loved him, as one loves a souvenir in a shop window. You rehearsed how to make a man out of a male child. His role and your stage directions were pre-established.

He is five years old when he draws his first fantasies on the walls of his nursery. Fantasies in a neat room, between four white-painted walls. On the one wall he projects his father, has him standing there wide-legged, always prepared, laden with TV, refrigerator and washing machine, in his back hand the new car. You'll knock the games out of him, fantasies on a white wall, where you can't find a single speck. Then he draws a lion on the wall, that his father is strangling with his bare hands.

That boy, with his strange ideas.

Until he has the lion bite. Now he draws his two guns, shoots from the hip with both hands, and finishes off his father, who dies his movie death.

You'll laugh.

A silly game.

That boy.

Now you are dead. Died of a heart attack.

Three days later your friend finds you and notifies your son.

She cleans out your wardrobe and piles the old clothes on the floor.

What can I do with them, says your son, and gives them to charity.

The housekeeper says, she thought she was being poisoned.

My mother always had strange ideas, says your son.

He bought your role as the eccentric old lady.

He gives the knick-knacks in the window to your friend.

At your funeral he's carrying soft white paper-thin slices of eraser in his coat pocket; he has his secretary with him. He says he will mourn for you. A son, says the midwife, and I hear her announce date and time, note length, weight and sex.

Seven pounds. A lightweight. I imagine how he'll grow up.

He's a few minutes old, and already you're laying your plans.

I'm figuring out the possibilities of making the person I love out of him.

You dismiss the future of the western heroes. Colts and notches are out.

Computers and robots are interchangeable, my son.

When things become serious, you won't let them draft you, you and the others. I think through the possibilities. Is that why you've brought him into the world, to change it?

Rafael Cadenas

DEFEAT

I who've never held a job
who've felt unsteady before all competitors
who lost the best qualifications for life
who barely arrived somewhere before wanting to leave (thinking
    that a change of place was a solution)
who've been rejected in advance and aided by the cleverest people
    in a most derisive and humiliating way

who lean against walls to keep from falling down completely
who am an object of laughter even to myself
who've been excluded at the altars of those more miserable than I
who'll be the way I am all through my life and often suffer ridi-
    cule this coming year for my absurd ambition
who tire of being advised by others more lethargic than I ("You're
    very apathetic, bestir yourself, wake up")
who'll never be able to travel in India
who've accepted favors while giving nothing in return
who drift from one end of the city to the other like a feather
and let myself be led by others

who have no personality nor want to have one
who all day long hide my rebellion
who've never gone to join the guerrillas
who've never done a thing for my nation
who don't belong to the FALN, despairing of all those things and
    others whose enumeration would be endless
who cannot leave my prison
who've been discarded everywhere for being useless
who could in fact not marry or go to Paris or have one peaceful day
who will not recognize the facts
who always drivel over my life history

who've been an imbecile and even worse since birth

138

who thought my father was eternal
who've been humiliated by professors of literature and asked
one day how I could help and got a horselaugh for an answer
who'll never be able to make a home, be a success in life, be brilliant
who've been cast off by many people because I rarely talk
who am ashamed of things I never did
who've reached the point of running down the street
who've lost the social circle I never had
who've come to be a general laughingstock because I live in limbo
who never could find a soul to tolerate me

who've been excluded at the altars of those more miserable than I
who'll be the way I am all through my life and often suffer ridicule
    this coming year for my absurd ambition
who tire of being advised by others more lethargic than I ("You're
    very apathetic, bestir yourself, wake up")
who'll never be able to travel in India
who've accepted favors while giving nothing in return
who drift from one end of the city to the other like a feather
and let myself be led by others

who have no personality nor do I want to have one
who all day long hide my rebellion
who've never gone to join the guerrillas
who've never done a thing for my nation
who don't belong to the FALN, despairing of all those things and
    others whose enumeration would be endless
who cannot leave my prison
who've been discarded everywhere for being useless
who could in fact not marry or go to Paris or have one peaceful day
who will not recognize the facts
who always drivel over my life history

who've been an imbecile and even worse since birth

who lost the thread of conversation I was making and could not
   find it
who don't give way to tears when feeling the urge to do so
and who am late for everything

who've been destroyed by so much progress and regression
who long for perfect immobility and flawless haste
who am neither what I am nor what I'm not
who have a satanic pride in spite of everything although at certain
   times I've shown humility to the extent of likening myself to stones
who've lived for fifteen years in the same circle
who've felt predestined for something beyond the ordinary yet
   have accomplished nothing
who'll never wear a necktie
and cannot find my body

who've sensed my perfidy in flashes yet could not topple myself, sweep
   everything aside, and from my aberration and my indolence and
   drifting create a new tranquility, but stubbornly commit the suicide
   within my reach.
I'll get up from the floor still more ridiculous to keep on laughing at
   others and myself till Judgment Day

Chimako Tada

DEAD SUN

A child comes crawling into
a world not yet wrinkled, dripping
glistening drops all over.

The child turns a somersault;
an hourglass too is turned, to
mark the start of new times.

The child picks up stars to skim across the waters,
while fish from prehistoric times laugh, waving their fins,
drenching the feet of the gods with their splashings.

The child gradually grows up; now
his world full of footprints is
heavy with memories. Then
he gives a long yawn, and
is off somewhere never to return,
with a dead sun stuffed in his pocket.

Translator LEONIE A. MARX

HICCUPS

BENNY ANDERSEN

As far back as I can remember, I have enjoyed hiccuping, and my only regret is that I cannot bring about the hiccups in the way one evokes other pleasurable sensations. They choose their own day and time. To be sure they can arise in connection with rapid consumption of cold liquids, but don't think that I can get them going by swilling cold water or beer. That usually only causes a sick stomach; hiccups can't be forced.

But when the miracle finally happens, I have to watch out. First of all I must be careful not to attract attention, and since hiccups almost always arrive when I am at a party with many people, the situation is difficult, especially since the highest degree of enjoyment is to emit a real loud, uninhibited hiccup. So I try to hold it in first gear, and for the time being it just rumbles a bit in my throat now and then or manifests itself through a sudden jerk of the head which can be camouflaged with ordinary nods or by tossing my hair back as if a fly were bothering me. Afterwards I may discreetly look around for a way out so that I can smuggle my hiccup out into the hall, into the garden or to the bathroom where it can finally sing out, but alas, only seldom do I get that far, for as a rule some sharp ear or eye has observed me: "Oh, you have the hiccups—I can cure that."

The cold water with which one usually starts the treatment is still all right. In the beginning I was nervous about that, but now I know that the hiccups aren't damaged by it, just as little as by vinegar with sugar in it and whatever else one comes up with as the unfailing

142

remedy. I calmly drink these things, joylessly, in order to show my good intentions. For I'd just as well not say that I should like to keep my hiccups; people think that I want to avoid imposing on them and find me only the more touching and helpless: "That is really admirable of you to pretend that it doesn't bother you, but we'll help you, just rely on us."

Now come the hard tests: I stand on my head; I stand on one leg with a glass of water on my forehead; but I submit to everything in order to keep a good relationship with the other guests, and I do want to be invited again, not because the party interests me especially but because being together with many festively clad people puts me into that vibrant mood which constitutes such fertile ground for my hiccups.

Next I count backwards from fifty with my mouth full of water, and blushing I dry the drops of water off my jacket when, at twenty-four, a powerful hiccup blasts the water out of my mouth. But people smile encouragingly; the fact that I am a difficult case only increases the suspense. It would indeed be sad if the hiccups had capitulated already because of a sip of water; no, this is better than any party game. The gentlemen take off their jackets and heatedly debate what one now should resort to; the ladies rush in and out with pitchers full of splashing cold water; after a while the floor is a mess.

But at a certain moment it becomes quiet, everyone is looking at me silently with sparkling eyes. I move up against the wall and lose a hiccup for it is clear to me that they are going to scare me. That has, to be sure, never damaged my hiccups, and I really have nothing against people suddenly shouting "Boo" behind me, if only I don't know it beforehand. But the fact that I know it makes me nervous. From what direction will it come, what can they come up with, who is going to start? Frightened, I stare at them; indeed, I'll give a start in acknowledgement if they will only hurry up and get it over with.

But now they can see I am on guard. There is a continued silence; to be heard are only my recurrent hiccups which I now let have free rein, at least to enjoy them to the fullest as long as I may. But I can see the worst is on its way. They all know there is one remedy which never fails, and one they have kept till the end, after everything else was unsuccessful. They look at each other—who wants to take the initiative? There is no risk connected with it; the money is safe enough. Finally someone takes out his wallet, pulls out a ten-crown note and holds it up: One more hiccup, and it's yours. This is terrible. I try with all my might to hold the next hiccup down, in order not to offend anyone and not rob the man of his ten crowns which he does not dream of being in danger. I know it only makes things worse to hold back the hiccup, but what can I do aside from gaining time and hoping for a miracle—that suddenly the doorbell will ring or a thunderstorm will break loose or there will happen something entirely different which can distract their attention. I press my tongue back into my throat like a cork with the result that the hiccup, when it finally comes, takes a running start all the way down from my kidneys and blasts itself a way out into the open with unbelievable power, so that I bang my head against the wall.

Everyone looks down into his coffee cup without moving or saying anything. For a moment the challenger stands paralyzed with his ten-crown note before flinging it over to me with a contemptuous air. And I am forced to take it. It isn't even of any use to say I am sorry; there is nothing to do. Everybody ignores me from now on. I can only wait for an opportunity to sneak out the door, downstairs and away, hiccuping sorrowfully.

After such an experience I keep to myself for a long time, but sooner or later my craving, not for company, but to hiccup, becomes so urgent that I again start to seek association with others and to ingratiate myself into social circles; now the question is to find some people who don't know me and my unfortunate inclination.

It is difficult in a smaller town constantly to reestablish a circle of acquaintances, I therefore have plans to move to the capital; there should be plenty of possibilities there.

Translator HERMAN P. DOEZEMA

Francisco Pérez Perdomo

ALL IS NOT A DREAM

It says nothing to me
It enters my room against my will
demolishes me
overpowers me
clothes itself in my skin
I feel its entrance
cold and silent
its skinless brutal body
as it takes refuge there from the night
and drifts through the stillness of dream
as if conquered by strange fatigue
Its fevered nose excites me
like a fugitive wave its breath drowns me
Its hands enter my hands
settling in my gloves
It pierces me
Carves my memory
And disappears consumed and fixed like lightning
My fratricidal power

José Angel Valente

tr. WILLIS BARNSTONE

THE ADOLESCENT

Great light already slips by your shores,
no one remembers the invasion of frost.

Her dreams no longer are enough to make
her right in being sighs to everyone.

You sing through the air.

Now her dresses turn green.
Now no one knows anything.
                                No one knows
how or why or when she was.

THE BET

To you whom I don't owe a thing
but the rude meddling of death,

to you from whom I have nothing
but a thin foil of undelivered love,

to you who did not walk with me in the night,

I give you a door not a threshold,
two faces, four blind alleys,
one lost bet.

PROHIBITION OF INCEST

Quadrangular stone.
                      The owl rests
in the lubricity of his thought.

Same as the secret bundle in the stomach.

So a woman's body splits apart
in two bloody forms.
Memory of childbirth at dawn
as if filled with saline air
and fatigue of having run far through the sandpits.

Quadrangular stone.
                      Broken time
in bodies that were before
and will be later,
while the lover who was recently engendered
enters the body of the woman mother
with the scream of possession.

And the same rite.
                      And the same body.
And the solar prohibition
of loving what we have engendered.

Translator Leonie A. Marx

SCHIZOPHRENIC PICTURES

SVEN AGE MADSEN

I
   write I
No words. Is sufficient with words issuf
   must continue, the attempt, must, gladly.
   It.

I
   write I.
   Always something.
   I now see clearly. I now see clearly. I now see clearly. I now see clearly. I now see clearly. I now see clearly. I now see clearly. I now see clearly.
   Nothing is superfluous,   is superf.
   Time, inscrutable, is lacking, always something, is now clear, time which, always something, will naturally, naturally I should, worth the effort, unless.
   Now see clearly, now clearly, now.
   I have written I.
   The beginning, in one word, time, one other, one.
   Nobody can deny that.
   The beginning could.
   I.
   Nothing, is the least essential.

Again, the beginning, not too often, help, time is running, first and last, everything goes, from first to, running out, the quickest, too easy, the situation.

It is.

Minutia, it is, conscious, could, incidentally.

The remainder, time naturally, naturally, unforeseen, I mean, time, reduce and expand, time and thereafter, few are lacking, until is exploited, talk about, minutia, quite simple, everything, the report.

Or rather.

Without hesitation, certainty, my other, without exaggeration, the assignment, not without firmness, yes exactly, result, sults, to confuse, this test, I feel, therefore should nothing.

The greatest possible exploitation, realize clearly, the day's length, from the one extreme to, sleep without suffering, more precisely, sleep, now realize clearly, the assignment, but I don't exist in order to, without suffering, an oversight, surely, so they say, now things are going, reservation, unless, well, before or, demand of me, result, I enjoy, insistence, the suffering, oversimplified form, additional effectiveness, last line, additional effectiveness, went well, sluggishly, but.

Now.

Not regressing.

Thereupon, becomes, maybe.

Neither.

Certainty, essential, that which can be demonstrated, the matter, if that word, an attempt, the investigations, everything can, exercises too, I need, chances, to be used, to be put in, if only order, essential. which can be demonstrated, the matter, if it, occurs to, thought, me.

Uncert. Rather.

Nothing can continue, not why, time,

I

remember I.

Easier, even if I, in the beginning, important, expansions follow, limitation, worth serious consideration, but I don't exist, words could, help, not, mind's, farther away, correction, perhaps without me obv naturally, naturally, idea, somewhat more difficult, no danger, even if the solution, big words, the result.

Is,

theory the report words should support will organism for food trap except for perhaps words before again distance certain write slowly up rest.

The conclusion, with, the thinking, indeed only just thin, without criticism, naturally, naturally, difficult to imagine, a comparison which only, in brief, time should not however, a prerequisite, the whole thing is not without.

Then I remember, the first time, I, see now clearly, repetition, of the words, could certainly, the first time, from.

Time.

Some pain, exaggerated, followed by, and this, sooner or, the result, I should then, since.

Nobody deny.

Renewed idea, hidden.

Work, so to speak.

The first assumption, if not, at most right in between, incidentally, difficult to, my own knowledge, opinion, perhaps, a sort of failure, or, the first, one could, instead of.

A new thought, too much, perhaps a new, a few, again perhaps.

I want now to.

In that I here, without complaint, a simple action, have written.

When I, from one time to.

I wouldn't want, good is not, a bit of fear, without a reason, certainty, again and, badly, reluctantly deny, no objection, arrange, too easy.

Not quite clear.

I see now, unless.

No exactly, this.

Important, absolutely, a lot, ill-founded, I should remember, from the start, naturally it became, naturally, incoherent but clear, and I therefore, excursio, incidentally, to give up, but no reason.

The work, the size, the proofs are, my hand. I.

The rest is

Translator HARRY HASKELL

THE RUPTURE OF SOLITUDE

MANUEL CAPETILLO

In the room, a star and a yellow flower. Far away in the distance, a cube of iron. The cube of iron was a thousand meters high and a thousand meters wide. It was cold and moved slowly. It spun leisurely, drifting away from the yellow flower and the star. Surrounded by shadows, it was dark and without light in the center; only stillness and silence, the murmur of a faint wind coming out of who knows where, a chair in the middle with its feet in the air and a small man sitting in it. The small man was old, skinny, and hungry with long bony hands and curved nails. He was dressed in tails, a white shirt and a bow tie; he was also wearing leggings. His hair was very long and straight and hung over the tails of his coat. They swayed together like the pendulum of a clock. I don't know how the chair remained in the center of the cube, but the man sat up straight, bound by an endless chain fastened together with locks; you could only see the paleness of his face, the long hair, the thin hands, one foot and the tails of his coat; everything else was covered with chains. He wasn't very cold. His eyes were open, dreamless; he was looking straight ahead, never turning to look around; he had no reason to, he saw nothing.

In addition to the faint wind, you could hear the small man breathing and the beating of his heart as it palpitated from time to time. His thought roamed from one corner of the room to the other and returned to spin through his head before it left again.

151

The tranquility and the silence were curious. You could hear a sound, a long, penetrating note. A pure sound, perfect, unique; a disturbing sound, a sound that enhanced what was in the center of the cube; it was meant for him and he rejoiced upon learning that he wasn't deaf. It was a low note, too low and too loud; as it ascended one step it seemed more pleasing to the small man.

The cube, spinning slowly, moved away from the yellow flower and the star; the cube, spinning slowly, returned to the yellow flower and the star.

There was a low note, it ascended one step and entered the star. The small man saw from a distance, in the corner of the cube, a star giving off a beam, just one beam that passed through the feet of the chair. He could see it clearly, it was white. The star was white, its beam was white, and the note was now not so low. The star was in the corner, the small man in the center, and the beam was stretching over to the other side. You could see a yellow point at the other side, a yellow point that was coming closer.

There was a note that was not very low, a white star, its white beam, and a yellow object. It had come very close and was in front of him. It was a flower, a huge flower, bright yellow, and the white beam illuminated it. The small man remembered the color red, but not the color yellow, and he liked this very much. And the flower, not for its color, but for being there, was a flower meant for him.

He once had chains, now he has a note that is not very low, a white star, the white beam of a star, and a yellow flower. His thought travels from one corner to the other, returns so he can hear a note and see a star, a beam of light and a flower.

With the note, the light and the flower, his heart beats more quickly, he breathes more heavily, and the locks unfasten themselves. He is free, he walks around. He seems weak, but runs easily: he wants to be where he finds himself. He runs through the cube, he examines it: it is an iron cube; he touches it, passes his fingers over every centimeter of its surface: it is cold. He measures it: a thousand meters long, a thousand meters high, a thousand meters wide. He runs, gets tired and wants to leave the iron cube. He seizes the star and the flower, records the note in his mind, gathers momentum and leaves.

Drago Ivanišević

GAMES AT THE EUROPEAN MASKED BALL

THE FIRST, THE MAIN GAME

First sharpen the knife well,
a knife is best sharpened on a brother's throat,
then drink a glass of wine or whiskey,
to drink or not to drink to the war
is all the same, one can do without all that,
then carefully cut the mother's throat,
lay her on her back and lie down next to her
and place your head on her bosom,
then carefully, so as not to hurt the joints,
slowly take off all the nails from your fingers,
sharpen the fingers well, like pencils,
then drink several glasses of wine or whiskey
and let the tears flow, cry for the mother,
for a long, long time, until sated,
then with the sharpened fingers
mix blood with tears
and draw many longitudinal lines on the shirt,
(the shirt can be white, black, or multicolored)
the rest will then be easy.

Michel Butor

Selections from *Exploded Meditation*

THE ROOF

On the sand I draw a house, complex and remote, a room for my friend, our project of society, wings to carry us, a forest to hide us, a rock to teach us, an incline to direct us, a terrace to cradle us, a cellar to slake us, a garden to intoxicate us, her looks to decide me, her palms to heal me, her nails to till me, her silence to seed me, her words to harvest me, her calm to contain my rejuvenation.

SLEEP

Stretched out on the sand, his weight increases, he submerges; rents open between his ribs through which he inhales minerals; he submerges still farther, his hands become flat and trenchant, he has disappeared beneath the sand; for a time passers-by still see a depression, as if someone there had scooped a hole at high tide, and the water had seeped away hours before, then a wind had sprung up and leveled it all out, while his eyes have taken on a crystalline consistency, and his respiratory system has been entirely transformed, his skin converted to carapace, his digestive tract to grinders that permit him to live within the terrestrial mass where he submerges, swimming very slowly between veins and strata, drinking from phreatic streams, seeking a gentle lava woman to whom at last he would give children of granite.

THE INSECT

On their wing sheaths the breeders, through controlled mutations, have succeeded in obtaining the plot of the city streets; and that is why each family cherishes a nest of them in its garden. For every excursion they provide themselves with one of these flying guides, perfectly tamed, who return at the slightest opening of the pollen capsule to which they are accustomed; but there are so many of them buzzing about the streets, the arcades, the corridors of moving sidewalks, that these days there is no longer the slightest danger of becoming lost. It is an ornament and a game. The breeders of other cities are working night and day to attain equally spectacular results; but for the most part upon opening the chrysalids they find no more than designs which albeit harmonious bear no relationship to their city. One of the most ingenious researchers, however, has estab-

154

lished that a variety found in Siberia bears the plan of a village in South Africa, save for one alley-way; and they say that in a region of Persia a city-planner, amazed by another that he is trying to acclimatize, derived from it the master plan for his entire province.

THE RUIN

The conflagration lasted several days. Beams hang across the breaches. One can make out what used to be windows, steps, a porch, or even a balcony with its columns. The bluebird came to sing its plaint at that tower. In the cellars casks now calcified once held the ripening wine that cooked as it poured out, tingeing with its intoxication the sinister smell that pervaded the ravines. A dragon has made its home beneath the ruptured vaults; those who venture into these devastations divine his scales by the light of the moon and the fangs gleaming within his tarry maw. A petrified hooting, as the sorcerers of my race come seeking terrifying neums to intensify the incantations with which they surround the distillation of their philters. The ancient moats are strewn with stray bones.

BREAD

The way in which the surface curves under the injunction. Space is kneaded, risen, baked, gilded in its black and white, savoury, crusty, nourishing, exposed on the white board, giving off its odor in the light room, in the light street, the light cave, the light abyss. He had had to work the fields of ink, sow the seeds of ink, watch their germination, their flowering, their maturation, harvest the ears of ink, thresh them, mill and unite with this flour of ink the yeast of the brush while the oven of eyes with all its embers heated conjunctions. Famished workers we, here is the darkness of the sky changed into oven to bake the bread that we are, here the darkness of the sky changed into light abyss so that we may devour it with our eyes.

Gabriel Zaid

tr. Sergio Mondragón and Sandra Smith

THOUSAND AND ONE NIGHTS

After the movie theatre
past midnight, in a state of strange drunkenness,
I listened to the heartbeats of my car
to avoid listening to my loneliness.

Music, inebriating sounds of music.
Serpents at the heart of night.
The demons of the steering wheel want to fly
but God did not give wings to cars.

In the forbidden garden of night
trees and rivers
strange fruits of amber,

jade and ruby
they all say no,
say yes.

REVEREND MALTHUS ON THE BEACH

Let's assume that it happens once a week
and that out of three billion people on earth
one third is of age.

In each case three cc's.

Three million liters weekly
irrigate the Garden of Eden.

Life carries its water to the mill.
Humanity harvested in three thousand tons.
And all this turns into seeds again.
If this carnal species were only edible!

Translator Vytas Dukas

NOTHING COMES EASY AT FIRST

VIKTORIA TOKAREVA

Fedkin woke up during the night because he felt that he was a fool. He lay and stared at the ceiling. The ceiling was as white as a sheet of paper; he, himself, painted it twice a month. Fedkin loved to paint ceilings more than anything in his life—to stand on something high and move the brush from one side to another.

Outside daybreak began.

Fedkin washed up and sat down at the table and his wife served him breakfast. Everyone eats breakfast, and everyone also has a wife. Fedkin's wife was not a very clever one, but, at the same time, she was not a fool. She walked in the kitchen with a face shining from cream, and her hair done in a tail with a rubber band from a drug store package.

"Zina," said Fedkin, "You shouldn't have married me. I am a fool."

"It's O.K.," said Zina.

"What is O.K.?" said Fedkin puzzled.

"The most important thing in this life is to find your place in it; to find equilibrium between desires and capabilities."

When Fedkin went out on the streets that day, he knew everything about himself. He walked slowly, breathed, and looked around. If he were more clever, he probably would have recited poetry, something like: "October came, the trees discarded last leaves from their naked branches. . . ." But Fedkin didn't know Pushkin, and he was just thinking, "God, it is so good . . ."

In the waiting room of the office building people were sitting, smoking, and nonchalantly moving their arms. They always came here to chat and pass the time. At first all were worried and even suffered from nerves. But after a year they relaxed and even found pleasure in their indefinite state.

Fedkin had no secretary and therefore people entered his office directly from the hall. He sent everyone to his supervisor, and the supervisor sent them to the next one, a higher supervisor, who had two doors and a secretary. There the client was detained and sent back to Fedkin. This was like a water cycle in nature: water evaporates, rises to the sky, falls from sky to earth, etc.

Fedkin entered his office. The door momentarily opened slightly, and a skinny and nervous young man looked in. He always nibbled matches and his fingers were brown from them.

"Hello," said the young man. "Do you remember me?"

"Of course," said Fedkin, "What is your name?"

"Lesin."

"Can you interpret dreams?" Fedkin asked suddenly.

"My grandmother used to say, that if you had a bad dream, you should say 'Where went the night, there went the dream'. . . ."

"Where went the night, there went the dream," repeated Fedkin.

"No, not now. Too late now."

"Have a seat," said Fedkin. He tore off a page from the calendar and began to paint it evenly with ink. It seemed to him that he was painting a ceiling.

Lesin looked on and waited until it would be possible to present his problem, but Fedkin had heard a lot about this problem and was not interested.

"You have parents?" he asked.

"Of course," said Lesin slightly surprised.

"Very good," praised Fedkin. "Aren't you ashamed you haven't worked for the last two years?"

"But you don't give me . . ."

"I?"

"Of course. In order for me to start to work, a paper must be signed and you've refused to sign for the last two years."

"I cannot help you at all," confessed Fedkin.

"Why?"

"Because I am a fool."

"In what sense?" Lesin was lost.

"Intellectually."

"I understand." Lesin's instant credence offended Fedkin.

"But it is you who is a fool."

"And what do I have to do with it?"

"Take up something else."

"Why do I have to take up something else?"

"All my life I have been occupied with things I do not like," said Fedkin.

"And how do you feel?"

"Bored."

"And what did you want to be?"

"A painter."

"I think it is a mechanical job," Lesin said cautiously.

"You try it," Fedkin was offended, "try to paint the ceiling white and I am sure it will come out patchy. I also want you to know my paint brushes are from France." Fedkin began to talk about his paint brushes; it was very interesting. Lesin was listening and nodding, then he advised, "Then drop everything and be a painter."

"Drop whom?" clarified Fedkin.

"Everybody."

"I can't drop everybody. I can't drop my wife. In her youth she had many proposals, but she married me. How would she feel in her old age to be a painter's wife? What would her friends think . . ."

"If she loves you, she will understand." Lesin's face became solemn, and his voice was breaking. Apparently, someone didn't understand Lesin.

"She would understand, but friends . . . they will see right away that I am a fool. From an executive down to a painter. . . ."

"But you can arrange it so they will fire you. . ."

"They won't fire me," said Fedkin thoughtfully, "I am not a thief, not an alcoholic. . ."

"A fool, this is very serious. You just underestimate. . ."

"All the same," Fedkin was upset, "they won't fire me for that. . ."

Fedkin's supervisor was a woman. Women, as Fedkin saw it, were created for love and family, and not for a job. Since the supervisor was created for both, she therefore helped her grandson with his homework over the phone. She called this caring for him from a distance.

The door to the office was left open a bit. You could hear the supervisor screaming, "Equals mass times speed squared, divided in two. Why do you call me at work rather than looking in your textbook? What will happen when I die?"

"Hello," said Fedkin politely.

"What a madhouse." The supervisor got disgusted and threw down the receiver.

Fedkin moved his eyebrows understandingly. For fifteen years she had screamed at her children in the same fashion, called her home a madhouse, and asked what would happen when she died. Nothing changed during all that time. And in general, Fedkin noticed, people don't change with age.

"What's with you?" asked the supervisor, thinking about taking care of her grandson from a distance.

"I would like to leave the job."

"You got offended?"

"No."

"Then what happened?"

"Simply I am not on a par intellectually."

"Who said?" The supervisor was edgy.

"No one. I discovered it myself."

"Did you discover it a long time ago?"

"Today. Since this morning . . ."

"And I knew about it all the fifteen years that you worked for me. And I beg you not to tell this to anyone. Otherwise, I will be a fool, not you."

"You think about yourself?" Fedkin got offended. "You're thinking about yourself when the matter is definitely official business."

"One fool cannot hurt official business."

Fedkin went to another supervisor. This boss was gray and handsome, but short. He resembled Napoleon Bonaparte and behind his back he was called not Mikhail Ivanych, but Michel.

Michel was constantly in a hurry and constantly fell behind in everything. When he had visitors he rose from his chair and smiled. In Stanislavsky's system there are approaches, lower and upper. Michel took the one in between so that the visitors sometimes became confused as to who really was the boss.

"Hello, Michel Ivanych," Fedkin started.

Michel smiled. "In two words, please," he asked, "I have only a minute and a half."

And Fedkin counted two fingers on his hand and said, "Me fool." Exactly two words.

"Continue," demanded Michel.

"That's all."

"If you understand that you are a fool, that already proves that

160

you are not a fool."

Fedkin wanted to contradict, but Michel had no more time. "That's all," he said, "I must fly to India."

Fedkin walked slowly along the corridor, and thought how repulsively the walls had been painted, how sloppily the ceilings had been done. And if this had been done as it should have been, then the bosses and all who came by would probably have been in a better mood—beauty changes a mood. And during the fifteen years—spent on who knows what—he could have painted many ceilings. But that time is now gone.

In the corridor behind low tables on small red wicker chairs, people were sitting, smoking and talking, nonchalantly waving their arms. Some of them he had seen here for a year or more.

Fedkin wanted to go in his office, but somehow he didn't, instead sat down on the red wicker chair.

"You told them?" quickly asked Lesin, now addressing him in a familiar thou form.

"Yes."

"So?" The others asked with curiosity.

Fedkin made a disappointed sound with his tongue. He looked really upset.

"Nothing comes easy at first," they warned Fedkin.

"Nothing comes easy at first," confirmed Lesin.

"Don't give up!"

THE HOT CENTER OF THUNDER

RUBÉN ALONSO ORTIZ

tr. H. E. FRANCIS

The Mother:

My husband doesn't like my company, or this house either, and he hasn't run off with Perla García for good because he thinks that in ten years he'll be over sixty-five and she'll already have run off for good with his best bet, she'll have taken his last cent, then we'll be alone. I'm sure that moment will come and I'm going to destroy his every word, break every silence he tries to make. He sold half the ranch to buy her that house she lives in, and of the ten thousand head of cattle his grandfather left when he died, all that's left, at best, is a thousand skinny cows, because nobody is capable of looking after them well; and there's still this old house that's going to collapse in the first big blow, this house the pioneers of Formosa built, and now it's full of leaks and falling apart. I'm tired of paying certain debts of his, but now I think my earnings as piano teacher can't go that far and I'm going to leave it completely up to him to repair—alone. I'm going to save my money for the day I get even with him.

Vicente said Formosa is the hot center of thunder, the only place in the world where the moon that sometimes floats on the river can be broken. My loneliness gave way to curses the night the life drained from his body. That very hour I lost my desire to turn my face toward the sun. This morning my husband refused to visit his grave. At least my daughter excused herself because she had to teach. She's at the age when her only hope is Alberto, especially in this city, where there are few bachelors but plenty of pretty girls. She's almost certain that if she

162

doesn't marry him, she's going to be a virgin all her life. But my daughter has no need to worry—Alberto's not going to marry anyone else here, but he's not going to marry her either. This morning at the cemetery, he told me he's going back to Buenos Aires to work in his brother's clinic. Only he and I know that three years ago, on a day just like this, Vicente was killed by his own father—on a day like this, blood gushed out of his mouth and cut off the sound of his voice.

My daughter thrives on blaming Vicente for all her failures. She knows that the night my husband ran over Vicente's body, he had been quarreling heatedly with Alberto. A neighbor told me that it was a terrible argument, judging by the shouts and crying she managed to hear. I always thought Alberto had a lot to do with my son's death. Or why was he always so crushed and nearly crazy? And why didn't he ever mention marriage again after that? Vicente came out crying, running as if someone were chasing him with the intention of killing him that night. I'm not forgetting that Doctor Alberto Irala came to Formosa to visit my son for a week and never went back to Buenos Aires. My daughter keeps slandering Vicente, but at times we get together and try to break down the barriers between us.

It was no secret from me that Vicente visited Perla García pretty regularly. I knew that my son had her as often as he liked and that she loved him to distraction. That's why when Vicente died she cried as much as I did, or more. I should have thrown her out of my house then and there, but in my despair I couldn't recognize her very well when she bent over my son's body and kissed him several times. It was one of her unforgettable indecencies.

Here, they accuse me of a lot of things, but really *I'm* the one who ought to set them straight, because it was my husband who ran over my son's body. I always thought he didn't hold back, that night, on purpose, because by doing it he eliminated a rival who was too young and good-looking. He could have avoided killing Vicente but he didn't do it because he knew that Perla García sucked the passion out of the younger, and was satisfied with the juice he smeared over her body. I was beside him in the car and we both saw clearly what Vicente was doing, I shouted *Stop*, but my husband chose to kill him.

The Father:
I knew Vicente better than anyone, but never enough to know why he seemed so horribly tired, pale, and consumed at times. It was as if he had an incurable disease, one that threatened death from time to time. The curious thing was that he insisted on hiding it all, but I

knew that when he wore dark glasses it was because he had bloodshot, watery eyes, like a drunk's. When he persisted in winning Isabel Peña's love, his enthusiasm caught us all in the flood; but he began to paint with more violence and to write mad sentences: that sadness strikes us like dead birds; that things come from the country of insupportable tensions; that there is a palpitating solitary, transcendent monster who will masticate his heart and swallow his skeleton. . . . The fact is his idyll lasted less than three months; then no one even mentioned Isabel Peña's name in this house, no one knew why they had stopped speaking.

Vicente was proud, but his mother dominated him, overshadowing him, blinding him, making him tongue-tied, and he finally chose hell because that was the only way to free himself from her prison. If it hadn't been my car, it would have been the next one he met. He had chosen hell and wanted to be blind, brainless, his mouth crushed.

Perla García looks a lot like him. She too is marvelously young, enthusiastic, and a little impetuous. I knew Vicente visited her as one of the ways of rebelling against his mother's impositions, but I'm also sure my son was always correct with her. They accuse me of rushing the end of that night because I was jealous, but here we know that's one of my wife's great inventions. The mass they are going to pray today for Vicente's soul satisfies her desire to appear the perfect saint. The blessing of the Church is no longer important to my son because he had the privilege of not being afraid of blood or hell. He chose the form of his own eternity.

The Sister:
Vicente didn't even respect my desperation. Never could I stand his compassion or his tenderness or his violence. He was never afraid I'd tell our father he slept with Perla García here in this house, using our beds and filling the rooms with cries and interminable whisperings. He wanted to frighten me with his bestial vitality, his wild pig's ferocity. Alberto could not free himself from Vicente—that was the great humiliation of my life. My brother insisted on showing me that the object of my love was the dirtiest and unworthiest, but nobody was capable of telling Vicente himself what *he* was: a lump of shit, a degenerate, a destroyer with no character. If it had not been because one night it occurred to him, simply to be more original, to throw himself in front of our father's car, I might have married Alberto three years ago; we had even ordered from the printer the two hundred invitations we were going to send out, but Vicente wanted to kill himself, and he did. He made father run over his head. We knew that Vicente

164

killed himself, and if I managed to talk, to tell the truth, today we wouldn't have a mass for the dead prayed over by the bishop, because suicides are condemned, and Vicente is a suicide who doesn't deserve mass said by the bishop! He doesn't deserve anybody's prayer! But "the accident" happened three years ago and today we're going to observe it solemnly.

Alberto lived for my brother. Often I came to think he courted me to see Vicente more often, but Vicente treated him badly at times, which calmed me and then I'd admit again that he preferred me. At last I realized that my brother did what he wanted with Alberto, and still does. I too argued with him that night. I begged him to leave Alberto in peace, I shouted it was his fault we couldn't get married, and he answered frenetically that an impotent man can't marry a frigid woman—he even shook me and knocked me down. It was the only time I could prove that his body was red-hot and his arms capable of clutching even a bitch in heat. I thanked God for all I felt during those moments and I wouldn't look away from the dark flesh of his face when he began the actual motion—before the final thrust, I ran my hands madly over every inch of his body, and after the great convulsion came, he got up and ran out to meet our father's car and I lay there stretched out on the floor, marked by the fire of his violence or his tenderness. When I found out he was dead, my hope flared up again and I went on desiring his death.

Unsi al-Haj

IS THIS YOU OR THE TALE?

my history goes back
to a fifth century since
I was baptized in my mother's presence
from whom I inherited the feeling
that whoever escapes four walls
commits
every treason

my history goes back to the time
when the head of the family
defied the Sultan in
Constantinople
and I wanted to be within things
for a while
by way of necessary aggression and violence
like an old statue

my history goes back to Eil and Baal
they printed me in Gilgamesh
and I was raised
in Ugaret
Sur Seidun Byblos
visited with me Greece
Persians ornamented me and Hebrews
bought passages from my works
Egyptians simplified me in their drawings
of the living
Astarte and I
through mascara were
merged together
I lived by the river
gods slaughtered me I them
I carried my little grandmother
on my back and fled
in the valleys she said
like a parrot
better if you

had buried me
when I did
I was born and died in Beirut

my history goes back downward
to storms blowing from books
and sitting for hours among crowds
to what is not of me
and as my age is counted in years
likewise
as drops of pearl
I wander outside this necklace

is this me or you
is this you or the tale?
after a while musicians will disappear
poet officialized behind buttons
cities of soul
flee through the chimney
psalms and roofs blown away
and stars of desperate longing to reach them

my sorrow is great
for a history steeped
in destiny
steeped in mish-mash
marching through chance through danger
marching through our fictions
marching in holes in inner pockets
marching in birthmarks
and astrology

marching in Too-late
marching through pallor of lips
on the slope of the eyes
which doesn't need
to be invented again
but only reconsidered

Translator H. E. FRANCIS

NEST IN MY BONES

ANTONIO DI BENEDETTO

I am not the monkey. I have different ideas, although they have put me, at least in principle, in the same situation.

My father brought him home as he did the palm tree. He has plenty of land and plenty of money. He set out the little palm and it seemed fine while it was young and beautiful. But when it went on stretching and stretching, he tired of it because it was graceless and hairy, unadaptable, he says—but because he lost sight of it, I believe, because he wasn't in the habit of raising his eyes to the sky, at least toward the side where the palm raised its head. He looks toward the river mouth, where the storms begin, since on the storms depend, for good or ill, the harvest.

Nor did it occur to him that the baby monkey would not adapt, not only because of questions of climate, but because it would be impossible to adjust to the family, and my father wanted it to be like a member of the family. Perhaps he wasn't completely wrong as, favored by certain considerations in which my father occasionally proved himself intuitive, the little simian did something to earn the place promised him. But his place, definitely, was the palm. My father did not always use play, food, and affection—above all, he deprived the monkey of food and did little to educate him properly. The monkey fled, taking refuge in the palm, as the son returns to his mother. He descended only to steal or eat whatever anyone's compassion had left at the foot of his home. He lived alone, just as alone as the rickety crown at the height of the palm. He turned unsocial and meditative, torpid in everything that did not have to do with getting food. Perhaps from bad humor—because the announced hothouse was never built—my father had the plants cleared from the entire sector where slowly, like a nostalgic sigh, the palm extended. Palm and monkey fell, and the monkey hid among some boxes and chests until the dogs, excited by the blood of a beheaded chicken which flopped about in agony, hurled themselves on him without anyone's opposing them.

I am not the monkey but, ordered by my father because of slight infractions, in childhood I too was often prohibited from the table. I don't have a palm, but I made a palm of my house—rather, of the rooms and of the dirt plots which could be my palm, or of some walk, some book, and some friend. My palm had, in fact, many branches; and therefore, perhaps, I had the possibility of thinking that I must not be like the monkey. Perhaps everything depended, as in the case of the simian and the palm, on birthplace and on final inadequate destiny. I don't know. Perhaps I should have been born in another country and perhaps it wouldn't be like this. It's possible that I shouldn't have been born in this period. But I don't mean by that to say that my birth had to have been in the Middle Ages or in the same years as Dostoievsky's. No. Perhaps I should have been born in the twenty-first or twenty-second century. Nor do I believe that it will be easier to live then, although it's possible that it will be. To make it possible, since it's impossible to be born a century ago, I have wished, as far as my strength permits, to be of some use.

When I learned the uselessness of the monkey, I could attempt what seemed to become a useful destiny, at least for others. His empty skull suggested the exploitation of my own. I wanted to make of it—it was simple to do—a bird's nest. My head filled with birds—voluntarily and happily on my part and theirs. I rejoiced indeed in the felicity of the firm nest, secure and protected, which I could give them; and I rejoiced in many other ways. For example, when I made an appearance (with a scheme of disguised calculation and anxiety), apparently somber, at my mother's somewhat joyful canasta tea, insulted and losing her self-possession, she asked how I could do such a thing as begin to whistle in the midst of that gathering of women? And I said, my lips scarcely parted in a pitying smile at her ignorance, that it was not I who whistled; and in that woman I stirred the candid surprise of one who witnesses the passage of a tangible, perishable musical god.

It has not always been so, only several years, perhaps several months. With the change I have come to doubt somewhat that making one bird happy I shall make happy all the families of future centuries. If we all put our heads to the service of general happiness, perhaps it would happen—but our heads, not merely our hearts.

I applied mine, and it had happy swallows, canaries and quail. The vultures which have nested in my head are also happy. But I can no longer be happy. They are unceasingly voracious and have sharpened their beaks to eat up even the last bit of my brain. Now on bare bone still they peck—I don't say with rage, but as if fulfilling an obligation. And even if their pecks were affectionate and playful, they could never be tender. They hurt fiercely, they make the bone ache, and they extend my pain and torture in a hysteric, rending, and endless cry. I can do nothing against them—no one can—since no one can see them, since no one ever saw birds who whistled. And here I am, my nest overflowing with vultures which—diligent, insidious, and perennial—crack with every peck of each one of their thousand pecks every bone in every part of my whole skeleton. Here I am, hidden among the trunks, in wait for one of those who once fed the monkey to take pity on this trapped creature and excite the dogs.

But, please, let no one who knows my history give way to horror, but overcome it and not leave off if he forms some good plan to people his head with birds.

Michael S. Harper

PHOTOGRAPHS: NEGATIVES:
HISTORY AS APPLE TREE

Nightmare begins responsibility.

The Indian is the root of an apple tree;
history, symbol, presence: these voices
are not lost on us, or them.

THE NEGATIVES

She agitates
the quart developing tank
in total darkness,
our windowless bath;
the cylinder slides
inside against the film
for ten minutes
at 70 degrees.
I can see the developer
acid in the luminous
dial of my watch:
she adds the stop-bath.
The hypo fix
fastens the images
hardening against light
on her film and papers.
I imagine her movement
at night as her teeth grind:
I know she dreams the negatives.

171

UTILITY ROOM

She shades the prints bathed
in what iron water there is,
artesian iron spring water;
pictures of winter green
blue in darkness,
the second hand stops.

She shakes the developing tank
as a uterus
mixing developer
to the negatives
where no light appears;
I hold her hips
as saline and acid
pock up images.
I see my children
on these negatives
in a windowless room.

A simple enlarger,
a bulb with a shade,
images born through her lens
packed on the contact sheet;
fatted negatives under thick
condenser glass,
prints from her uterus,
cramps from her developing tank.

Jayne Cortez

PHRASEOLOGY

I say things to myself
in a bitch of a syllable
an off tone wisp remarkable
in weight and size
completely savage to the passing of silence
through mass combinations of moisture
uncaked in pockets of endless phraseology
moving toward sacred razors
like air like untangled bush
over a piece of dead scar
instant in another smashed ear lobe
shivering between word echoes of
word shadows
jugular veins of popular contradictions
well dressed & groomed in the mirror of language
transparent and useless against
the impulsive foam of
a spastic

Jayne Cortez

I AM NEW YORK CITY

i am new york city
here is my brain of hot sauce
my tobacco teeth my
   mattress of bedbug tongue
legs apart   hand on chin
   war on the roof   insults
pointed fingers   pushcarts
   my contraceptives all

look at my pelvis blushing

i am new york city of blood
police and fried pies
   i rub my docks red with grenadine
and jelly madness in a flow of tokay
my huge skull of pigeons

my seance of peeping toms
my plaited ovaries excuse me
this is my grime my thigh of
steelspoons and toothpicks
   i imitate no one

i am new york city
of the brown spit and soft tomatoes
   give me my confetti of flesh
my marquee of false nipples
   my sideshow of open beaks
in my nose of soot
   in my ox bled eyes
in my ear of saturday night specials

i eat ha ha   hee hee and ho ho

i am new york city
never-change-never-sleep-never-melt
   my shoes are incognito
cadavers grow from my goatee
   look i sparkle with shit with wishbones
my nickname is glue-me

Take my face of stink bombs
my star spangle banner of hot dogs
take my beer-can junta
my reptilian ass of footprints
and approach me through life
approach me through death
approach me through my widows peak
through my split ends my asthmatic laugh
approach me through my wash rag
half ankle   half elbow
massage me with your camphor tears
salute the patina and concrete
of my rat tail wig
face up   face down
piss into the bite of our handshake

i am new york city
   my skillet-head friend
my fat-bellied comrade
   citizens
      break wind with me

Curtis Lyle

TAMPA RED'S CONTEMPORARY BLUES

we are stranded here against a dark blue and shaded night
peering into these intelligent rooms
                              through the forested eye
of thirteen great atlantic owls
conjuring while conceived in the original blue bottleneck
of Tampa Red

black-inked leaves teardrop and fall toward
the unbearable street or sit dumbfounded
                              in corners
of chimerical ceilings
where we place our three eyes
                              under the melting pot
of ludicrous passion
and await that rude performance called the initiation
of the world, the opening of blistered and boiling water,
the translucent floodgates of incorrigible time
engaged in a dialectic
                    of wheatstraw and steel
or riding the australian crawling logs down market street,
speed boats contending
                    in the black plum trees, huge and scuffling
feet tangled in the buckling and bladed blood
of steaming and involuted roots

the initiation of the world, dark hands moulding charcoal
into the artifice
                    of bleeding stars, the mouths intent
and drawn-out
against the still life impression
                              of our own navels
where innumerable fish owls seek the obscure identity
of woman

the initiation of the world, absolute and libertine fishermen
dying
of freedom, their ox heads sighted beneath carnivals
of shitty peasant women, rancorous and fucked-up mules thrown
into a fulcrum
of wild nuts
and beaten under this composition
into a primeval cross
of woodcut carbon

the initiation of the world, perspiring and yellow moons
amid a sad procession of trees, through the sad night
an innocent man's blood caught in the sun
against the crucifixion
of evil and sad women, in the sad night

an alchemist composing cold and erotic ducks, under a sad tree
of the night we are waiting for a report
from Charlie Parker
waiting tables in Spain, 1939
or Diego Rivera, upside down scratching his ass
while beginning the construction of the new
and profoundly imaginary world, between shadows and mountains,
between drunken women and hod carriers, between some silver
altar piece and the portrait of a miserable stable
hoarding the angelic and allegorical eyeballs
of the heroic Zapata
we are waiting for Bud Powell
and the corn stalk
of nude prisoners
fleeing his persecuted and percussive piano
we are waiting for horses and their vestige, the child-figure
who will come out
of his solitary egg dancing
and bringing us an essay concerning the moon
we are huddled and waiting, western and cowboy drunk
between the one colour of our malleable landscape
to see if this poem just rides off into the sunset
or really succumbs to a frightening and logical end

Quincy Troupe

AFTER THE HOLOCAUST

we sat on the edge;
a bituminous razor-bladed thought
stretched like madness beneath us
a buzzard licked its beak perched
on top of a portable gas chamber;
below, millions of yellow
slick bones stared questions
from the blood covered courtyard;
a clown danced on the point
of a poison needle in the square
the soldiers armed with laser beams
and atomic ray guns
discussed overkill as a form
of new scientific philosophy
raped women at deathpoint
sewed human eyes
into the snakes
that was their hair;
and suddenly from the gate
a loud shrill trumpet blares;
it is the new king who was invented
in a test tube and marketed
as a necessary household item
to cure the life
that flows from people's lungs;
his face is powdered white
and his lips are painted red;
he smiles and waves the head
of an Indian; his subjects scream
and ask for the head of a poet;
a mockingbird is shot

off of the note of a flute
falls and is quickly beheaded;
the buzzard swoops down
eats up the rest of the poet's body;
we shake our heads to see
if they are still attached to our bodies
and go on writing poetry
as we sit on the edge of the dead

Clarence Major

MARRIAGE BY CAPTURE

we upheld every moment
        until two years later
her father came back from a holy war
        worked extracting toloache but
it didn't help him tho he came across
        with the dowry after all this time
doubt if he expected from me
        a lobolo 'cause even if he had
he'd have been out of luck, anyway
        he never tried to understand
his bright girl child he so busy
        a violator of her spirit and
never liked me anyway so the dough
        was a surprise, and the strange
thick bunch of 326 toxic white bell-shaped flowers,
        an equal shock, said
they'd improve *our* style and make sacred our strokes,
        get to that—
but you know I ain't got no use for formal religion,
        I suspect he got converted
beyond hope in the war and tho I stole his daughter
        turned her to a *true* believer,
doubt if we will ever figure what to do with these
        jimson weeds except maybe start a cult
make folks pay to chew them save the bread
        to send our crumbsnatchers to college

Ossie Onuora Enekwe

THE JOKER

I come from a land
where the sun smiles in the day,
the moon at night,
and electric has not killed the stars.

In the coming of Winter,
I was scared of ice,
slip and fall,
turtlenecks, coats fat
with hair or feathers,
and all that make men
walking birds, for none
ever spoke of Winter as a Joker.

In Manhattan, this winter dawn,
from my cabin . . . down the lift.
"What! White smoke as my breath . . . .
Like a dragon in the fables!
Must have burnt my lungs
somehow, somewhere at night . . . .
Must see a doctor."

But then before me hurry
men and women, boys and girls,
their dogs on leashes,
their cats like babes in their arms;
all shoot white clouds through their nostrils
into the mist like pipers in a crowd.

Dogs and cats
like their masters or mistresses
shoot white clouds into the air!

Dennis Brutus

Pray
if you believe in prayer
for those shipwrecked by love

else pity them;
the sunburst of your compassion
may heal their broken stems
may restore their crushed tendrils

they live in a drought-shattered continent
where the children are skeletal ghosts,
their music the hoarse death-low
of emaciated expiring beasts;
they cannot shutter their ears to the guttural rattles

those who should free them live in suave hotels
where chrome waiters glisten and glide
where magic is a signature on an authorized check
where rich food is discarded garbage
insulting the nostrils of famished children
where hope is a dead rat among the putrifying viands

in the cerecloths of devious strategems
the healers are paralysed
in the formaldehyde of their wise inertia
our viscera grow noisome and decompose—
our tears are maggots battening on our corneas
acid rains hiss as they corrode our membranes

Forgive us our anorexia, our anomy, our acidie
forgive us our arid eyes, our unresonating ears
our vanished mouths;
forgive us and pity us
permit us our oblivion of grief
and the dry abrupt lusts
that spasm us

We have soared among cloudpeaks
and splintered our hearts on their marble whiteness
we were sodden in the drizzling harmattan of tears
now we sear, sere, in the sirocco of lost hopes

we have known the rocks and the shoals
the organing breakers and the talismanic spray
we have stood transfigured and effulgent
we have known the jagged edges and the taloned reefs

Pray,
if you believe in prayer,
for those shipwrecked by love;
or pity us:

for still it will not rain

Daniel P. Kunene

COALESCENCE

Pealing bells
    piercing ears
    splitting drums
       to
A deaf-muteness
    like
A blunting narcosis

Torn membranes
Crying blood

Stilled drums
Nor ear nor tongue
For Afrika

Deafening clamour of clanging steel
    Draining life
       from
              Black bodies
Now limp
    like
             Impotent phalli

Then
    A recessional of the bells
    Reluctantly the clangour
        falls into retreat
        finds refuge in convalescent homes

Drums once more pierce the sky
Reviving, advancing,
Trousered thighs
Flail mine-booted feet
Percussing with rattles
    of coca-cola caps

Shirted torsos
    heave in unforgotten rhythms

Snapped-off buttons fly
Heads rise
Eyes stare
Nostrils dilate

The royal salute thunders:
Bayede Baba
    Hail Father
Bayede Nkosi
    Hail King
Bayede Kristu
Son-of-Elephant-in-the-Sky

Baye . . . . de

Lucille Clifton

IN SALEM

to Jeanette

Weird sister
the Black witches know that
the terror is not in the moon
choreographing the dance of wereladies
and the terror is not in the broom
swinging around to the hum of cat music
nor the wild clock face grinning from the wall,
the terror is in the plain pink
at the window
and the hedges moral as fire
and the plain face of the white woman watching us
as she beats her ordinary bread.

NEW BONES

we will wear
new bones again.
we will leave
these rainy days,
break out through
another mouth
into sun and honey time.
worlds buzz over us like bees,
we be splendid in new bones.
other people think they know
how long life is
how strong life is.
we know.

Nikos Engonopoulos

NEWS OF THE DEATH OF THE SPANISH POET FEDERICO GARCÍA LORCA ON AUGUST 19, 1936, IN A DITCH AT CAMINO DE LA FUENTE

art and poetry do not help us to live:
art and poetry help us
to die

all that noise
and investigations
and endless talk
around the mysterious and shameful circumstances
of the execution of the hapless Lorca
by the Fascists
which every so often
idle and conceited pen-pushers impose on us
are worthy
of contempt

let's face it everyone knows
that for a long time now
—especially in our own wretched day and age—
it has been the custom
to murder
poets

Modern Dance: An Interview

ALWIN NIKOLAIS

Mundus Artium: Improvisation plays an important part in the development of your dancers. Can you train someone to improvise?

Nikolais: Improvisation, whether it's good or bad, depends upon the skill of the person doing it. We talk about sanity and insanity. Certainly an insane person could improvise, and certainly does, but we're talking about improvisation from an esthetic point of view, where you place yourself in terms of extending into an environment to receive the impressions of what rests therein, and then with whom you make conversation, just as we're making conversation now. In the instance of my dancers, they're trained to do this. Not everyone can do it, because not everyone can open himself to that extent. To my mind, improvisation takes great sanity; sanity in terms of sensitivity, being present and aware of, and making choice of, even though the choice is so swift that you don't have any consciousness of choice. Improvisation is unpredictable; I can tell my dancers to get up and improvise without giving them any subject, and the catalyst to the occurrence is a mystery; the curious thing is, if they try to do the same things twice, realizing the success of previous gestures, it'll be absolutely dreadful.

Mundus Artium: How do you relate improvisation and the actual performance on the stage?

Nikolais: I am convinced that we're concerned with communication here. Communication requires contact, it requires an interplay. I think perhaps it's easier to do an improvisation than an actual performance. The individual himself is originating the talking, whereas in the performance, the expertise of the performer to interpret the words of somebody else becomes the challenge at hand, and is not always successful. Performances vary greatly—for instance, I can have a group that can travel all over Europe and there are certain pieces that will be absolutely fabulously received and the rapport between audience and performer extraordinarily good—let's say in Paris or Berlin—but take that same piece to Rome and it's like playing tennis against a wet blanket. That tension doesn't exist, it's impossible to create. That these dancers might succeed better in an improvisation than in a performance is a matter of a difference between a performing skill and an improvisational skill, and also to a certain extent on the choreographed structure as against the rather free, more spontaneous and immediate live thing of an improvisation. In my pieces I use a lot of improvisation in the thing itself, but after many performances they tend to get set.

Mundus Artium: What then do you emphasize in the training of your dancers?

Nikolais: I try to find their own individuality first, and that's not easy. You have to strip away all the surface junk—a twitch, for example, is not basic personality, it's some unfortunate thing that happened to it. It takes many years to erase all that junk. That's the process of any teaching, isn't it, to get rid of all the junk. Usually the beginner is wonderful, very interesting. I get refreshed going back to beginning people, they teach me something new. Also, they refresh my own theories. And then there's an intermediate ugly duckling period, where they're so boring, so dull, so educated, you could kill them. All of a sudden something will happen, if it ever does, to relieve them of all that junk, and suddenly an artist appears. You never know if its going to happen or not, you can't predict it.

Mundus Artium: How does the dancer or an actor see himself in relation to his audience?

Nikolais: The artist has to make love to his audience. In reality, it's simply the fact of opening the channels, which is really what love is, basically—that you enter into me and I enter into you—not in the sexual sense, but we make ourselves available, one to the other. Then when you do that, plus make yourself available to the situations of other things that surround you, then the interplay between all this is evident. You start closing it off, and you start going towards insanity, and catatonics. I know that with my performers, I have to say, it is not sufficient that you be entirely imbedded in the thing you do—you must also be aware that that process is one that must be empathetically transferred out, so your edge is different, the leaning of the motion is different. It's all very well that I sit here and weep, but to tell you that I'm weeping I must edge it over. There's an electrical edge to the body that says, "Doll, I am telling you I am weeping, and I want you to know that I am weeping, and for what reason I am weeping"—this is a different thing. It's like twisting; I can twist for the sake of twisting, but if I twist for the sake of looking I must also lean. I think you must lean psychically as well as physically towards the persons to whom you're speaking. It's a very simple thing—if I'm talking to you, my voice is carrying to you, but if I become very eager, I will lean physically and psychically toward you; the outpouring is done from every part of the body, including the ankles. A great performer will do this; he'll lean toward his audience, and that's what they call presence, projection or whatever.

Mundus Artium: How long would dancers continue to dance privately, without an audience?

Nikolais: I think perhaps the dancer would do it longer than the actor. It's curious, but the dancer's ego is less than the actor's. I have succeeded in changing dancers because of this awful thing of giving up the motion as a decoration of self, rather than lending the self to motion. It's a very touchy thing with a dancer, and yet once they discover that when they

188

	do that, they themselves are more brilliant, in their own personal shining, but it's a dreadfully hard lesson to learn—one can hardly succeed in doing it.
Mundus Artium:	You talked about drama as the art of emotion and dance the art of motion. Are they related to each other in any way?
Nikolais:	Yes! Emotion, psychologically, I suppose is caused by change—if there's no change, there's no emotion. But I don't know really when motion becomes emotion—I've talked about this to psychologists—my theory is that motion precedes emotion, and that emotion occurs as a result of motion. But in terms of drama—drama is created mostly out of conflict and resolution, whereas dance is not created out of conflict and resolution. I suppose—if I can go back to the music of Bach—it is not conflict; it's the dynamics of juxtaposition of sounds; whereas most of our history of drama is created through actual psychical conflict. And I think that drama is in a great mess right now because it doesn't know how to resolve the continuation of the art without dropping that process. The minute it does, it goes into abstraction, which is dance. So we might better study dance than drama. But the actor really practices situations of conflict and resolution. I think probably we're trying to get away from conflict and resolution.
Mundus Artium:	Do you think, as a future projection, that we'll come to a point where dance, drama, and electronic music will come much closer together than they have in the past? Perhaps a new kind of opera?
Nikolais:	Well, I think that opera might find the solution sooner than drama, but I don't know how. Certainly the sounds of the composers working now—I must say I'm rather ignorant—not ignorant, but I haven't had the time to see many things, particularly the European electronic composers. I've done several pieces using the voice, and the dancers do learn after a while to work the voice into an agreeable sound structure. But it's very difficult. For instance,

we do this thing called Scenario, and it's all made up of motion. There are scenes of anger, of sadness, of terror: they're all very playful, and should have the edge to it of rather frightening comedy, in a way, although we don't mind if people laugh at the time they're crying. It's a disturbance. But the thing is to find esthetic structure in these things, and of course the great opera composers did. I wouldn't discount that completely. I just think this is not the time for it now. Also I'm very much against finding *the thing*, because the thing you find now may also be unserviceable the next year. I find that happening to some of my works too, that whereas they were terrible exciting at one time, this next year they might not be, and you can sort of sense it in the audience, that, no, they don't want this any more; they'd like something else.

Mundus Artium: Could multi-media show a new direction?

Nikolais: In a period of time when no one believes the one sense, I think multi-media is necessary, because we are living in such a cacophonous world, we have to go back to that primal business of being bombarded on all the senses, so they, like hundreds of scouts, bring in their varied messages, so they can be computed together. I think this is the reason why we go for this now, and that I sense seeing is not believing any more—what you see you don't always believe. The ear is the thing of hearsay— what you heard is not always the fact. Psychologically all this has changed now. Now we have to hear, see, taste, smell, touch—otherwise we don't believe. But I think that each one should make its own statement. I would like sometime to really work on, let's say, motion that goes one way, then sound that goes another way—each is speaking of the same subject, but not necessarily independently, recognizing the other, but fortifying each other by the dimensions of their statement. I think this is one way it could be done.

190

DISCUSSION OF MIKROPHONIE I,II and PROZESSION

TRANSLATOR *Sandra Smith*

KARLHEINZ STOCKHAUSEN

MIKROPHONIE I and *MIKROPHONIE II*

In the following two texts I will try to summarize briefly the processes I invented and used for two of my recent works. At this time, the sober description of the technical procedures seems to me more informative than a discussion of my aesthetic goals.

Through the use of modern technical processes of sound amplification and sound transformation, I have renewed banal things like a tomtom (one of the oldest musical instruments which was used in Asiatic music), or an electric organ together with choral singers whose sound effects and musical possibilities seem to be known to everyone, and thus made possible heretofore unknown musical experiences.

Thus, when I describe how I have experimented and articulated in my composition the results of the experiments, I am conveying my attitude toward everything that surrounds me: to transform and bring into a new context with the help of the techniques of my epoch what seems to be old, banal, in order to make free again the magical power that is inherent in every "instrument," above all every old one, and in time is buried alive, and thus to reawaken areas in us which have long been asleep and seemed to be dead.

What I have done in *Mikrophonie I, Mikrophonie II* and other works in the last years anyone can transpose into the area in which he is active: even into the office, even into the arrangement of an apartment, into cooking, the sex life, etc.

In the first work in which I united instrumental and electronic music, *Kontakten* for electronic sound, piano and percussion, from 1959-60, a four-track tape of electronic music is played over a loudspeaker during the performance of two instrumentalists. The tape runs through uninterrupted from beginning to end; the musicians read the score, where the electronic music can be followed exactly, and they play the instrumental part, which is also noted in the greatest detail. At that time, after several rehearsal attempts during the preparation for the performance, I had to drop my original plan to have the musicians react to the electronic music in a way that would vary from per-

191

formance to performance, and also to make the reproduction of the electronic music dependent on the actual performance of the instrumentalists by stopping and starting the tape recorder, by variations of the dynamics, by closing and opening single channels. I was not satisfied with the results, and decided on a score I would clearly determine in all details. Since then, however, the thought of uniting electronic music and instrumental music even more closely has not left me, perhaps even to find a solution in which an insoluble fusion and regeneration between the two realms would take place.

I had already formulated theoretically several times since 1960 the separation and supplementing of a sound generation by instrumentalists and a simultaneous sound transformation by electronic apparatus also attended by musicians, with a simultaneous reproduction over loudspeakers, as a possible synthesis of instrumental and electronic music. In recent years there has been quite a number of attempts—especially in the realm of light music—to strengthen instruments with the help of contact or normal microphones, and thus to alienate the sound-colors, to distort them, provide them with an echo, etc. Musicians performing light music call such results, appropriately, "gags." I always found such effects superficial, since they only add to the arsenal of the usual instrumental colors a few new variants which again, after a short time, seem just as banal, just as obvious, as the previously used instrumental sounds. Such purely quantitative expansions of instrumental effects have a fashionable character like the seasonally determined "gags" of the merchandise industry; and whoever wants the sound expansion in electronic music understood as simply a matter of increasing the usual sound-color palette by a few thousand new sound variants is, in my opinion, missing completely the actual qualitative significance of structural sound-color composition. I have never been able to do anything with the argument that a sound or certain sounds were "used up," "worn out." Now, as always, it is a matter of the relationship, already felt by Schoenberg, to be worked out between the inner structure of a sound used in a composition and the structure of the work this sound is fitted into; it is a matter of the function of a sound-color in the organism of a composition.

The goal of my considerations was clear to me: instrumentalists should produce a structured initial material, differentiated in all musical characteristics; the instrumentation here would be, at first, of subordinate significance, provided that it contained a sufficient complexity for the transformations intended for it. The specific musical qualities of this material would be provided by the fact that the performers would be professional interpreters who employ all their musicality and performing experience in the interpretation of this initial material, including the expansion of their individual realm of decision and reaction to each other on the grounds of experience with ambiguous instrumental compositions of latest development. These already thoroughly worked out musical structures should, in a second, autonomous process, be re-articulated in *all* sound qualities, and again, by musicians who should modulate the sounds recorded by microphones with appropriate electronic apparatus. In the summer of 1964, I composed two works: first the *Mixtur* for orchestra and ring modulators, in which five instrumental groups of a normal orchestra are recorded, singly, by microphones during the performance, the microphones are connected with ring modulators, and in these modulators, by means of sine generators which are attended by musicians according to the indications in the score, are changed into sound-colors, rhythm, volume and pitch, and then, simultaneously with the orchestral sound, are reproduced over five loudspeaker groups.

After the completion of the score of *Mixtur* for orchestra, four sine generators and ring modulators (1964), I tried as far as possible to compose also flexibly the process of the microphone recording. The microphone, which up to now had been used as a rigid, passive recording device for the most accurate sound reproduction possible, had, in addition, to become a musical instrument and, by its own service, influence *all* the sound characteristics: thus be able to produce, autonomously, pitch in harmony and melody, rhythm, dynamics, timbre and spatial projection of the sound, according to the composed indication.

My next work after the score of *Mixtur* was *Mikrophonie I* for tomtom, two microphones, two filters and regulator. A few years before, I had bought myself a large tomtom for the composition *Momente*, and set it up in the garden. In the summer of 1964 I made a few experiments by agitating the tomtom with the most varied instruments, which I collected in the house—of glass, cardboard, metal, wood, rubber, artificial materials—and connected a hand-controlled, strongly directional microphone to an electric filter, joined the outlet of the filter with a volume regulator, and made its outlet audible over loudspeakers. My collaborator, who was in the living room, at the same time improvised changes of the filter setting and the volume. Simultaneously we tape-recorded the results. The recording of this first experiment is for me a discovery of greatest importance. We had made no agreements; I used some of the collected instruments as I saw fit and thereby listened to the surface of the tomtom with the microphone, the way a doctor listens to the body with a stethoscope; the technician also reacted spontaneously to what he heard as the product of our common activity.

On the basis of this experiment I then wrote the score of *Mikrophonie I*. Two performers activate the tomtom with the most varied materials, two more palpate the tomtom with microphones; in a corresponding notation, the distance between microphone and tomtom (which influences dynamic and timbre), relative distance of the microphone from the point of activation (which determines the pitch, the timbre and above all the spatial impression of the sound between far distance, faded, and extremely close), and the rhythm of the microphone movement are prescribed to them. Two additional performers each attend an electric filter and a volume regulator, and they again shape timbre and pitch (by the adjustment of the filter), dynamic and spatial effect (by the combination of filter adjustment and volume regulation), and rhythm of the structures (by the prescribed temporal alteration of the two apparatuses).

Thereby, three processes of sound structurization, dependent on each other, reacting to each other, and at the same time autonomous, are united, which were composed synchronous or temporarily independent, homophonous or in up to sixfold polyphony.

The score consists of thirty-three independent musical structures, which for a performance are combined by the musicians according to a prescribed scheme of connection. This scheme indicates the relationships between the structures. Three musicians (a tomtom player, a microphonist and a filter-and-volume regulator attendant) are one unit, and play at any given time one of the aforementioned thirty-three structures. At a certain point, they give the other group their cue to begin the next structure; the latter group returns the cue after a prescribed time, and so forth. The relationships between these structures are determined at any given time in three ways: the subsequent structure, in relation to the preceding, must be similar, different, or opposite; this relationship should remain constant, increase, or decrease; the subsequent structure (which usually already begins during the preceding) must have a supportive, neutral or destructive effect in respect to the preceding one. The scheme of connection, then, gives three indications for every combination of two structures; e.g. similar ones are to support constantly, or opposing ones are to destroy increasingly, or different ones are to be neutral decreasingly, etc. According to these prescribed criteria, then, the musicians select the sequence of composed structures, which are themselves composed according to such points of view. Although the relationships between the structures, the scheme of connection, remain the same for all performances, in order to guarantee a strict and directed form, still the versions of the structure sequences can be very different. *Mikrophonie I* was premiered on December 9, 1964 in Brussels, and is dedicated to Alexander Schlee. The German premiere took place on June 11, 1965, on the "Westdeutschen Rundfunk" with the following interpreters: first and second tomtom players, Aloys Kontarsky and Fred Alingo; first and second microphonists, Johannes Fritsch and Bernhard Kontarsky. I was first filter and dynamic regulator, second filter regulator was Jaap Spek, and second dynamic regulator was Hugh Davies (Spek and Davies shared the two duties, since Spek had to take over control of the technical processes at the same time).

MIKROPHONIE II

After *Mikrophonie I* for tomtom, two microphones, two filters and regulator, I composed *Mikrophonie II*. In this work a further attempt at a synthesis of song and electronic music is undertaken. In *Mikrophonie II* a transformation of the song with the help of electrical apparatus takes place during the performance. Twelve chorists (six sopranos and six basses) sit in a half-circle on the podium during the performance, backs to the audience (they could also sit in the middle of the hall and be surrounded by the audience). Groups of three singers —three first sopranos, three second sopranos, three first basses, three second basses—each have a directional microphone in front of them. The chorus director sits in the center of the half-circle, facing the audience, and directs single levels of the music, which is polyphonally composed throughout. Next to him sits a timer, who indicates to the chorus the duration of the thirty-three musical moments with appropriate hand movements. Behind and above the chorus stands a Hammond organ; the organist sits facing the public.

The technical principle of sound composition is as follows: the circuits of the four microphones are connected to four so-called ring modulators, and the electric outlet of the Hammond organ is also connected to all four ring modulators. In these ring modulators, now, the sounds of the chorists and the tones of the Hammond organ are modulated so that the frequencies fed in are suppressed, and the sums and differences of the frequencies come out of the modulators. One music modulates the other. Transformed sound arises only when both—organ and chorus—produce sound simultaneously. The sound mixed in the four modulators is conducted through volume regulators whose outputs are connected with four loudspeaker groups. The loudspeakers are behind the chorus on the podium, thus the original sound of chorus and organ mixes with the modulated sound coming simultaneously from the loudspeakers. At the premiere in the large broadcast hall of the Kölner Funkhaus, I attended these regulators from the gallery of the hall. Here I had to open or close the four loudspeaker inputs, according to the score, and I could influence the ratio of the mixture between natural and transformed sound. It is important to me that in *Mikrophonie II*, the transformation of the choral sound takes place in different degrees, and that often untransformed and more or less transformed levels are mixed at the same time; or there are transitions from natural to artificial sound, and vice versa. In comparison with purely electronic music, music like *Mikrophonie II* offers directly perceptible possibilities to compose relationships in a scale from natural to artificial sound, from the familiar (nameable) to the unfamiliar (unnameable).

One of the most important reasons to follow such sound composition is—as with all new, above all electronic, music—to compose a unique, unmistakeable world of sound, and not to uphold any longer the old contrast that says that in composition it doesn't depend so much on the What, for example the material (in this case chorus- and organ-sounds), but only on the How, on what one composes with such sounds. In a work like *Mikrophonie II*, the "what" cannot be separated from the "how": I never would have composed the *way* I composed, if the "what" didn't already have quite specific characteristics, valid only for this work, which led to certain kinds of "how;" e.g. when using ring modulators, one must compose quite definite kinds of structures: as simple superimpositions as possible, many controlled notes, easily perceivable, not too fast levels, since the ring modulation makes very dense symmetrical spectra out of simple sound-processes, and thus can easily lead to a preponderance of noises or to stereotyped articulation of the sounds. The notation in the score changed often in the course of the work, above all during the rehearsals, since many mutual effects between natural and transformed sound were unforeseeable. Finally a score resulted which makes it possible for every single chorist and the organist to react to each other according to context. There were extraordinary demands on the chorists. Every one had not only to sing well, but also, proceeding from my instructions, to himself invent melodic, rhythmic and dynamic articulation in different variations. The organist had to determine from the context the moment and the degree of the electronic transformation through volume change.

From this kind of notation with words and few notes for the singers and the organist, a lively exchange among all the members can arise, if one finds inspired musicians and above all a chorus director like Herbert Schernus, who rehearsed the work *Mikrophonie II* for the Cologne premiere. The sopranos were Mimi Berger, Meta Ackermann, Frigga Ditmar, Ulla Terhoeven, Helga Hopf, Monika Pick; the basses Arno Reichardt, Dietrich Satzky, Hermann Steigers, Peter Weber, Friedrich Himmelmann, Werner Engelhardt. Alfons Kontarsky played the Hammond organ. Johannes Fritsch was the timer. Chorus director Herbert Schernus took care of rehearsals and direction; Hans-Georg Daehn was conductor. The work is dedicated to the American Judith Blinken. As text I used "Einfache grammatische Meditation," 1955, by Helmut Heissenbüttel (Walter-Verlag, Olten and Freiburg/Br.), supplemented by linguistic "insertions" I found in everyday speech. In a few places in the composition, reminders of my earlier compositions *Gesang der Jünglinge, Momente, Carre* appear in the distance (reproduced in performance by loudspeaker). The premiere took place in a public concert "Musik der Zeit" in the large broadcast hall of the Kölner Funkhaus on June 11, 1965.

PROZESSION FOR TOMTOM, VIOLA, ELECTRONIUM, PIANO, FILTER AND REGULATOR

I composed *Prozession* in May 1967 for the ensemble I regularly make concert tours with: Fred Alings and Rolf Gehlhaar (tomtom), Johannes Fritsch (viola), Harold Bojé (electronium) and Aloys Kontarsky (piano).

The tomtom—as in my composition *Mikrophonie I*—is picked up with a microphone, and the viola has a contact microphone. These two microphones are connected with two electric filters and regulators that I attend during the performance; the two regulator outputs lead to four loudspeakers in the four corners of the hall, so that I can have the filtered sounds of these two instruments wander back and forth between two loudspeakers each.

The score formulates a musical process with methods similar to those I have already used in *Plus-Minus, Mikrophonie I* and *Mikrophonie II*. The musical events are not notated in detail, but rather are variants from my earlier compositions, which the performers play from memory. Specifically, the tomtom player and the microphonist call upon *Mikrophonie I*, the violist calls upon *Gesang der Jünglinge, Kontakte* and *Momente*, the electronium player upon *Telemusik* and *Solo*, and the pianist upon *Klavierstücke I-XI* and *Kontakte*. I play filter and regulator with a technique similar to *Mikrophonie I*.

197

In the score of *Prozession* the degree of modulation is prescribed for every player with which he reacts to the event that he himself just played, or to an event that one of the others played. Thus an "oral tradition" is formed between my earlier music and this *Prozession*, as well as from one performer to another, in the moment of performance.

After the players, in the first rehearsals, reacted mostly to themselves and constantly brought new events into play, we have now—after several performances—arrived at a framework in which the players react very strongly to each other, whereby single events run through chain reactions of imitations, transformations and mutations, and often all the players unite for long periods of time into a single musical net of feedbacks.

The instruments for *Prozession* are prescribed in the score; they can, however, be replaced by other appropriate ones, and draw on the additional compositions of the authors as sources.

The premiere was on May 21, 1967 in Helsinki. Other performances followed on the 24th in Stockholm, the 26th in Oslo, the 29th at the Bergen Festival, June 1st in Copenhagen, June 3rd in London. In connection with the following performance on August 26, at the "Internationalen Ferienkursen für Neue Musik," Darmstadt, the first recording was made there for Vox-Turnabout, New York, on September 2. During this recording we played three versions; we chose the third. It was played uninterruptedly. The stereo recording is—without cuts and without the slightest change—a record of the live performance. This record is just as important as the score; it should serve as study— or informational material for future performances of other ensembles in the same way as the printed text, which aims at a newly beginning oral tradition.

The work is dedicated to Judith Blinken.

NEW ROMANTICISM:
AN EMERGING AESTHETIC
FOR ELECTRONIC MUSIC

LARRY AUSTIN

The increasing availability of electronic music instruments is helping to bring about a new understanding of the nature of the medium.
Growing competency with such sonic materials and increasing sensitivity to their flow has freed composers to concentrate on important
problems of content, expression and context, necessary to solve for an
emerging aesthetic for electronic music. Though music made by machines would seem to preclude what we normally think of as "expressive"—passion, sensibility, emotive power—the paradoxical is often
the case: a sensitive, warm, human quality is revealing itself in new
electronic music.

Of course, composers of electronic music have all along been
cognizant of the difficulties of being truly expressive in this medium
of machine music. Composers Pierre Boulez, Morton Feldman, and
Hans Werner Henze, for example, were all early experimenters in
electronic music, but were disillusioned early. Boulez stated in 1957
that "The machine has enormous capabilities, but its skill is very
small when compared to that of the interpreter. . . We are interested
much more by the possibilities given by the fantasy and inspiration
of the human interpreter than by precise mechanical realization."
Other notable composers like Karlheinz Stockhausen, Milton Babbitt,
and John Cage persisted in the medium, overcame early limitations,
and helped to develop the enormous potential of electronic instruments.
Along with design engineers and technicians they worked patiently to
improve the performance and flexibility of the machine. On the improved machines impressive techniques for treating sonic materials
were refined, equal and occasionally even superior to certain expressive powers of human performers, not the least of which was the
obvious virtuoso advantages these new machines had over the human
performer.

Electronic music practitioners today are exploring and developing
viable techniques in fascinating areas: the phenomena of moving sound
sources in space; the psychological and physiological effects of sound

on man (psychoacoustics); the synthesis of vocal sounds with the computer; the control of sound with brain waves; and, along with other important research, the development of new theories of perception, so necessary for the creation of a value system for electronic music. By extending their inquiries over many more aspects of sonic experience, they create new sounds to hear and new musics to enjoy. This curiosity about the nature of sound stems mainly from the new practitioners' attitudes about and their success with the technology of electronic music systems over the past decade. Born at the beginning of this age of electronic and computer music, they know these instruments as an integral part of their immediate musical heritage. They are actively engaged in creating new music with these instruments in the way that, for example, the piano—after its invention in 1709 by Cristofori—gradually gained the status of a repertory instrument. The difference seems to be that what took composers and performers two hundred years to nurture for the piano, is being accomplished for electronic music instruments in a much shorter span of time. New electronic music created in Stockholm yesterday, for instance, can be sent to California for playback tomorrow. Evidence of the enormous spread of electronic music information and the resulting international mutual influence is seen in the rapid development and increased use of electronic music instruments over the past five years, particularly in the portability and reliability of solid state synthesizers and multi-channel tape recorders. The new *Arp-2600 Synthesizer*, for instance, is a complete mini-studio, weighing only thirty-five pounds, extremely reliable and easy to operate with functions that would have involved a good-sized classic studio a decade ago. Other mini-studios are the custom-made *Buchla Electronic Music Systems;* the other popular U. S. mini-system—the *Sonic VI,* the *Electrocomp,* the *mini moog;* the English-made *Putney Synthesizer;* and the most recent entry, the Finnish-made *Digelius,* a digitally operated instrument complete with memory bank. The synthesizer's companion instrument, the tape recorder, has improved as well. For instance, with the successful development and manufacture of a reasonably priced, portable, quarter-inch, four-channel (separate and in-line) tape recorder (called "quadraphonic"), it has now become feasible for the independent practitioner to experiment with the complex compositional concepts involved in the discrete placement and movement of sound sources: moving sounds in circles, figure-eights, or in random patterns; placing sounds in specific positions in space, creating "sound sculptures," such as slowly evolving sound-mobiles or quickly whirling sound textures or dense sound masses;

creating sonic environments which conform to and complement a given space. Such "sound-in-space" compositions can easily be recorded and played back on these new four-channel, portable machines, opening up even more possibilities for the creation of new musics. It is a fact that, because of rapid advances in the technology of electronic music instruments over the past few years, new musical concepts and techniques of much importance are being developed, often non-traditional and unconventional (e.g., "event-complexes"—non-linear, overlapping, layered, turned-back on themselves, and tautly inter-related). Stravinsky, nonplussed by such tendencies among the youth, wryly remarked in a New York Review of Books interview in 1967: "The young musician takes his degree in computer technology now, and settles down to his Moog or his mini-synthesizer as routinely as in my day he would have taken it in counterpoint and harmony and gone to work at the piano." Quite right. Young composers formerly worked for compositional fluency primarily with the piano and its sound materials; today their composing instrument is often mainly the synthesizer.

The intense concentration by electronic music practitioners on "made-up" sound materials often manifests itself in the kinds of music being created today, for "sound's sake": "sonic flurries," "soundscapes," "sonic rituals," "sonic apparitions," "sound bathing," "sound gardens," "spatial harmonies," "electronic symphonies" . . . in short, a celebration of electronic, sonic abundance. Contrast these current fantasies with the preoccupations of the sixties: experimentalism; minimal and conceptual art; graphic notation; serial and chance techniques exploited to extremes; "process-perceptions;" open forms; free group improvisation . . . necessary explorations in gaining requisite technical fluency for today's romantic, sonic outpouring. As a result, currently emerging attitudes among younger composers seem genuinely motivated by a deeper understanding of the nature of music as pure "aural information." In electronic music this sort of attitude provides an ideal situation for the budding composer: whatever one is talented, sensitive, and rigorously informed enough to do and wants to do is seemingly possible to realize on the synthesizer or the computer and, of course, practical to present in whatever context one chooses. What better situation for the new practitioner?

Today, electronic music is no longer casually dismissed as a series of "bleeps and blurps" occasionally tickling the fancy with crude resemblance to conventional instruments or echoes of the sounds of the machine world we live in. As its acceptance as an important part of the music scene makes steady progress, the main prejudice against the medium—that electronically-made music is inferior in expressive power to human-made music—is being disproved. For the uninformed, however, electronic music must still symbolize the modern frustration that the machine, rather than extending man's powers of creative expression, has instead turned on its creator and subjected him to a tyranny of technological dependence. Electronic music, to this time, may indeed have seemed to many tradition-bound music lovers like an awful nightmare of a mad, de-humanized sound scientist intent on getting rid of all "imperfect" human-made music, replacing it with his own "perfect" machine-made music. Such fears would be silly to mention, of course, if it weren't for the fact that, even for many sophisticated professional musicians, electronically-made music is thought to pose a real threat. With amazed credulity we witness a lone electronic music practitioner combine synthetic instrumental *and* vocal sounds to "perform" great works from the standard repertory—music made by machine which normally would have taken, say, fifty musicians hundreds of man-hours to prepare for a performance or a recording. The most famous example of the astonishing prowess of such electronic music practitioners is Walter Carlos's synthetic renditions of Bach's orchestral music on the Moog Synthesizer, a recording which quickly became a hit. Thoughtful observers of the musical scene realize, however, that lurking fears of economic deprivation for professional musicians are short-sighted, developing from a misunderstanding of the nature of the electronic music medium itself. The essential point to remember is that serious composers of electronic music look upon their medium as being a complement to the other music media, not a competitor with and certainly not as a replacement for human-made music. Electronic music has its own meaning, its own validity, and is developing its own aesthetic value system, hopefully allaying unwarranted fears and prejudices among the music community. Electronic music will flourish in the future because of its worth as art, not its questionable worth as an imitator of other musics or its toy-music novelty. The bases for judging the essential worth of this or that piece of electronic music were laid two decades ago, the beginning of the modern era of electronic music.

PRECEDENTS

Two years after World War II the first tape recorders, banks of wave generators, modifiers, and various electric music instruments became available to pioneer investigators in New York, Paris, and Cologne. The electronic music compositions that resulted were mainly of two classes: *musique concrète* (also called "tape music" and "music for magnetic tape"), pre-recorded sounds electronically and mechanically modified, and assembled in novel fashions, most often in collage; and *elektronische Musik*, sounds generated exclusively from banks of wave generators, combined and modified into tape pieces, whose compositional principles derived mainly from then-current post-Webern serialism. A third direction was the combination of these two classes: "pure" electronic sounds with "live" and/or pre-recorded sounds. These initial investigations resulted in significant electronic music compositions, including John Cage's *Williams Mix* (New York, 1952), Karlheinz Stockhausen's *Studie I and II* (Cologne, 1953-54), and the tape portion of Edgar Varèse's *Desert* for chamber ensemble and tape (New York, Paris, 1953-61).

After 1953, studios were established in many national radio broadcasting centers in Europe, including Milan, London, Geneva, Gravesano, Utrecht, Brussels, Berlin, Darmstadt, and Warsaw, as well as an important studio in Tokyo. In the United States, culminating from the tape music research accomplished by Vladimir Ussachevsky and Otto Luening at Columbia University in the early fifties, the Columbia-Princeton Electronic Music Center was established in 1958. There, the following year, the Mark II RCA Synthesizer was installed, beginning the current era of the completely self-contained electronic music machine. Meanwhile, at the universities of Illinois and Toronto, experimental electronic music studios had been equipped and were in operation, beginning a movement in musical higher education in the United States which was to have major influence on subsequent research, composition and instruction in electronic music.

In the early sixties two more classes of electronic music were developed: "live-electronic music," originated by John Cage and David Tudor and performed regularly since then as music for the Merce Cunningham Dance Company, and "computer-generated music," first used successfully by Lejaren Hiller at the University of Illinois and later by Milton Babbitt and his associates and students at Princeton. The proliferation of electronic music by the mid-sixties throughout the world was astounding: over 5000 tape music compositions were extant and catalogued by then.

Through the sixties, as younger composers became aware of the exciting potential of the electronic music medium, important conclusions about its nature were being reached: machines don't *have* to sound like conventional instruments, imitating their musics and techniques (the unfortunate and misleading term "synthesizer" originates from the conception that electronic music instruments must necessarily have as their highest goal the successful imitation or "synthesis" of the sounds and timbres of conventional musical instruments); machines don't *have* to deny their elemental nature, e.g., the constancy of the electrical current which powers them; since machines don't have to breathe, phrase, or count like human performers, machines don't *have* to mimic known musics, basing their validity on such classic conventions as antecedence, consequence, gestural content, sectionalization, or even the use of the 12-tone tempered scale. Consequently, younger composers began to explore new approaches to musical content, leaning more and more toward organic evolution of material and away from classical concepts of structure that had been an inherent part of the evolution of conventional instrumental music to that time. They were finding that, rather than imposing past contexts of other musics on the new medium to gain requisite compositional fluency, they would allow the sound materials of electronic music to reveal new compositional contexts, naturally. "Work with the materials and the instruments, and the appropriate contexts and techniques will reveal themselves." This self-instruction method was the necessary pragmatic approach, since no tried and true procedures for creating this new music existed at the time.

THE OUTLOOK

Working regularly with the sonic materials of electronic music is much more practical today than a decade ago. If an aspiring practitioner can't actually afford his own mini-synthesizer or tape machine, he can probably rent time on one; or he can have access to well-equipped studios in various educational institutions; or, more and more, he can simply construct the requisite equipment himself. The trend is for the practitioner to construct electronic music instruments himself, using as a guide circuit diagrams and instructions found in popular electronic magazines, handbooks, and various specialized electronic music publications. After gaining practical experience from building a few such instruments, the young practitioner often experiments with designs of his own or others. Young composers are thus becoming knowledgeable about how electronic music instruments are designed and made and about the potential for further refinement of their technology and control, finally leading to the design and invention of aesthetically viable, totally automated music machines.

Composers have always been fascinated with the invention of music-making machines: canons, fugues, perpetual motion pieces, tape loops, the Composetron, the Theremin, the Melodium, the Melochord, the Elektronium, computed compositional sub-routines, all sorts of electronic music-making devices. Nowadays, the already highly automated synthesizer is adding more and more features to make the materials of electronic music automated: memory units, sequencers, sample-and-hold devices, random sound generators, etc. Since the advent of space-age electronics, with the possibility of hundreds of functions contained in one tiny electronic part (the "integrated circuit"), this compulsion to create composing machines has led many younger practitioners to do their own research and development of equipment, acting as their own technicians and design engineers. They purchase electronic parts originally designed for commercial computers (or rockets), for instance, adapt them to their own use and, through a varied process involving instinct, rigorous self-instruction, improvisation, trial-and-error, and a sort of electronic alchemy, invent "black boxes" sometimes capable of rendering music of incredible sonic complexity and musical interest.

New composers of electronic music are expressing a new-found romanticism, not unlike their nineteenth century counterparts. The important difference is, however, that the visions of a Berlioz, a Liszt, a Wagner, or a Busoni are not just idle dreams of creating musics: "sonic visions," the "sounding space," the "sounding mass". . . Such dreams are perhaps realizable today. In a 1967 conversation recorded in the first issue of the magazine "Source," German composer Karlheinz Stockhausen and California composer Robert Ashley discussed with me their feelings about new music. At one point in the conversation, expounding about deeply moving music, Ashley said, "It's beautiful, because it's really aural magic." I added, "It happens with ecstasy," as Stockhausen responded, "It's just incredible. You get goose skin and everything. And you cry. You fall in love." Compare our reactions to the music of our time with Liszt's comment that, "Music embodies feeling without forcing it. . . " or Hegel's 19th century book on aesthetics saying that, "The special task of music is that . . . it becomes alive in the sphere of subjective inwardness . . . the musical work absorbing us completely and carrying us along with it . . . exerting an elemental power lying wholly in the element of *sound*." The new romantic movement in electronic music exhibits these same qualities of feeling, subjective inwardness, love of sound, and complete emotional absorption.

NEW ROMANTICISM:
AN EMERGING AESTHETIC
FOR ELECTRONIC MUSIC
Part Two

LARRY AUSTIN

NEW CONTEXTS

New contexts are always being developed for the presentation of various musics, but most especially for the relatively new medium of electronic music. Conventional concert halls are often unsatisfactory for the proper presentation—the proper sounding—of much electronic music. This is particularly true when such music involves movement of sound sources as part of the composition, or when environmental factors such as lighting or seating arrangements play an important part in the total effect of the composition. Consequently, a great deal of experimentation has gone on during the past decade to find better contexts for the presentation of electronic music. One outgrowth of this activity is the increasing number of "sound exhibitions" being presented in galleries about the country, the most notable one having been the exhibit called "Sound" at the Museum of Contemporary Crafts in New York in the fall of 1969. The movement "out of the concert hall" and into the gallery, private soiree, or other space, plus the general disaffection among artists with the socio-economic situation around the concert-giving business, is converging with an increased interest in and use of film, experimental television, and radio, presented in all sorts of theatrical and environmental contexts. Electronic music, because of its newness, is inexorably mixed up in all this experimentation. From its beginning twenty years ago electronic music has been confronted with the problem of reconciling the conventional music audiences simply to *listening* to two or more speakers on a stage, without the pleasant diversion of watching performers realize the piece. Most composers—intensely concerned with controlling the presentation of their works and the perception of them—realize that they have now become responsible for the visual as well as the aural. Out of this need for control over the visual and the theatrical contexts of presentation, then, has come "mixed media" or "multi-media" or, lately, "intermedia." "Intermedia," a term coined by avant-garde critic-composer Dick Higgins, suggests the special interaction and mutual complementation of the sonic, graphic, spatial, cinematic, poetic, choreographic, and theatrical. Whatever one terms this development, it is clear that electronic music is, indeed, becoming more refined and consistent in its contexts of presentation and, consequently, audiences are becoming more appreciative of the significance of the medium.

Audiences today want to know about who makes electronic music, how they do it and what value systems these practitioners have developed for judging its worth. Instances of growing popular acceptance of electronic music are proved by the great number of records sold of a purely electronic music composition like Morton Subotnick's *Silver Apples on the Moon*. Evidence of growing critical acceptance of the medium is found, on the other hand, in the fact that three recent Pulitzer prizes in music were awarded to composers of electronic music: the first, Leon Kirchner's *String Quartet No. 3* with taped electronic music, the second, Charles Wuorinen's electronic music composition, *Time's Encomium*, created on the Columbia-Princeton RCA Mark III Synthesizer. Wuorinen's work was, in fact, the first exclusively electronic composition to receive the Pulitzer prize. The most recent prize went to Mario Davidovski, for his *Synchronism For Piano and Tape* (1972). Future contexts for electronic music, particularly those associated with the visual arts, will no doubt include productions on cable television for special audiences as well as the possibility of intermedia productions made for the new cassette television viewing.

CONVERGENCES

At the same time that electronic music is finding more appropriate contexts for presentation, and its sister medium—intermedia—is achieving new levels of excellence, other related movements also seem to be converging. One, text-sound compositions, involves poets who are working not only with written poetry but also with electronic realizations and modifications of its aural and oral materials—with its sound. In so doing they are developing impressive acuity for sonic materials and are taking good advantage of modern electronic technology, in a way bringing back to life the ancient art of spoken poetry, but with modern transformations. The most important text-sound poetry is being created by a Swedish group in Stockholm, calling themselves *Fylkingen*, literally "flying wedge." In a recording from their 1969 festival is a fine example of their work: Lars-Gunnar Bodin's *From any point to any other point*, a text-sound composition. In notes written for the work, Bodin says: *"From any point to any other point* is the last piece of a trilogy. The two other compositions are *Cybo I* and *Cybo II*. The text material in these pieces refers entirely to discussions and reflections about sciento-logical and technological views of the world. The texts form a range from 'pure' objective descriptions to my more personal reactions or ex-periences from this field. *From any point* is the most abstract piece in this trilogy. The text has been modified and transformed electronically, sometimes to a degree where the semantic meaning is lost, and only the rhythmic structure remains. In the last section of the piece, the speech element is reduced to a certain 'oral behavior.' I have called this section 'electronic menagerie.' "

Painters and sculptors, too, are becoming increasingly involved in *temporal* and *sonic* considerations indicating yet another convergence of the time and space arts. Conversely, as I mentioned before, composers are exploring visual, graphic, spatial, environmental and theatrical concepts for inclusion in their works, producing theater pieces, sound sculptures, films, environments, even plays. Indeed, we might say that, eventually, the classical distinctions between the fine arts—music, paint-ing, sculpture, dance, theater, poetry, prose—could once and for all blur, finally resolving to the really basic distinctions: the *time arts* and the *space arts*, perhaps with the kinetic and visual joining the two.

STYLE CONSCIOUSNESS

Proof that the medium of electronic music is reaching maturity is revealed in the fact that, through the past two decades, an international movement for the medium has developed and is gaining momentum. As higher standards of excellence in techniques and materials are achieved, schools of electronic music composition are delineating themselves. For instance, we can certainly identify a California school of electronic music composition, centered mainly among composers and practitioners in the San Francisco Bay area and extending to work going on in San Diego and Los Angeles. Or we can point to the pioneer American schools of electronic music composition at the Columbia-Princeton Center or the Experimental Music Studio at the University of Illinois. Each has its unique approach to the techniques and materials of electronic music. Or we can distinguish those practitioners who adhere to one or the other type of synthesizer, such as the Moog composers, the Buchla owners, the Arp enthusiasts, the few who use the Italian synthesizer, the *Synket*, the new *EMS Synthi 100*, or the Finnish digital machine, the *Dimi*. We can name the numbers of electronic music composers who employ digital computers to generate their compositions at institutions like Stanford University, the University of Florence, Utrecht, in Paris or Oberlin or at Buffalo or Stony Brook. And, of course, there is the continuing tradition and improvement of the pioneer electronic studios in Europe and Japan. Finally, and certainly not the least important, are the individual composers who have distinguished themselves in the medium and who are greatly influencing others to follow their lead, forming constellations of influence in this or that "style" of electronic music. All these schools are not only intent on finding their own characteristic basis for expression—their style—but also on healthily influencing one another through the wide circulation of tapes, scores, writings, films, mutual performances, broadcasts and commercial recordings.

Along with and as a result of all these convergences a "style consciousness" is more and more evident. In my view, the currently more mature awareness of the nature of electronic music and its instruments is manifesting itself less in the sort of formalized, classic humanism, which flourished in the recent past, than in a freely associative, informal, highly fantasized expression, what I have earlier referred to as a "new romanticism." Early in the search for viable techniques of composition, much electronic music became highly systematized, of necessity de-emphasizing the knotty problems of expressiveness inherent in the medium. As techniques for producing electronic music became better understood, and a basic electronic music language began to achieve assimilation, fluency in the medium quickly developed. As composers became fluent, they began to acquire the requisite technique to think about style and expressiveness and, of course, became much more sensitive to musical content and its subsequent perception, appreciation, and analysis. The electronic music medium has in some ways gone through a whole history of music in a comparatively short time: after the initial amazement of discovery and experimentation in the medium led to improved systems and instruments and the subsequent introduction of associated visual media, there came the most important events —the widespread use of solid state synthesizers, available to virtually any composer-practitioner and, happening today, the development of valid systems of judgement of the music through informed critical analysis.

Proof of a mature and flourishing electronic music style can be illustrated easily by the effect it has had on conventional instrumental music. Certainly, Stockhausen's *Kontakte*, composed in 1958 for piano, percussion, and taped electronic music, is the first and one of the best examples of the possibilities of the interchangeability and interinfluence of electronic music with instrumental music. An example of the interinfluence of electronic and orchestral music is Gyorgy Ligeti's *Atmospheres* for orchestra, which has not one electronically produced sound but which has often been mistaken for idiomatic electronic music by many uninitiated movie-goers when they heard this music used as a film score for *2001: A Space Odyssey*. The long, sustained, non-diatonic masses of micro-tonal sound produced by the orchestra are easily mistaken for electronic music. It happens, in fact, that Ligeti had, just before the composition of *Atmospheres* in 1961, completed three electronic music compositions in the Cologne Studios and had, most probably, heard a performance of Stockhausen's *Kontakte* there. It is indeed instructive to make a comparison between Ligeti's orchestral and electronic music. First, listen to *Atmospheres* and its electronic-like masses of sound and, then, listen to *Artikulation*, with its gestures and flourishes of "notes" so typical of instrumental music of the post-Webern school of the late fifties. (The practice of exchanging techniques among media is time honored, of course. It happened in the 17th century, for instance, when composers assigned fancy, ornamental passage work to voices, passages that were normally typical of instrumental music of the period. Recently, incidentally, young electronic music practitioners have been rediscovering the unique qualities of conventional instrumental sounds and are turning to this "new area" with great excitement and enthusiasm.)

THE PROCESS OF INSTRUCTION

How have younger composers acquired new fluency and expressiveness in electronic music? Through the sixties two otherwise opposite approaches began to converge: one, the systematic, the formalistic, the analytical, the Stochastic approach, where value is placed primarily on refining precise control over tested compositional techniques and materials; the other, an almost compulsive denial of conventional technique in favor of intense experimentation with materials, creating new contexts for the discovery of yet newer techniques and materials. Younger composers, today dissatisfied with both such exclusive approaches, choose instead to seek more expressive, less empirical approaches for creating their works, working for convergence of approaches, a more pluralistic attitude. Their music seems less and less prone to adopt either anti- or hyper-technical approaches to material and thus seems to me to be on much firmer aesthetic ground. The important accomplishment today is that a tolerance for different approaches is being nurtured, more dialectical, less empirical. Certainly, with continued progress made in approaches to the medium, a better chance is offered than ever before for building a discriminating and thoughtful audience for electronic music.

However, if we don't continue to instruct our audience about the significant electronic music that can be made with our ever-improving machines, there is the danger that the medium will become inexorably associated with the banal and cheap through commercial exploitation in the mass broadcast and recording media. The temptation is there, certainly, since electronic music involves much lower costs of production than conventional acoustical instrumental music. However, if our potential audiences have sets of values for perception and appreciation of electronic music to refer to and to rely on, they can easily distinguish the banal from the truly innovative, the ugly from the beautiful. Before that wonderful day arrives, in the process of acceptance of electronic music, however, there will have to be full acceptance into the musical halls of learning, where future musicians and arbiters of musical taste are trained. As it improves in excellence, electronic music will be made a legitimate part of the musical world and function in what I call the classic "syndrome of art"—composition: performance: appreciation: analysis: composition. . . (A piece of music is created through our understanding of and fluency in a particular musical medium; the work is then realized through performance; if it is well-made and well-performed, its audience perceives and appreciates the relative significance—even the beauty—of its concept and realization; beyond this point, a smaller, specialized group seeks to understand the techniques involved in its production through style analysis; and the smallest number—sometimes only the composer himself—profoundly understands its value through informed critical analysis, suggesting new insights and uses for the initiation of another concept for a better art work, thus recycling the syndrome of composition: performance: appreciation: analysis: composition: . . .) Since the audience is such an important part of the syndrome of art, their education about electronic music is extremely important. That responsibility belongs more to our educational institutions, where long-range programs of instruction in electronic music are being developed. It is lamentable that, as yet, only isolated programs of instruction in electronic music are being carried out today in our educational institutions. The institutions devoted pri-

211

marily and traditionally to training professional performers and composers of music—the conservatories, the schools and departments of music—are still for the most part ignoring the existence of this important music medium and are, I feel, shirking their responsibilities to provide competent personnel, modern equipment and rigorous courses of instruction in electronic music, even though there is a steadily growing demand for persons with such specialized competence and talent. Without a comprehensive and highly specialized education, future practitioners of electronic music will be ill-equipped to handle the materials and future instruments of electronic music. I expect though, that, in time, such problems will be solved and the new kind of artist-musician will emerge: the new music practitioner, the new music expert, the new music artist-scientist.

Finally, one of the most hopeful signs for electronic music is that a great many more people have developed appreciation for and even critical acuity in the medium. Discriminate tastes and higher standards are being developed, because electronic music has taken on value. Music lovers hear and appreciate beauty in this music. It's here to stay.

BETWEEN CATEGORIES

MORTON FELDMAN

Oscar Wilde tells us that a painting can be interpreted in two ways—by its subject or by its surface. He goes on to warn us, however, that if we pursue the painting's meaning in its subject, we do so at our peril. Conversely, if we seek the meaning of the painting in its surface—we do this also at our peril. I will not be as ominous as Oscar Wilde, though this problem does exist when we separate one integral part of any work of art from another.

Music, as well as painting, has its subject as well as its surface. It appears to me that the subject of music, from Machaut to Boulez, has always been its construction. Melodies or 12-tone rows don't just happen. They must be constructed. Rhythms do not appear from nowhere. They must be constructed. To demonstrate any formal idea in music, whether structure or stricture, is a matter of construction, in which the methodology is the controlling metaphor of the composition. But if we want to describe the *surface* of a musical composition we run into some difficulty. This is where analogies from painting might help us. Two painters from the past come to mind—Piero della Francesca and Cézanne. What I would like to do is juxtapose these two men—to describe (at my peril) both their construction and surface, returning for a brief discussion of the surface, or aural plane, in music.

Piero della Francesca is compounded with mysteries. Like Bach, his construction is his genius. We are looking into a world whose spatial relationships have adopted the newly discovered principles of Perspective. But Perspective was an instrument of measurement. Piero ignores this, and gives us eternity. His paintings indeed seem to recede into eternity—into some kind of Jungian collective memory of the beginning of the Christian ethos. The surface seems to be just a door we enter to experience the painting as a whole. One might almost say—despite all the facts against it—that there is no surface. Perhaps it is because Perspective itself is an illusionistic device, which separates the painter's objects in order to accomplish the synthesis that brings them into relationship with each other. Because this synthesis is illusionistic, we are able to contain both this separation and unity as a simultaneous image. The result is a form of hallucination—which della Francesca is. All attempts at utilizing an organizational principle, either in painting or music, have an aspect of hallucination.

Cézanne, on the other hand, does not recede into an arcane time world. The construction of the painting, which might begin as a pictorial idea, disappears, leaving little trace of a unifying organizational principle. Rather than taking us into a world of memory, we are pushed into something more immediate in its insistence on the picture plane. The search for the surface has become the obsessive theme of the painting.

The Abstract Expressionist painters carried Cézanne's surging surface another step forward into what Philip Pavia characterized as "raw space." Rothko discovered further that the surface did not have to be activated by the rhythmic vitality of a Pollock to be kept alive—that it could exist as a strange, vast, monolithic sundial, so to speak, with the exterior world reflecting upon it still another meaning—another breathing.

I'm afraid that the time has now come when I will have to tackle the problem of just what the surface aural plane of music is. Is it the contour of intervals which we follow when listening? Can it be the vertical or harmonic proliferation of sound that casts a sheen in our ears? Does some music have it, and other music not? Is it possible to achieve surface in music altogether—or is it a phenomenon related to another medium, painting?

While thinking about all this, I went to the telephone and called my friend Brian O'Doherty. "Brian," I asked, "what is the surface of music I'm always talking to you about? How would you define or describe it?" Naturally, O'Doherty began apologetically. Not being a composer—not knowing that much about music, he was hesitant to answer. After a little coaxing he came up with the following thought:

> "The composer's surface is an *illusion* into which he puts something real—sound. The painter's surface is something *real* from which he then creates an illusion."

With such excellent results, I had to continue. "Brian—would you now please differentiate," I said, "between a music that has a surface and a music that doesn't."

> "A music that has a surface *constructs* with time. A music that doesn't have a surface *submits* to time and becomes a rhythmic progression."

"Brian," I continued, "does Beethoven have a surface?"

"No," he answered emphatically.

"Does any music you know of in Western civilization have a surface?"

"Except for your music, I can't think of any."

Now you know why I call Brian O'Doherty.

When O'Doherty says that the surface exists when one constructs with Time, he is very close to my meaning—though I feel that the idea is more to let Time be, than to treat it as a compositional element. No—even to construct with Time would not do. Time simply must be left alone.

Music and painting, as far as construction is concerned, parallel each other until the early years of the 20th century. Thus, Byzantine art, at least in its uncluttered flatness, was not unlike the Gregorian Chant or the Plain Song. The beginning of a more complex and rhythmic organization of material in the early 15th century with the music of Machaut was akin to Giotto. Music also introduced "illusionistic" elements during the early Renaissance by way of inaugurating passages of both soft and loud sounds. The miraculous blending or fusing of the registers into a homogeneous entity, as in the choral music of Josquin, could also be said of the painting of that era. What characterized the Baroque was the interdependence of all the parts and its subsequent organization by means of a varied and subtle harmonic palette. With the 19th century Philosophy took over—or to be more precise, the spectre of Hegel's dialectic took over. The "unification of opposites" not only explains Karl Marx, but equally explains the long era that includes both Beethoven and Manet.

In the early years of the 20th century, we have (thank Heaven!) the last significant organizational idea in both painting and music— Picasso's analytical cubism, and a decade later, Schoenberg's principle of composing with the 12 tones. (Webern is even more related to Cubism in its formal fragmentation.) But just as Picasso in Cubism was a summing up—an analysis of the history of formal ideas in painting that extended his own future—this tendency also characterized the great names of music at that time. Schoenberg—Webern—Stra-

215

vinsky—are more the history of music than an extension of musical history.

Picasso, who found Cubism in Cézanne, developed from this a system. He failed to see Cézanne's more far-reaching contribution. This was not how to make an object, not how this object exists by way of Time, *in* Time or *about* Time, but how this object exists *as* Time. Time regained, as Proust referred to his work. Time as an Image, as Aristotle suggested. This is the area which the visual arts later began to explore. This is the area which music, deluded that it was counting out the seconds, has neglected.

I once had a conversation with Karlheinz Stockhausen, where he said to me, "You know, Morty—we don't live in Heaven but down here on Earth." He began beating on the table and said: "A sound exists either here—or here—or here." He was convinced that he was demonstrating reality to me. That the beat, and the possible placement of sounds in relation to it, was the only thing the composer could realistically hold on to. The fact that he had reduced it to so much a square foot made him think Time was something he could handle and even parcel out, pretty much as he pleased.

Frankly, this approach to Time bores me. I am not a clockmaker. I am interested in getting to Time in its unstructured existence. That is, I am interested in how this wild beast lives in the jungle—not in the zoo. I am interested in how Time exists before we put our paws on it—our minds, our imaginations, into it.

One would think that music more than any other art would be exploratory about Time. But is it? *Timing*—not Time, has been passed off as the real thing in music. Beethoven, in such works as the *Hammerklavier*, illustrates this perfectly. All the mosaics, all the patch quilt juxtaposition of ideas happen at the *right time*. One feels one is being continually saved. But from what? Boredom perhaps. My guess is that he is saving both himself and ourselves from anxiety.

What if Beethoven went on and on without any element of differentiation? We would then have Time Undisturbed. "Time has turned into Space and there will be no more Time," intones Samuel Beckett. An awesome state that would induce anxiety in any of us. In fact, we cannot even imagine this kind of a Beethoven.

But what does Cézanne do as he finds his way toward the surface of his canvas? In Cézanne's modulations, intelligence and touch have become a physical thing—a thing that can be seen. In the modulations of Beethoven we do not have his touch, only his logic. It is not enough for us that he *wrote* the music. We need him to sit down at the piano and play it for us. With Cézanne there is nothing more to ask. His hand is on the canvas. Only Beethoven's mind is in his music. Time, apparently, can only be seen, not heard. This is why traditionally, we think of surface in terms of painting and not music.

My obsession with surface is the subject of my music. In that sense, my compositions are really not "compositions" at all. One might call them time canvasses in which I more or less prime the canvas with an overall hue of the music. I have learned that the more one composes or constructs—the more one prevents Time Undisturbed from becoming the controlling metaphor of the music.

Both these terms—Space, Time—have come to be used in music and the visual arts as well as in mathematics, literature, philosophy, and science. But, though music and the visual arts may be dependent on these other fields for their terminology, the research and results involved are very different. For example, when I first invented a music that allowed various choices to the performer, those who were knowledgeable in mathematical theory decried the term "indeterminate" or "random" in relation to these musical ideas. Composers, on the other hand, insisted that what I was doing had nothing to do with music. What then was it? What is it still? I prefer to think of my work as: *between categories*. Between Time and Space. Between painting and music. Between the music's construction, and its surface.

Einstein said somewhere that the more facts he uncovered about the universe, the more incomprehensible and alien it seemed to become. The medium, whether it be the sounds of a John Cage or the clay of a Giacometti, can be equally incomprehensible. Technique can only structure it. This is the mistake we make. It is this structure, and only this structure, that becomes comprehensible to us. By putting the "wild beast" in a cage, all we preserve is a specimen whose life we can now completely control. So much of what we call art is made in the same way—as one would collect exotic animals for a zoo.

What do we see when looking at Cézanne? Well—we see how Art has survived; we also see how the artist has survived. If our interest lies in discovering how Art has survived, we are on safe ground. If our interest lies in how Cézanne, the artist, survived, then we're in trouble—which is where we should be.

I have a theory. The artist reveals himself in his surface. His escape into History is his contruction. Cézanne wanted it both ways. If we ask him, "Are you Cézanne or are you History?" his answer is, "Choose either one at your peril." His ambivalence between being Cézanne and being History has become a symbol of our own dilemma.

Yves Bonnefoy

THE DIALOGUE OF ANGUISH AND DESIRE

I

Often I imagine, up above me,
A sacrificial face, whose rays
Are like a field of ploughed up earth.
Its lips and eyes are smiling,
Its brow is clouded, a sea noise tiring and deep.
I say to it: Be my force, and its light increases,
It dominates a country of war at dawn
And a river which calms by meanderings
This seized and quickened earth.

And I wonder now why all this time was needed,
And all this trouble. For the fruits
Reigned already in the tree. And the sun
Lit up already the country of evening.
I see the high plateaux where I can live,
This hand which holds another hand of rock,
This respiration of absence which raises
The masses of unfinished autumn ploughing.

II

And I think of Koré the Absent; who took
The glittering black heart of the flowers in her hands
And who, unrevealed, fell, drinking blackness,
On the meadow of light — and shadow. I understand

218

That sin, death. Jasmines, asphodels
Belong in our land. Shores of water
Limpid, green and not too deep make the shadow
Of the heart of the world tremble there . . . Why, yes. Take.
The sin of the cut flower is forgiven us,
The soul is all arched round some simple words,
The grey shading is lost in the ripe fruit.

The iron of the words of war disappears
In the joyous matter of no return.

III

Yes, it's that.
A dazzle in the ancient words.
The crests
Of our whole life in the distance like a joyous
Sea, made clear by a sword of living water.

We no longer need
Agonizing images in order to love.
That tree over there suffices us, which, through light,
Passes beyond itself and knows no more
Than the nearly said name of a nearly incarnate god.

And all this high country the One, rising, burns,

And this wall's rough plaster that time, simply, touches
With its hands of no sadness, that have measured.

IV

Oh you,
And my pride is there,
Who are less in your own light, better loved,
Who are strange to me no longer. We have grown, I know,
In the same dark gardens. We have drunk
The same difficult water under the trees.
The same severe angel has menaced you.

And our steps are the same, freeing themselves
From the brambles of forgettable childhood
And from the same impure imprecations.

V

Imagine one evening
Light is late over the land,

Opening its proferred hands of storm, whose
Palm is our place of hope and of anguish.
Imagine that the light be sacrificed
To save a mortal place, and under a god
Far-off, no doubt, and dark. The afternoon
Has been purple and simply drawn. Imaginings
Have torn in the mirror, turning their bright
Silver smiling face towards us.
And we have grown a little older. And happiness
Has ripened its bright fruits in absent branches.
Is a nearer land there, my pure water?
Are these roads you go along in barren words
To become, on a shore then your home forever,
Music "in the distance", pass through "in the evening"?

VI

Oh with your wing of earth and shadows wake us
Angel vast as the earth, and bear us
Here, to the same part of the mortal earth,
For a beginning. May the ancient fruits
Be our thirst and hunger, now assuaged.
The fire be our fire. And the waiting turns
Into this hour, this stay, and this near fate.
Iron, ultimate seed,
That sprang up in the fallow of our gestures,
Our curses, our pure hands,
That fell apart in grains which welcomed the gold
Of Time which, like the circle of near stars,
Is both beneficent and vain,

Here, where we are walking,
Where we learned the universal language,

Open, speak to us, tear yourself apart,
Burning crown, heart's luminous beating,
Sun's amber.

Angel Gonzalez

POETICS

Writing a poem: marking the water's skin.
Softly, symbols
change shape, are enlarged,
express what they want,
the breeze, the sun, the clouds,
swell up, tighten up, until
man sees them
—wind calm,
sunlight high—
or sees his own face
or—pure transparency, deep
failure—sees nothing.

Angel Gonzalez

ORDER

Prudent poets,
like virgins—when there are such—,
should not take their eyes
from the sky.
And, you, daring stranger
who watches men:
study the stars!
(Time, not History).
Avoid
obscene clarity.
                    (*cave canem.*)
And edify mystery. Be pure.
Do not name. Do not reveal.
Let your dark word flow into the night,
shadowy and senseless,
like the moment of your life.

Angel Gonzalez

COUNTERORDER

This is a poem:

Here it is permitted
to hang posters,
throw trash, piss
and scribble phrases like:
Whoever reads this is queer,
I love Irma,
Kill the . . . (silence),
Free sand,
Murderers,
etcetera.

This is a poem.
Keep the strophe dirty.
Spit into it.

The endless afternoon is responsible,
today's tedium,
the changeless stupidity of time.

Angel Gonzalez

CALAMBUR

Then,
        in summer twilights,
the wind
brought an unstable odor of stable
and of grass whispering like a river

from the countryside to my street

that flowed along pale shores of dream
with its song and aroma.

Remote echoes,
sounds unfastened
from that murmur,
threads of a hope
unraveled little by little,
fade away sweetly into the distance:

Already yesterday passes whispering like a river
carrying what is dreamed downstream,
toward the blank shore of oblivion.

Angel Gonzalez

EVERYTHING IS CLEAR NOW

Hope—once so dilligent—
has not come to visit us for some time.

Lately it has been distracted.
It always arrived late, and called us
by the names of long-dead relatives.
It watched us with eyes that saw through itself
like those mirrors that lose their quicksilver.
It touched us with imperceptible hands
and we awoke full of scratches.
It also gave us coins later found worthless.

But now, not even this.
It has been so long since it came
that I even thought:
                    Could it have died?

Later I realized
it was we who were dead.

THE CORPSE IN THE PARLOR

DALTON TREVISAN

tr. Jack E. Tomlins

Lying on her back in bed, staring into the darkness, with her hands folded over her breast, she mimicked the corpse in the parlor. The afternoon had passed quickly: it was a novelty to have a dead man in the house. That night Yvette would not have to listen to his eternal argument with her mother: he was convinced that Yvette was not his child. She could hear her mother scratch herself as she sat beside the dead man: the anxious scraping of fingernails over a silk stocking. She recalled the face of the caller who had come to pay his respects to the deceased, how he had afterward slapped at the cuff of his trousers. He had not wanted his clothing to absorb the dead man's cloying mustiness: every corpse is a bloom of a different perfume.

The night breeze rustled the window curtain and gave her arms gooseflesh, but she did not pull up the blanket from the foot of the bed. She could smell the sweetish odor of the wilted flowers and of the tapers at the four corners of the casket. As the wick sputtered, it made the shadows leap against her bedroom door. The man's particular fragrance hovered beneath the mingled odors of the house. There in his casket, his chin caught up with a white handkerchief knotted at the top of his head, he was beginning to stink.

She heard her mother dragging her house slippers over the floor as a different scent, momentarily overpowering the others, reached her dilated nostrils. Her mother was burning incense. At that moment it would have been easier to die than to elude the corpse. The burial had been set for the following morning, and until then the man's odor

224

would furtively spread through the house, seep into the fabric of the curtains, take root under Yvette's fingernails. The caller had slapped uselessly against the cuff of his trousers. He would be obliged to send them to the dry cleaner's.

The dead man had decided to take leave of his home with consummate lack of grace. The burned-out ash of his last cigarette lay undisturbed in his ash tray; his coat hanging on the back of his chair still reeked of his sweat. How could they hide his hat hanging there on the hatrack, his hat whose brim had so often been turned back by hands now lifeless and folded across his chest. If the girl raised her head, she would be able to see his pajamas outside the window, hanging on the clothesline. His striped pajamas with stains that no water could wash clean. If she looked in the mirror, it was his ashen face that she would see.

It was not her mother's slippers dragging across the parlor floor: it was his as he leaned against the door to listen to Yvette and her fiancé whispering in the hallway. Suddenly his rocking chair would begin to move again, at the slightest recollection of him. His rocking chair with the cane bottom distended from the weight of him. No matter how frantically she swept the floor, she still found his broken toothpicks in every corner: he had always had a toothpick hanging from his mouth. After digging at his rotten teeth, he would slowly draw a whitish line with his toothpick across his puffy nose. He would roll his bread into little balls and flick them with his fingertips. Yvette had found them in the folds of his napkin, among the lacy fingers of the potted fern, lodged in the frame of the Last Supper.

He had taken his own good time in dying. For months on end he had rocked back and forth in his chair with his pajama top open because of the heat, revealing a mass of chest hair so long that it coiled into wiry gray ringlets.

"That girl has no feelings," he railed at his wife. "She looks at me like she wanted me to hurry up and die and be done with it."

He had spent his life as a traveling salesman and had wasted little time with his family, and one fine day he simply came home to die. He sniveled from room to room in his striped pajamas, which he never changed. She could hear his felt slippers as he came near and leaned against the door to listen to the little sounds Yvette and her sweetheart made in the hallway. As he eavesdropped he would chew his toothpick behind the closed door. The girl would cough to let him know that she was aware of his spying, and when she came in again she inevitably found that he had dragged himself back to his rocking chair. She took small vengeance in polishing his shoes, always his shoes. Why polish them if she knew he would never wear them again? She left them resplendent, never waiting for his gratitude, and every week his unused shoes reappeared as smudged as before. There they were now, lined up straight, on top of his wardrobe. If her mother offered them to the milkman or to the baker, the dead man would climb the steps again to reclaim them and the girl would recognize his footfall on the stairs.

It began the afternoon Yvette was dusting the furniture. She was wearing slacks rolled up to her knees, and she noticed that he was looking at her legs. She could imagine his thoughts: "That girl with her birdlegs . . ." From behind his paper he spied on her out of the corner of his eye. The page trembled so violently that is was impossible for him to read. He dropped the page and screamed that she should go change her clothes and not run around the house half naked:

"Cover up your legs. Even if they were pretty, which they're not!"

She was thirteen years old, and since the salesman had returned for good, she never left the house except to go to school, and only then in that dreadful blue uniform. She and her mother were the man's prisoners, he in his woolen socks (even in summer), with the little balls of bread on the tablecloth, and his broken toothpicks in every corner.

"He's just upset because he's sick," her mother implored. "Please be patient with him!"

Yvette did her homework in the parlor. He dozed or read the paper; her mother drudged in the kitchen. Bent over her notebook she suddenly felt the hair on her arm stand erect: he was staring at her. He wasn't asleep; nobody could sleep when his eyelids were moving. He wasn't reading the paper; who could read a paper with his hands shaking like that! The girl went to her bedroom to finish her lessons. From there she could keep an eye on the rocking chair in the parlor. She lifted her eyes from the book and listened hard like a hunted animal . . .

She smoked on the sly in her bedroom. The chair creaked when he rocked and annoyed her so she could not study, but the man who could barely drag himself along by holding on to the furniture knocked at her bedroom. He knocked so hard that it frightened her and she opened the door. He immediately saw the cigarette, still burning where she had thrown it on the floor. With the live ash he burned Yvette's arm, and he made such a hideous face that she did not dare to call out for her mother.

"Don't scream, you tramp. If you do I'll kill you!"

She began to wear only long sleeves so she could hide the red welts on her arms. At mealtime he never took his eyes off her and, if she wanted a second portion, she got up and went around the table for it so she would not have to address him directly. Between them, her mother ate without lifting her eyes from her plate.

When he could not bear it any longer (he rocked in his chair so furiously, why in the name of God didn't he just go flying out the window?), he scratched on her door. He held a cigarette in his hand. It was the only time he ever smoked. He slowly lifted her sleeve, and the girl bit her lip with all her might to keep from crying out. She bore the burn of the cigarette until it crumbled to shreds between the man's fingers.

She always woke up at night when she heard them arguing in the next room. He had been on the road for years and insisted that, in his absence, his wife had enjoyed numberless affairs. Bellowing, he demanded to know what the girl was doing under his roof, since he was not her father. The poor woman sobbed and swore that she had been faithful. In the morning, Yvette looked at herself in the mirror to see whether she could find any family resemblance. It was strange. She was the very image of her father: the same dark hair, just like his before he fell ill, the same large mouth and full lips.

Her mother asked her to take the patient his tea in his room. The doctors had given him up and he could not possibly last much longer, a few days at most. She begged the girl to treat the dying man with kindness. Why not take his tea to him in his room. Yvette's heart softened and she took the tray from her mother. She stopped short at his door: he was only a pityful old man who was afraid of dying.

Before he died, he begged her to forgive him and kiss him on his forehead as a token of her pardon. He spoke with his eyes closed; his eyelids fluttered. As she leaned down, he suddenly grabbed her and kissed her full on the mouth. It was worse than being burned by his cigarette. She ran to the bathroom and rinsed out her mouth and brushed her teeth with such frenzy that her gums bled.

He could now barely stand the pain of his wracked body and got out of bed only by leaning on his wife's shoulder, in order to reach his chair. He was too weak to rock it. The eyes in his helpless body followed the girl. She never again returned to his room. Her mother never asked why. When he saw that she was beyond his reach, he roared:

"Who's your old man? Which one of your mother's lovers was your old man? Tell me his name. Come in here, you tramp!"

In revenge the girl took to wearing too much make-up. When her fiancé whistled at the front entrance, the chair fell silent. The salesman returned from the transports of his crazed mind. From the dark hallway Yvette could see him in her imagination, craning his neck, trying in vain to sort out the voices. She laughed a little too loudly so the spy could hear through the door. Her boy friend thought she was crazy. When she came back in, her lips were stripped of the lipstick the boy had kissed away. She deliberately crossed through the parlor so the man could lean from his chair and see for himself the dark circles under her eyes and her disheveled dress.

At dawn Yvette was awakened by their shouting. Clinging to his chair he was in such acute pain that he could not sleep. His wife rocked the chair for him while he demanded to know the names of her lovers. Sleepless with his pain the dying man idly observed the spectacle of his waning life. In her bedroom the girl lit her lamp; lately she could not get back to sleep without a light. Waiting for sleep to come, she fervently prayed that he would die.

Her fiancé had whistled from the hallway and Yvette went to meet him. The man in the striped pajamas had reached his final agony. They kissed so long that her mother had to come to the hallway to get her: she could feel the scratch of his beard with every kiss. Lying in bed with her hands folded over her breast, playing dead, her heart pounded with delight, she fell asleep. Then the man climbed from his casket and came into her bedroom:

"What are you doing, tramp?"

"I'm sleeping."

"Don't you have a mathematics examination in the morning?"

"Yes."

"Why aren't you studying then?"

"You're dead, father. I don't have to take the examination."

When Yvette awoke, she could still hear their voices. She opened her eyes: one corner of the mirror shone in the half light. She could hear her mother in the parlor, scratching herself. She had caught the dead man's fleas, for sure.

She sat on the edge of the bed and outside the window she caught a glimpse of the pajamas, covered with stains, flapping in the breeze. He was dead. She heard her mother dragging her slippers along the corridor toward the kitchen.

Standing beside the casket, Yvette rubbed her lips against the back of her hand. His kiss burned her tongue. She waited a long moment; it was not an easy matter to escape the dead man. She lit a cigarette and gazed at the old man through the gray smoke. She saw the handkerchief tied about his chin, the handkerchief which kept the drool from oozing from his mouth. Was he staring at her with his half-open eyes, through his long lashes? No. This time his eyelids did not flutter. Yvette swallowed the smoke; she was mad with pleasure. He was really dead. In the kitchen, her mother made coffee in preparation for the wake.

The girl leaned over and examined the man: his eyelids, his beard, his mouth. She raised his sleeve and, pushing aside the black beads of the rosary he held between his fingers, she pressed the red glow of the cigarette against her father's flesh. Very slowly she burned a hole in his hand.

Vasko Popa

THE GAME OF THE ASHES

tr. VASA D. MIHAILOVICH

Some are nights others are stars

Each night lights up its own star
And dances a black dance around it
Until the star burns up

Then the nights divide themselves
Some become stars
Others remain nights

Again each night lights up its own star
And dances a black dance around it
Until the star burns up

The last night becomes both star and night
It lights itself up
It dances the black dance around itself

Vasko Popa

ECHOING

tr. Vasa D. Mihailovich and Ronald Moran

The empty room begins to growl
I retreat into my skin
The ceiling begins to squeal
I fling it a bone
The corners begin to yelp
I fling them a bone each
The floor begins to howl
I fling him a bone too
One wall begins to bark
I fling him a bone too
And the second and the third and the fourth wall
Begin to bark
I fling each one a bone
The empty room begins to roar
And I am empty
Without a bone
Into a hundredfold echo
Of the roar I turn
And echo echo
Echo

Tadeusz Rozewicz

THE SURVIVOR

tr. PAWEL MAYEWSKI

I am a twenty-four year old
survivor
from slaughter.

These are synonyms:
man and beast
love and hate
enemy and friend
darkness and light.

Man's death is an animal's death;
I saw fourgons laden with butchered bodies
that shall never be blessed.

Values are sounds:
virtue and crime
truth and falsehood
beauty and horror
courage and cowardice.

Crime and virtue are analogous;
I knew a man
who was both
virtuous and vicious.

I am searching for a teacher
let him restore my speech and hearing
let him give words their due again
divide anew darkness from light.

I am a twenty-four year old
survivor
from slaughter.

Mario Luzi

tr. I. L. SALOMON

LAS ANIMAS*

Fire everywhere, the gentle fire of brushwood,
fire on the walls where a feeble shadow flaming
hasn't the strength to imprint itself;
fire rises even beyond the pinnacles and sinks
to the hill across a length of ashes,
fire in flakes from the branches and trellises.

Here not before not later but at the proper time,
now that everything about the festive
and sad valley loses life and fire,
I turn round; I count my dead,
the procession seems longer, trembles
from leaf to leaf as far as the first stump.

Give them peace, eternal peace, carry them
to safety away from the ashes and flames
of this whirlwind that presses
strangulated in the ravines, is lost
on trails, flies uncertainly, vanishes,
makes death what it is, no more
an end, struggle done with and lifeless.
Give them peace, eternal peace, quiet them.

Down there where the cutting is thicker
they plow, push vats to the springs,
whisper during the stilled mutations
from hour to hour. In a corner
of the garden a puppy stretches himself and dozes.

---

* Note: Jorge Guillén told me that in Spain the day of the dead is called *Las animas*.

A fire so gentle is hardly enough,
if enough to illuminate as long as
this undergrowth under life may last. Another,
only another could do the rest
and more; to consume these spoils,
to change them to light, clear and incorruptible.

Requiems from the dead and for the living, requiems
for the living and dead in one flame. Poke it:.
night is here and overspreading
stretches its quivering cobweb between the mountains;
soon the eye will no longer serve; what remains
is awareness for light or the dark.

Translator JONAS ZDANYS

Henrikas Radauskas

THE TASKS OF MIRRORS

When midnight comes, mirrors begin to work. The autumn night is long, the glass is smoky and lazy with age, it's a long time until day, and they have no reason to hurry. The first leans over, and in him is reflected the shape of someone lying on the rug with a black stain on his temples, and the mirror gently hands him over to the next one, and the second pours him over to the next one, and that's how they work until dawn when, in the last mirror, all that's left is a dark stain, but that, too, eventually disappears.

Meanwhile all the sleepers in the town dream that they are being born and just can't be born and that they choke in narrow corridors and fall into ravines where they begin to rush about,—they'll kill themselves and kill those on the bottom and scream but can't scream and wake up, drenched in sweat, and hear a fading blow of a bell stretching toward a damp cotton-stuffed sickly November morning.

Eugène Guillevic

ROCKS

tr. TEO SAVORY

I

They would not know
if we spoke of them
And they never have anything to keep
except size.

Except forgetfulness of the tides
and of red suns.

II

They have no need of laughter
or drunkenness.

They do not burn sulphur
in the darkness

Because they have never
feared death.

They have made a guest
of fear.

And their madness
is clear-sighted.

III

And then the joy

Of knowing the menace
and enduring it.

While on their margins
a pebble, scratched

By wave and wind,
leaves them, during their siesta.

IV

They do not have to carry their face
like a punishment.

They do not have to wear their face
where all may be read.

V

Dance is in them,
flame is in them,
whenever they feel like it.

It is not a spectacle in front of them:
it is in them.

It is the dance of their intimate
and lucid madness.

It is the flame in them
of the ember's core.

VI

They have no desire to be a temple
of delight.

But the menace is always there
on the outside.

And the joy is always there
from within them,

Joy whether the sea is grey
or a decayed blue.

VII

They feel the ouside,
they know the outside,

At times perhaps they might feel blessed
by the limitations of it:

Total power
is not their weakness.

VIII

Sometimes in their night
there is a groaning
long resounding,

And their grain is drowned
in an overwhelming fright:

Then they no longer knew
that they had a voice.

IX

The time comes when a block
pulls away and falls,

Falls and loses breath
in the liquid sea below.

Then they were no more
than lumps of pebbles,

A place for the dance,
worn out by the dance.

X

But the worst is always to be
outside of the self
when the madness
is no longer lucid:

To be the memory of a rock, thrown
outside towards wave and sea.

Bertalicia Peralta

SILENCE

Silence is the substance of a drop
           of water that does not fall
it creates or it does not create

silence also can endure
           in time without enduring
silence is in the end
object of subtleties
like light / authentic
like water / rigid
like certainty / undiscovered

weakness of the mind
clamor of night
           the vapor of a glowing eye

silence like death
           like love
           is everything
or is not

Bertalicia Peralta

LIKE A HOLLOW SNAIL

Here a man echoes
like a hollow snail

without house / wine / or blood
in the absence of loving union
it happens

from revelation and dream
he is nourished / he is alone
he sings alone
      and echoes
like a hollow snail

Alfonso Chase

SOLAR MUSIC

> *There is nothing but the earth and the senses of people.*
> *Nothing that will endure the pulsating veins.*
> *The spirit is only the flesh,*
> *the soul is only the bones.*
> *They invented the soul to shame the body,*
> *the only dwelling place for dream and reason.*
> ANNA DE NOAILLES

A man. A woman. Two senses woven together.
Two shadows without memory.
Above the sky I recognize a world free of oblivion,
seasons without time, the air stirring over the water,
and life, the mirror of itself
passing its knife back and forth in my hands.

A man. A woman. The abyss.
A city in flames that glows
in the unbounded darkness of your hands,
forms that meditate or rise up in the nights
to take refuge in the body:
dark signs searching for the essence in words
cast aside the wisdom of proverbs.

A man. A woman. Two worlds alone
in the monotonous spinning of the air.
A tree with its roots towards the sky,
a caterpillar that struggles against the air
as new shadows build into the touch
the freedom that flows,
the hands that invent themselves
in the ageless time that is reborn in the pores.
In the beginning you and I are
the air, the streets: the hours,
the anguish of being the others, so distant from ourselves,
invaded by mad unstable dreams,
asking for freedom of the body, the word.

Time that circles and is no longer time.
Death that springs forth and is never life.
Speeches. Men cutting off their hands
in a vain attempt to escape the body.

Desire. The blood that flows is not the blood
that strengthens the heart or warms the touch.
Death. Conferences. Buildings.
I am born in myself. Bombardments.
You are born within me, your skin expands.
A thread of air. The shadow of a tree.

To be born, never resting. The racing of time toward life.
You destroy primordial desire,
displace the four cardinal points
and then hide yourself at the crossroads:
the child playing games.
You create the endless geometry of water, death,
you rise forth, throw yourself against the multidimensional object
while the children dance, the moon plunges into their throats.
The orphan city explodes.

II

The void. Always the blind voyage,
always the laughter on fire, always the decayed word,
always the bridge reaching out, always the dry tree.
The word in flames. April in flames passing over time.
A sun that shines brighter. Central Park, London, Mexico,
Buenos Aires, Washington, your body, San José.
A solemn sun, dying,
the timid grass that appears
on forgotten manuscripts or clippings of old newspapers.
Mutual guilt. Slave labor.
War. An immobile shoe
balances the room.
The extermination of natural order: language.

Only silence exists, only the body,
only the battle with the word,
and the defeat of not finding
its image in the air.
The body, accessory to this mystery:
a fixed light forever confronting its fire,
a new purpose, long, complacent, singular,
intent upon gathering one drop of the universe's blood,
something lost among the dreams of trees.
Time, always time,
a dog lifts his jaws to the sky
and licks the wound of the fleeting air.

III

At sunset you hide beauty,
the original shadow, the transparent lonely face.
There in the panting of the darkness, the daily terror,
the meaningless tears,
oh, you, orphan presence of mirrors
suddenly beating in the silence
that falls on the furniture of this room.
Music, music, music, the same music,
the same sound constructing voices
in the silenced rebellion of the throats.
Enraged days talk about each other,
everyone flees through the streets,
the light goes on creating green pines, stones, houses.
Older hands disrupt the balance. Everything crumbles
into foam, noises, orgasms, melodies.

The mirror, the world, the voices.
Confusion of bodies that are suns.
Distant orders, blessings over cannons,
gases that are angry rivers that flow into
the patient blood of children, leaves,
birds of water, silence.
How effortlessly I sink under your eyelids,
pass through your dreams, your body,
swarm of lies and hot coals.
The bridges collapse with empty words,
decisions pretend they are not decisions.
A flower loses its petals, magnesium flash,
waves, streets, oblivion,
the everpresent hammer, pounding out cries,
suffocating the air, splattering out the world,
curiously reborn between my hands.

Memories. Skin. Newspapers. War.
The world breeds murmurs,
the precise excuse, a city that thrives on bitter words,
I love you, I deface you, I abhor you, don't leave me,
the breaking point that encloses,
spring that flourishes in the mirror,
the summoned truth of this music now alive
drumming out sounds over the body.
I am the river of blood that bores
into the rock, the wing of a bird, the night.

IV

At dawn I remember you
in your childhood already spent
among the phantomless streets
that pursued the mist of my town.
The dawn unfolds, it is tenderness,
it is the battle of the tree that throws out its branches,
that pursues, corners, is nothing,
that propagates, explodes,
that loses itself upon losing me in the intricate mask of day.

Memories. Shadows. Words.
I fasten myself to the universal hand, to the sun,
to the multitude that demands meaningful changes
that are born within themselves, that are one,
because abundance suffocates, contracts, destroys me
like an ax against the earth.

I watch myself suffering and I live
under the rain inhabited by your voices.
August. January. May.
The same hand with identical fingerprints:
The child drawn into the night
with this blind brutal music
that grows alone between his fingers.

Oh, you, woman, lover, sister, shadow.
Small drop of joy that explodes noiselessly on the floor.
Childish inconsistency, decayed portrait,
burned leaf, barren corn,
watching you I see myself within your body:
presence around mouths that expand
to form words.

The bodies are stretched out over the earth.
The grain of silence shared under the trees.
The rain forever falling over love,
because it is April eaten away,
the voices of April that explode in the thin solitude of hotels.
Your mouth eaten away, consecration of insignificant acts,
larvae that die of suffocation,

handkerchiefs held high,
the spring is born in scars,
the bitter wind snaps off buds:
deliriums that I endure during intimate caresses.

Grains of pollen that the wind
scatters over the speechless city.
I am pursued by a language that demands the truth,
sacrifices, hopes, bodies.
The sobs of pruned trees
stripped forever of their miracles.
Oh, you, premonitioned and found,
word with green leaves, daughter of the sun, the wind
and the morning. The unleashed desire, the expectant night
that reigns over the face of the world.
Eyes that sharpen their glances. Brittle shadows
broken by your fingers.
Bodies I once knew
I hold this evening against the bed.
In and out of the body you are with me.
The premonitioned. The inevitable. The one who breaks away
in this supreme consecration of all that is forgotten.
I give you a pectoral moon,
you give me a sun, a cry, a word,
a strangled light that unfolds
over the curved world of my chest.
You name me. I name you
but yet suddenly you exist only in the poem,
oh, you, premonitioned, perpetual, sacrificed,
the one who tears apart the spring
and listens to herself like rain.
Tomorrow. Today. Forever.
The knife that cuts through the silence,
that unveils the eye of the needle
and enters the vast world
where tree and water were once together.
The new. The armour of the sun.
Oh, you, balance, murmur, excess:
pour yourself out over my body.

LOCATION OF THE HEART

JUAN TOVAR

tr. MARGARET SAYERS PEDEN

That day he gave them a more than usually difficult assignment; he scolded them for talking in class; he made sarcastic remarks about a teacher they admired. Any one of these things or all of them ("it was a long time ago," Nelly says), the fact is that their usual get-together to do their homework was dedicated to planning revenge. They could stick nails in his tires, but they would have to get permission to leave the school yard during recess and then they themselves (even supposing no one saw them while they were doing it) would become the first suspects. They could go break windows in his house, "I know where he lives," Aurora said, "let's go right now," but Cecilia and Nelly confessed that that idea frightened them also, and they didn't know how to throw anyhow. Aurora said something contemptuous, so the three of them turned to solving equations. The record ended, Presley naturally ("We were crazy about him"), and Cecilia went to change it. Then she left the room; when she came back she was carrying a little book from her father's library.

"Look."

They looked: the title, *Witchcraft*, and hands pushing some very long pins into a rag doll.

"Does it say how you do it?" Aurora asked with interest. They had found the revenge that Suarez Esponda would suffer.

Suarez Esponda was their literature master. A man of medium stature, fiftyish, robust but pale, he always wore slacks and a jacket, a bow tie, and enormous shoes. He had been educated in Germany, and "all he needed was to make us march the Goose Step." That was his nickname, of course, because of his Teutonic training and his big feet. It was natural for him to say: "Next week read *Faust* and bring me a report on it, ten pages minimum" and things like that. He grew indignant if they asked him to repeat, to explain in more detail, or to translate a quotation, or if a boy dared to put his feet on the desk, or if a whisper broke the absolute silence he demanded as background to his dry, precise voice. His weapon was humiliation, wielded with professionalism.

"You don't know who wrote *Mary Stuart*, Mr. Villalobos? But man, only a perfect imbecile wouldn't know who wrote that. Or don't you think so? Answer me! Yes, isn't that true? Only a perfect imbecile. That's you, then? Louder, so all your classmates can hear. That's it. And so you won't forget it, you will bring me one hundred sentences: I am a perfect imbecile. It's my fate, to be in a land of imbeciles trying to educate imbeciles."

In spite of his ridiculous qualities, Esponda was imposing and frightening: a great hostile force against which the girls had now found the perfect opposition.

The booklet on witchcraft is still sold in the cheap bookstalls, along with advice to the lovelorn and joke books. It is nothing but a hasty review of systems and formulas from throughout the ages, but on page thirty-eight Aurora, Cecilia and Nelly must have discovered a key paragraph: "Upon a small wax model, modeled as carefully as possible so as to recall the person whom one wishes to harm, one affixes hair, a tooth from the victim, or parings from his nails, then each day at a determined hour one transfixes the effigy with a pin in the location of the heart, pronouncing words to intensify the intent to do evil, even unto determining death."

Nelly promised to look for more information: her old nurse said she was from a town of witches and the girl made her tell one of her stories about an unpopular mayor who died six months after taking office of a debilitating illness no doctor could diagnose.

"And what *was* the matter with him, Nana?"

"What do you think? The little spell they cast on him."

"And how did they do it, huh?"

"Well, like they do, child."

"How?"

"Oh, there are several ways."

"Do you know any?"

244

"I know how, but it's better not to meddle with those things. The payment comes later. The spirits help you but they collect for it."

"Mmmmm. They do things with dolls, don't they?"

"Yes. Dolls, or pictures."

"Nails or hair . . . ?"

"Um hummm. Or anything that belongs to the person. Unwashed clothes, something in their handwriting. . . ."

"And pins?"

"Pins where you want the pain to be."

"And what else?"

"Water cooled in the night air. And earth. You bury it all to fix the spell. But why do you want to know?"

"Oh, no reason."

Cecilia found *The Medieval Roots of German Romanticism* by Suarez Esponda among her father's books with the author's photograph as frontispiece, and Aurora no longer had to continue struggling with the piece of wax she had obtained. Permission to use a sample of handwriting instead of nails, teeth or hair also made things easier. After class, the girls approached the Master to ask him to autograph his book. . . .

"Do you girls intend to read this?" Esponda smiled. "I don't think you'll understand much of it."

"Whatever's possible, Maestro."

"You *should* say im-possible, if the possibilities are those you demonstrate in class." Esponda put on his glasses and tested his fountain pen. "Is the dedication for all three of you?"

"Yes, Maestro."

In thick, upright letters, Esponda wrote: "To my esteemed students (and the three names, complete, without asking any of them), hoping that the road to knowledge will be for them a path of roses." Following that a quotation in Latin and then his elaborately baroque signature. They thanked him, struggling with the reaction provoked by the trite phrase. ("I felt I don't know what: it was ugly to think about what we were going to do with his book.") But Esponda relieved their conflict, neutralized their sentimental impulse, converting the inscription once again into an instrument for revenge:

"Don't think that because you buy my book I'm going to promote you. If you did it with that in mind, consider it a lost investment."

Near Aurora's home there was a sparsely-populated area: empty lots, construction sites, and an abandoned house which was to be their chosen place. Although midnight would have been the ideal hour, they made a concession on that point. Each one, backed up by the others, told her parents there was going to be a play at school (it was true, although the girls weren't in it) and that the rehearsals were at night. The first meeting was held about nine o'clock under a full moon. Nelly brought a gardening trowel and Cecilia a plastic flask of the specially prepared water; on the way they bought a pennys-worth of pins. With much trembling, in the light of the moon, they searched the abandoned structure to make sure no beggar was in-stalled for the night. It smelled of excrement—the next night Cecilia brought a pine-scented deodorant. They cleared a section in the area of what would have been a large hall. They dug a small grave in which to bury the picture and its inscription. Cecilia played with the pins, laughing nervously.

"Where shall we stick them?"

"In his legs," Aurora said, "and may it give him rheumatism."

They lacked an incantation. Rather than admit she hadn't been able to obtain one, Nelly decided to improvise. The important things were the intent and the intensity: she had never felt as close to God saying Our Fathers as she did when speaking directly to him in a prayer combining respectful formulas and repeated entreaties: All-Powerful God, please let me pass my algebra test. You who can ac-complish anything, please let me, please let me, please let me pass the algebra test, the algebra test, Merciful God. Now it was something like: Do him harm, do him harm, do him harm, oh great and powerful spirit, over and over again, the three girls chanting the three-syllable singsong, building in intensity until some kind of dark trinity seemed about to emerge. Nelly opened her eyes suddenly when she realized ("I swear") that something, a vast shape formed of moonlight, a face-less giant, was there among them, with one foot on each side of the grave. And her glance met Aurora's, frozen at the same point. Nelly lowered her head and opened her arms wide and raised her voice and the others imitated her—three young girls kneeling around a grave where their schoolmaster Esponda, in a library with a fireplace, gazed serenely towards the stars. Now there was no need for consultation, for reaching an agreement: they were of one mind, they were fulfill-ing a well-learned ritual. Cecilia took a few pins and passed around the rest. They pierced the calves of the portrait. Nelly sprinkled the magic water. Aurora began to fill in the grave. When the picture was covered, Nelly said Amen. Amen, said Aurora and Cecilia, and then silence, perhaps the chirping of crickets. The three remained on their knees around a little pile of dirt. They tramped it down a little, they placed a large stone over it. They left the trowel and the flask behind some bushes next to the brick wall and left, in silence.

"Tomorrow we'll have to bring a light," Cecilia said.

They nodded gravely. Only when they were back in the street with the streetlights and the cars did the spirit of play return.

"That'll give him rheumatism," Aurora said, and they burst out laughing.

Several days passed without Esponda's showing the least ill effect: the nocturnal ritual was repeated with slightly desperate insistence, with the rage of possible ineffectiveness, with sordid desire ejaculated in panting rapture. One of the last nights they rubbed earth on their faces; on their breasts, tearing open their blouses; on their legs, chanting, chanting, as if attempting to empty themselves completely, to surrender their vital energies to the spirits so as to contribute to the threatened revenge. The following morning Nelly wept when she saw where she had scratched herself pinning her blouse—she wept without knowing why, a lament that was not remorse although it might have seemed to be. As if it were no longer a game, she says, "it was—I don't know, like masturbating. I don't know if you understand what I'm saying." I think I do. To draw shameful forces from within ourselves, to allow ourselves to be possessed by them . . . and when the possession ends, the faceless monster we have evoked is there still, he takes a long time returning to the dark center where he dwells and one looks at him and says: Is this I? But more than that, it was masturbating in public, in a group, in front of mirrors.

Cecilia was the first to yield to the tension: she missed one night. Her companions waited for her a while, then returned to their homes without planning to meet the next day. The Holy Week holidays came shortly after that; they all went out of town with their families. And when they returned to school: there was a new literature master: Suarez Esponda was ill. Ulcerated legs. They made no comment among themselves, they pretended not to notice. As a matter of fact, they practically never spoke to one another anymore; when school was over each went her way and met with other girlfriends to do her homework.

One night, after one of these sessions, Nelly passed by the house that Aurora had once identified as Esponda's: large, old and gray, only the garden was not neglected. She looked for a while at the lighted windows before crossing the street and ringing. A blond, heavy woman appeared, the German wife of the schoolmaster.

"Ah, you come see Professor, he will be glad. Come, please."

Esponda was in the library, behind his desk. He greeted her by her proper name, invited her to sit down. He made a sign to his wife who then pushed his wheelchair over to the fireplace of the buried picture. Esponda looked at Nelly and raised his eyebrows slightly as if they were in class and he had just asked her a question.

"I came to see how you were getting along, Maestro."

"I thank you very much, although you might have come at a better hour."

"It's just. . . I was just passing by. . . "

"Yes, yes, and I appreciate it. How is school?"

"Well . . . the same as always. Will you be back soon?"

"I don't think so. This won't heal."

Esponda pointed disdainfully at the plaid robe covering his legs and sighed resignedly. Then he looked at Nelly with scorn.

"That must please all of you very much, does it not?"

"No, Maestro," she protested weakly: suddenly it seemed to her that he knew everything, "how could you think. . . ?"

"How? Easy: I'm aware of what goes on. I imagine all of you students are happy: Old Goose Step is out of combat."

Nelly blushed. Standing next to her husband, the German woman listened with an affable smile, looking from one to the other.

"That is what they call me, isn't it?"

"Some . . . but . . . "

"You will have to look for a more fitting nickname. That shouldn't be difficult. Lame. . . The Lame Duck. The . . . but you have more imagination for these things than I."

"Maestro, it isn't true. . . "

"What? *What* isn't true?"

Esponda struck the arms of his chair and leaned forward abruptly as if to rise. He grimaced with pain and fell back, a moan dying deep in his throat. His wife cried: "Willie!" and leaned over him speaking rapidly in German. He answered something, pushing her away. His face gleamed with sweat.

"Look, my girl, I know how things are," he said in a tired voice. "But never mind. You are either a popular teacher or you are a good teacher. I am, I believe I am, a good teacher. Not in vain. . . "

He made an incomplete gesture and allowed his wife to dry his forehead with a cloth. Nelly looked at the diplomas over the fireplace, the bookcases filled with books, the bust of Goethe on the desk, and then once again at Esponda and his wife.

"Oh, well," he said, "there's no point in talking about it. You came by to say hello to me and I appreciate it very much. Truly. And forgive me if I say good evening now, but it is late and I have work to do."

Nelly left in a daze, with an undefined urgency that little by little became more clear, then completely clear, when she found herself standing in front of the abandoned house. Everything was in its place. Nelly moved the stone and began to dig rapidly. The water-faded inscription, the portrait blotched with black stains—Esponda, standing in his library, looking straight before him with a pin piercing his heart. Nelly looked at him in incredulous fear, then cautiously she removed the pin, as one does a splinter embedded in live flesh. She pulled the pins from his legs. She picked up the photograph and raised it towards heaven, her eyes closed. God, make him get well; God, make him get well. It was not God who responded, but the form with no face, and the picture felt like a chunk of amputated flesh in Nelly's hands. She dropped it and fled.

Esponda died a few days later: heart failure. Nelly's attempt to save him did no good—or perhaps it was that Aurora or Cecilia, whichever one had stuck the pin in his heart, came back to continue the ritual. "Or maybe it was all just coincidence. I mean, if some of it's true it all has to be true, doesn't it? And there wasn't any punishment; as far as I know, nothing happened to any of us. Last year I saw Aurora and Cecilia at a class reunion; they're married, too, and well, and happy. Surely in the future, God won't want. . . Really, I still don't know what I think about it all."

Nor I, but I think I know how to end this account: with the image of a girl alone beside the ritual grave in the center of that unfinished, dilapidated building reeking of excrement; in the dark place of temptation to which something in her has yielded—a single voice mumbling ominous supplications, a single demonic possession enacting alone the frenetic gestures, the intense surrender to a solitary shame. It is almost unimportant how she arrived there. Was she pursued by the anticipation of the exercise of power? By a sense of violent abandon? Or was she inspired by the idea of atoning for previous descents into the temptation that awaited her, the temptation that enslaved her through its contact with those instruments of power and surrender? I don't know why when I imagine this scene I always see Nelly with her short hair and her sweet face looking at the photograph of the schoolmaster, slowly drawing a rusted pin from the legs and then suddenly burying it in the left side of his breast. I don't know why I see *her*. Doubtless because I do not know the other two.

Philippe Soupault

FACE TO FACE

You'll find me here one day or another
almost alone like all of us
facing all the lived out
forgotten and unknown weeks
facing the pyramid of Cheops
and the billions of years
facing the midnight sun
at the world's other end
reflected once more in the ponds of my youth
facing the dying sun
that's ours for only several billion years
to live just as long
as the billions of seconds that I have lived
which are left for me to live
perhaps to never know
and again if my memories are as exact
as the walls of Machu Picchu
facing the pyramids of Yucatan
and the twilights in front of my mirror
the future and the hope of every morning
of every evening of every night
because we have to live
because no one ever asked me to choose
my opinion or my life or my fate
because every night someone knocks at my door
because dreams wait at the edge of my bed
for rendezvous with friends who have vanished
dead or alive no one knows anymore
because little by little one by one I recognize them
as my best friends the clouds
children of madness
that I greet at the doorway
they have already vanished when we look at them
faithful companions of the sun
at the bedside of its daily agony
at the moment of its last sigh like a frayed flag
where we must uncover the profiles of friends
those who will welcome me

an outstretched hand
as before
hands stretched out
to the dawn
all all of you
those I've never forgotten
even those whose names I no longer remember
and who ride on the clouds slaves of the twilight
Face to face alone facing this agony
that daily never ends
because tomorrow is another day and other days
and already the night is advancing with its look of innocence
the same night always the same merciless
ushering in sleep or death
in spite of its planet that's been dead for so long
color of skeleton color of memory
witness for the best and the worst
and yet luminous like a reproach
always the automatic profile unrelenting like a calendar
mistress of the tides and mother of catastrophes
devourer of peoples fearless
that we in turn detest and admire
lovely like a mirror
unfaithful these days of rain and misery
days of boredom and melancholy
we must forget them
and find again traces of lost steps
guided by this insolent memory
insomnia's hangman
across all the fields where regrets are in flower
all the lost opportunities lost pains
before and after shipwrecks
when we no longer wait for rescue
nor anyone to trust
women and children first
those abandoned
and found again as if everything once more
were to begin again
shipwrecks mass-produced
like birthdays
but stranded here on this deserted beach
once more deserted

is a man who wanted to forget
who thought he had forgotten all
a man surrounded by all the shells
memories that the sea spits and vomits
a man who knows and does not know
if it's daybreak or dawn

It is dawn this flash this hope
this little girl playing with a hoop
when the sun comes up
the one jumping rope
when the clouds disappear
and are nothing more than dreams
then again uncertain flashes
fleeting like doubts
here's the invincible sun
mute conqueror of night
of sleep of insomnia
demanding silence
before the fanfares and all that follows
before the uproar and the morning bells
before the regrets the remorse
before the inventory of dreams and nightmares
before the ghosts of daily obligations
when we know we can't escape

Everyone has a turn in turn
at misery or joy
Every day we must know how to play
for better for worse
And not be impatient
because we all know
the moment will come
when we can no longer choose
our last word our last sigh

Last memory last cloud
dispersing like a good-bye
Goodbye bad day bad night
Hello good night and so on
A thousand good evenings of good evenings
A thousand good-byes
To take or to leave
A good death is the best you can wish
          for *Philippe Soupault*

Nadia Tuéni

EXILE

And here are countries slashed in colors by the wind: this living nature is bluer than a sun at its zenith. I enter the geography of stones, and with a stroke I discover the perfection of evil. In that place where one eye perceives another, tell yourself that the desert begins. The opened chest of the mountains captures the rain. Suddenly an alp more radiant than a pyre erupts from the sea.

New land leading from childhood to childhood, land that our fingers limit with a movement of love. Land of bone, hard lover, with beaches of madness, yet a breath traverses you from head to life, a breath dripping with all our tears.

And here are towns sculpted by storms, ringed with birds. Black plays sweet music on the windowpanes of day. The sea is a memory of old age. The moon is only lost time. Tomorrow my sky at a gallop will crush your thoughts, and from their ruins will ascend, soft as morning, exile.

INVENTORY

From all which is earth I accept the message. From that which is garden I accept the force. A smell of the future settles down upsetting a child on his way.

We will make suns behind the wall, within your eyes of painted moons and in your cool-running hands.

If death is perfect beauty, each life inherits a morning of birds, gentle and cruel.

From that which is day I will conceive the night (say nothing it is done). In your steps a white foreboding love.

This evening, between me and the first arrival, a word arches on the sky. Because from a cry I will build my life.

Takis Sinopoulos

WAITING ROOM

This is no place for pride
this is no place for ecstasy,
a long river of sluggish days
the night the fear and the chair,
you, searching for the staircase to the sky

I, groping my face with my fingernails
amid the silent ruins of hunger
in this place with the frozen fire
what am I waiting for?

What am I waiting for here where the fever mounts?
What if someone shouts for help from the street
if someone beats on the wall
if all the games won without God
go to the opposite side and sit down,
the continuation of darkness
the lamp that consumed the kerosene
the cigaret butts thrown on the floor
the clothes of strangers
still warm,
what if the miracle with elderly hands comes
the act
that suddenly turns into murder?

Why should I invoke the unblemished woman
who has been cleaning her kingdom all day long?
Why should I remember the pride worn thin by time
the quietness in the room, the warmth and the refusal?
The mouth was alive
truth was being nailed on the lie and was still writhing
freedom leapt from city to city

blood dripped
nakedness dressed itself with pretences
and I grew cold
as now you grow cold and frightened and hide yourself
in the house where silence creaks
and the darkness breathes deeply.

In this room the imagined rapes took place
the contrivance of love and desperation
here falsehood and the sky were invented
there is a hole in the chair
there is silence and time
there are still other contrivances, resemblances of relationships
resemblances of linked contacts
behind the wall the night weaves a world of shadows
exiled probabilities sleep in their net
the hour lurks in the pendulum
with a cold smile the ghosts are moving but do not move
approach and do not move
in this room where I remain motionless and wait
what am I waiting for?

Perhaps you will descend there, stumbling, where the houses vanish
there where the dawn lights up a million pebbles
perhaps you will descend still lower
there where the darkness digs the ground incessantly
there where half-lit faces swirl
there where the darkness designs
unending complexes unending works
in that unending place that exists behind things
where shape vanishes and motion vanishes
there where, nevertheless, you exist
your eyes dark your hands smashed
your body curved within time
within the night that burns
there where I remain motionless and gaze and wait
what am I waiting for?

255

Marco Antonio Montes de Oca

tr. LAURA VILLASEÑOR

AT SEA LEVEL

Radiances, miracles,
sudden busyness in the offices of air,
bells that soften into silence in octopus heads
in this universe where nothing changes
and where it's all the same if you cry or I sing,
all the same to rip or not the napery of leaves the holly weeps
and calm spreads over the forehead's furrows,
hiding the nadir of the consummate fable,
the nadir of all that sings or slyly winks
among placated visions and avalanching black rocks
that scatter roots of oracles, albums of fog where photographs
                             cough that never should be lost.
Let's lose ourselves with them! Let's lose ourselves like what
                         seeks its own orbit
in the torrential garbage of the stars
and finds only ventricles full of wings
and auricles sheltering other wings of greater power.
The half-dreamed hymn needs new transfusions,
more of the holy chlorophyll, incandescent sperm,
so that man can be again a minimal planet infinitely achieved,
an instant of numbered days, a firefly glowing with its own light,
a weapon incensed by peace in the hall of arms
and whose progeny does not bow under Niagara.
O spirits who will not live at sea level!
We have, we only have.
We have the delight and the rage and the longing.
We have the wheel that seizes its own motion
and a condor under each arm,
both aghast that nothing sates our desire for height.

Let's lose ourselves, then, like an amulet of ozone
among deep nocturnal pockets,
among air holes where a drop of water
rears its iridescent crown.
Let's lose ourselves, perhaps to rise again
when the green young virgin fruit goes to our head,
when the fierce countenance of beauty
finally turns to us
and the plied years, the incomparable insomnias
pasture visions lashed by rawhide flowers
and hands soiled from long caressing of statues.

Marco Antonio Montes de Oca

LIGHT IN READINESS

Creation is on foot,
its spirit arises among white dunes
and sprays from inexhaustible aspersoria
the orchards crushed by flint foot
or by the cold insolence of night.
The heavenly colors locked in the windows
widen the silhouettes of saints.
Above the wretched floor a plaster spring rears shadows
that wave their arms in anguished daring.
And the magic horn summons the creatures wasted with pain
for the marvelous vertigo to install their hour of redress
and for ash to awake leaping in bubbling gushes of grays.
The unique, splendid, irresistible creation
is on foot like an impassioned skeleton
and overflows all the sluices,
touches in every flame the door of raging fire,
and saddles galaxies that a great wizard must mount,
when spirit patrols the dawn
until it comes to the pillars of living time.

Mahmud Darwish

DON'T SLEEP

When the moon falls
Like broken mirrors
The shadow grows larger among us
And legends die.
Don't sleep, my darling.
Our wound has become medals,
It has become fire on a moon.

Beyond our window is a bright day
And an arm of satisfaction
When it embraced me and flew
I thought I was a butterfly
In necklaces of pomegranate blossoms.
Lips of dew
Spoke to me without words.
Don't sleep, my darling
Beyond our window is a bright day.

Roses fell from my hand
Without fragrance, without torpor.
Don't sleep, my darling
Birds are committing suicide
My eyelashes are ears of corn
Drinking night and destiny.
Your sweet voice is a kiss
And a wing on a string.
An olive branch wept
In exile over a stone
Looking for its roots,
Sun and rain.
Don't sleep, darling.
Birds are committing suicide.

When the moon falls
Like broken mirrors

The shadow drinks our shame
And we hide our escape.
When the moon falls
Love becomes an epic.
Don't sleep, darling
Our wound has become medals
And our hands on the darkness
Are a nightingale on a string.

Translator: Adnan Haydar

MEMOIRS OF EVERYDAY SORROW

Mahmud Darwish

I hire a taxi-cab to go home . . . .

I chat with the driver in perfect Hebrew, confident that my looks do not disclose my identity.

"Where to, sir?" the driver asks me.

"To Mutanabbi Street," I reply. I light a cigarette and offer one to the driver in recognition of his politeness. He takes it, warms up to me, and says:

"Tell me, how long will this disgusting situation last? We are sick of it."

For a moment, I assume that he has become sick of war, high taxes and mounting milk prices.

"You are right," I tell him. "We are sick of it." Then he continues:

"How long will our government keep these dirty Arabic street names? We should wipe them out and obliterate their language."

"Who do you mean?" I ask him.

"The Arabs of course!" he replies.

"But why?" I inquire.

"Because they are filthy," he tells me.

I recognize his Moroccan accent, and I ask him:

"Am I so filthy? Are you cleaner than I am?"

"What do you mean?" he asks, surprised.

I appeal to his intelligence; he realises who I am, but does not believe it.

"Please, stop joking," he tells me.

When I show him my identity card, he loses his scruples and retorts:

"I do not mean the Christian Arabs—just the Moslems." I assure him that I am a Moslem, and he qualifies his statement.

"I do not mean all the Moslems—just the Moslem villagers." I assure him that I come from a backward village that Israel demolished—simply razed out of existence. He says quickly:

"The State deserves all respect."

I stop the car and decide to walk home. I am overtaken by the desire to read the names of the streets. I realise that the authorities have actually wiped out all the Arab names. "Saladdin" has metamorphosed into "Shlomo." But why did they retain the name of Mutanabbi Street, I wonder for a moment? Then in a flash I read the name in Hebrew. It is "Mount Nebo," not Mutanabbi as I have always assumed.

I want to travel to Jerusalem . . . .

I lift the telephone and dial the number of the Israeli officer in charge of civilian affairs. Since I have known him for some time, I inquire about his health and joke with him. Then I appeal to him to grant me a one-day permit to Jerusalem.

"Come over and apply in person," he says. So I leave my work and I come over. I fill out an application and I wait—one day, two days, three days. There is hope, I rationalize; at least they have not said "no" as usual. And I continue to wait. Then I appeal to my friend once again, because by now my appointment in Jerusalem is imminent. I beg him for a response:

"Please say no," I plead with him. "Then at least I can cancel or postpone my appointment." He does not respond. Exhausted and disappointed, I tell him desperately that I have only a few hours left to get there.

"Come back in an hour," he says impatiently. I come back an hour later to find the office closed. Naively I wonder why the officer is so diffident, why he hasn't simply refused as usual? Finally, consumed by anger, I decide—not too judiciously—to leave for Jerusalem even at the risk of evading the State's "security measures."

Upon my return, I receive an invitation to appear before a military court. I queue up with the rest and I listen to the charges brought against the people before me. There is the case of a woman who works in a kibbutz and who has a permit which clearly forbade her to stop on her way to work.

260

For some pressing reason, she stopped and was immediately arrested. Similarly, some young men wandered away from the main street, only to be arrested. The court acquits no one. Prison sentences and exorbitant fines are automatic.

I am reminded of the story of the old man who, while patiently ploughing his field, discovered that his donkey had wandered off into someone else's land. Intent on retrieving his donkey, he left his plough and ran after him. He was soon stopped by the police and was arrested for having trespassed on government property without a permit. He told them that he had a permit in the pocket of his caba, which he had hung on a tree. He was arrested anyway.

I also remember the "death permits" which obliged farmers to sign a form blaming themselves for their own death if they stepped on mines in an area that was used by the army. The signatures allowed the government to shirk all responsibility for their death. Intent on earning their livelihood and unconscious of the dangers, the farmers signed these statements anyway. Some of them lived, but many of them died. Tired, finally, of the dead and living alike, the government finally confiscated the farmers' land.

Then there was the child who died in her father's arms in front of the office of the military governor. The father had long been waiting for a permit to leave his village for the city to hospitalize his sick daughter . . . .

When the judge sentences me for two months only, I feel elated and thankful. In prison, I sing for my homeland and write letters to my beloved. I also read articles about democracy, freedom and death. Yet I do not set myself free; neither do I die.

I want to travel to Greece . . . .

I ask for a passport and a *laissez-passer*. Suddenly, I realise that I am not a citizen, because either my father or one of my other relatives took me and fled during the 1948 war. At that time I was just a child. I now discover that any Arab who fled during the war and returned later forfeited his right to citizenship. I despair of ever obtaining a passport and I settle for a *laissez-passer*. Then I realise that I am not a resident of Israel since I do not have a residency card. I consult a lawyer:

"If I am neither a citizen nor a resident of the State, then where am I and who am I?" He tells me that I have to prove that I am present. I ask the Ministry of the Interior:

"Am I present or absent? Should you so wish, I can philosophically justify my presence." I realise that I am philosophically present and legally absent. I contemplate the law. How naive we are to believe that law in

261

this country is the receptacle of justice and right. Here, law is a receptacle of the Government's wishes—a suit tailored to please its whims.

Notwithstanding all this, I was present in this country long before the existence of the State that denies my presence. Bitterly, I observe that my basic rights are illusory unless backed by force. Force alone can change illusion into reality.

Then I smile at the law which gives every Jew in the world the right to become an Israeli citizen.

I try once again to get my papers in order, trusting in the law and in the Almighty. At long last, I secure a certificate proving that I am present. I also receive a *laissez-passer*.

Where do I go from here?

I live in Haifa, and the airport is close to Tel-Aviv. I ask the police for permission to travel from Haifa to the airport. They refuse. I am distraught, yet I cleverly decide to follow a different route and to travel by ship. I take the Haifa port highway, convinced that I have the right to use it. I revel in my intelligence. I buy a ticket, and without trouble pass through the passport checkpoint and the health and customs departments. However, near the ship they arrest me. I am again taken to court, but this time I am sure that the law is on my side.

In court, I am duly informed that the port of Haifa is a part of Israel—not a part of Haifa. They remind me that I have no right to be in any part of Israel except in Haifa, and that the port—according to the law—is outside Haifa's city limits. Before long, I am charged and convicted. I protest:

"I would like to make a grave confession, gentlemen, since I have become aware of the law. I swim in the sea, but the sea is a part of Israel and I do not have a permit. I enjoy the weather of Haifa, yet the weather is the property of Israel, not of Haifa. Likewise, the sky above Haifa is not part of Haifa, and I do not have a permit to sit under the sky."

When I ask for a permit to dwell in the wind, they smile. . .

I want to rent an apartment . . . . .

I read an advertisement in the paper. I dial a number.

"Madam, I read your advertisement in the paper; may I come and look at your apartment?"

Her laughter fills my heart with hope:

"This is an excellent apartment on Mount Carmel, sir. Come over and reserve it quickly." In my happiness, I forget to pay for the telephone call and leave in a hurry.

The lady takes a liking to me, and we agree on her terms. Then, when

I sign my name, she is taken aback.

"What, an Arab? I am sorry, sir, please call tomorrow."

This goes on for weeks. Every time I am rebuffed I think about the apartments' real owners who are lost in exile. How many houses have been built destined to remain uninhabited by their owners! Awaiting their return to their houses, the owners keep the keys in their pockets—and in their hearts. But if anyone of them should return, would he, I wonder, be allowed to use his key? Would he be able to rent but one room in his own house?

And yet they insist:

"The Zionists have not committed crimes; they simply brought a people without a country to a country 'without' a people."

"But who built those houses?" I inquire.

"Which demons built them for which legends?"

On that note, they leave me alone, and they continue to breed children in stolen houses.

I want to visit my mother during the holidays . . . .

My parents live in a small village an hour's drive from where I live. I have not seen them for several months. Because my parents regard holidays with emotion, I send a carefully-worded letter to the police department. I write:

"I should like to draw your attention to some purely humanitarian reasons, which, I hope, will not clash with your strong regard for the security of the State and the safety and interests of the public. By kindly granting my request for a permit to visit my parents during the holidays, you would prove that the security of the State is not contradictory to your appreciation of people's feelings."

My friends leave the city and I am left behind by myself. All the families will meet tomorrow, and I have no right to be with mine. I remain alone.

In the early morning, I leave for the beach to extinguish my grief in the blue waters. The waves bear me; I resign myself to their might. Then I stretch out on the warm sand, basking in the sun and a soothing breeze with my loneliness.

"Why does the sun squander its warmth so?" I wonder. "Why do the waves break against the shore? So much sun . . . so much sand . . . so much water." I contemplate the obvious truth.

I hear people speaking Hebrew. I understand what they say, and my grief and loneliness increase. I feel the urge to describe the sea to my girlfriend, but I am alone. With or without justification, those around me curse my people, while they enjoy my sea and bask in my sun. Even when they are swimming, when they are joking, when they are kissing, they curse my people. Could not the sea, I wonder, bless them with one moment of tranquility and love, so they would forget my people for a while? How can they be capable of so much hatred while they lie stretched out on the warm sand?

Saturated with salt and sun, I go to a cafe on the beach. I order a beer and whistle a sad tune. People look at me. I busy myself with a tasteless cigarette, and then I buy an ear of corn and eat alone. My wish is to spend the entire day on the beach in order to forget that it is a holiday and that my parents are waiting for me. Soon, however, I realise that it is time for my daily visit to the police in order to prove that I have not left town. The searing blueness of the sea and the sky blaze in my eyes as I leave the beach.

At the entrance of the police station, my little brother meets me and says:

"Hurry up and prove to the police that you are present; Mother is waiting for you at your apartment." I prove that I am present and reach home panting.

My mother has refused to celebrate the feast without me, and so she comes to my apartment bringing everything—the bread, the pots of food, the coffee, olive oil, salt and pepper.

In the evening she leaves. I kiss her and close the door behind her. I cannot take her across the street because the State does not allow me to leave the house after sunset—not even to bid my mother goodbye.

In my room, I become aware of my loneliness once more. I sit on an old chair and I listen to Tchaikovsky's First Concerto. Suddenly I cry as I have never cried before. For years, I have carried these tears and they have finally found an outlet.

"Mother, I am still a child. I want to empty all my grief onto your bosom. I want to bridge the distance between us in order to cry in your lap."

My next door neighbour calls to tell me that my mother is still cleaving to the door. I run out to her and cry on her shoulders.

tr. CHARLES SIMIC

Ljubomir Simović

ONE EVENING

I was a bell-tower and blizzard of birds,
the ramparts and the chalice thrown from the ramparts;
    now it's in the sea and the sea is in it;
I was the king cleaning the boots of a boot-maker.
I was a pigeon on a marble helmet,
a clearing and the rope-maker weaving the rope
and the criminal hung by that rope.

I was a soldier raising his glass like a flag
and another one in the stable
on the top of a nurse who embraces him fainting.
In the grass, with flowers high to horse's belly,
I was the horse and its rider, night through which they ride,
I was the fields, the messenger and his evil tidings.

I was everywhere and everyone, seeking how to throw off my back
these troubles and animals, violence and flowers,
evil and inclination to evil,
                        but early one sleepless
evening before a storm in Western Serbia I saw
a great flight of birds which, as they rose from a tree,
made it seem as if the tree had disappeared.

Robert Creeley

from PIECES

How that fact of
seeing someone you love away
from you in time will
disappear in time, too.

Here is all there is,
but *there* seems so
insistently across the way.

Heal it, be
patient with
it — be quiet.

Across the
table,
years.

HERE
Past time — those
memories opened
places and minds,
things of such reassurance —

now the twist,
and what was a road
turns to a circle
with nothing behind.

I didn't know what I could do.
I have never known it
but in doing found it
as best I could.

Here I am still,
waiting for the discovery.
What morning, what way now,
will be its token.

They all walk by
on the beach,
large, or little,
crippled, on the face
of the earth.

The wind holds
my leg like
a warm hand.

Translator KIMON FRIAR

Odysseus Elýtis

SLEEP OF THE VALIANT

They smell of frankincense, and their features are scorched from their passage through the Vast Dark Places.

There where the Immovable suddenly hurled them

Prone, on a land where even its smallest anemone were enough to embitter the air of Hell

(one hand outstretched, as though it were striving to grasp the future, the other under the desolate head, turned sideways,

As though it were seeing for the last time, deep in the eyes of a disembowled horse, the heaped ruins smoking)

There Time released them. One wing, the most red, covered the world, while the other was already tenderly moving in the distance.

And not a single wrinkle or pang of remorse, but at a great depth

The ancient immemorial blood beginning laboriously to dawn in the inky blackness of the sky,

A new Sun, still unripe,

Not strong enough to dissolve the hoarfrost of lambs on the living clover, yet dispelling, before a thorn could sprout, the oracle-making powers of Darkness . . .

And from the beginning, Valleys, Mountains, Trees, Rivers,

A creation of avenged emotion glowed, identical yet reversed, through which the Valiant now might pass, the Executioner slain within them,

Peasants of the infinite azure!

Neither the hour striking twelve in the abyss, nor the Polar voice falling vertically annulled their footfall.

They read the world insatiably with eyes forever open, there where the Immovable had suddenly hurled them

Prone, where vultures swooped down to savor their clay entrails and their blood.

SEVEN DAYS FOR ETERNITY

SUNDAY.—Morning in the Temple of the Calf Bearer. I say: May fair Myrto become as real as a tree; and may her lamb, looking my murderer straight in the eyes for a moment, punish the most bitter future.

MONDAY.—Presence of grass and water at my feet. Which means I exist. Before or after the glance that will turn me to a stone, my right hand holding high a gigantic azure Stalk of Wheat. That I may establish the New Zodiac.

TUESDAY.—Exodus of the numbers. Battle of the 1 and the 9 on a completely desolate shore, strewn with black pebbles, piles of seaweed, huge backbones of beasts on the rocks.
My two aged and beloved horses, neighing and rearing above the vapors that rise from the sea-sulphur.

WEDNESDAY.— From the other side of the Thunderbolt. The charred hand that will sprout again. To smooth out the world's wrinkles.

THURSDAY—An open gate: stone stairs, heads of geraniums, and further on transparent roofs, paper kites, fragments of pebbles in the sun. A he-goat slowly ruminates the centuries, and a smoke rises serenely between his horns.
At the very moment the gardener's daughter is being kissed secretly in the back yard, a flowerpot falls and shatters of the great pleasure.
Ah, if I could only preserve that sound!

FRIDAY.—"The Transfiguration" of women I have loved without hope. I cry out: Ma—ri—naaa! E—le—niii! Every stroke of the bell is a spray of lilac in my arms. Then a strange light, and two dissimilar doves that pull me up high to a large house wreathed with ivy.

SATURDAY.—Cypress tree of my race, cut down by sullen and silent men: for a betrothal of a death. They dig the earth round about and sprinkle it with carnation water.
But I have already proclaimed the words that magnetize the infinite!

Carlos Drummond de Andrade

tr. JACK E. TOMLINS

SADNESS IN HEAVEN

In heaven there is also a melancholy hour,
A difficult hour when doubt pervades all souls.
Why did I create the world? God wonders
and answers himself: I do not know.

The angels look at him with disapproval,
and feathers fall.

All the hypotheses: grace, eternity, love
fall, they are feathers.

Another feather, heaven is undone.
So gently, no roar betrays
the moment between all and nothing,
or rather, the sadness of God.

TO BE

The son I did not create
would be a man today.
He runs on the wind,
fleshless and nameless.

Sometimes I find him
as I find a cloud.
On my shoulder he rests
his never-never shoulder.

I ask my son,
object of the air:
in what grotto, what conch
do you rest abstracted?

There where I lay
his breath answers me,
you did not hear me,
though I called to you

as still I call
(beyond, beyond all love)
where nothing, everything
longs for creation.

The son I did not create
creates himself quite by himself.

tr. DUANE ACKERSON AND
RICARDO DA SILVEIRA LOBO STERNBERG

Carlos Drummond de Andrade

MOONLIGHT IN ANY CITY . . .

Moonlight left things very white.
The stars disappeared.
The houses, silenced, impregnated
not by dew, but by moonlight.
We walked endlessly, not anxious
not hurried.
We walked through the moon.
And we were two normal beings and two ghosts
at the same time.
Far away, the world
at that time covered by sun.
But would there be a sun?
We floated in moonlight. The sky
a diffuse brightness. The earth
less than the reflection of that glow.
We felt so clear! So calm!
We were dead and did not know it,
buried, walking the crypts of moonlight.

THE DUEL

HORST BIENEK

tr. MICHAEL BULLOCK

It wasn't a sudden fright that came over Gordon as he felt the door open, it was only a cold, bewildering pain in the chest; he imagined a door had opened in his body laying bare his heart and his blood vessels and exposing them to the cold night air. He was feeling with outspread fingers over his sweat-soaked shirt as the door clicked shut; the draught was gone and a slight quiver ran over his skin. Someone had come in, someone had just entered the room, he felt it quite clearly, there was someone else with him in this room, he smelled his clothes (a sweetish, musty smell like rotting fruit), he heard his irregular breathing, but he couldn't see anything, because this night was perfect in its darkness. Nothing else in this damned country was perfect, only the darkness, it walled him in, it buried him, it was trying to suffocate him. He opened his mouth and hurriedly sucked in the air, the air that the hostile Others also breathed with him, and a low whistle was audible as he did so. He knew that he was thereby giving himself away, that he was delivering himself up to reality, to the alien figure that had entered almost soundlessly like a piece of this accursed lightless night, which was dark enough to protect him, but also dark enough to conceal his murderer. But they hadn't come yet. . . No, they wouldn't get him that easily. If they came, they wouldn't creep into the room soundlessly,

272

almost timidly—they would march into the yard in hundreds, surround the house, the butts of their guns would batter down the door, and then. . .

But this man here can only be Ham, no one else knows about this hideout. It must be Ham, it's got to be Ham! "Ham," he yelled, and he noticed with dismay that at full strength his voice was no more than a hoarse whisper. Is it possible I'm scared? A feeling I've never known till now, but if this feeling of cold pain in my chest is fear, then at this moment I'm afraid, thought Gordon.

"Yes, it's me," someone said from the far end of the darkness. Gordon heard the familiar voice of his friend, and suddenly the darkness was no longer quite so dark, and he actually thought he could see Ham sitting in an old armchair, in the opposite corner of the room, facing him, four paces away, his hair hanging wet and tangled over his face, his clothes soaked with sweat and torn, in places incrusted with blood. When Gordon looked more closely there was nothing there but the foaming darkness, and a slight pain in his left thigh reminded him of his injury. So long as it doesn't get infected everything will be all right, he thought.

"Don't . . . don't switch the light on," said Ham from the other corner, his voice trembling slightly. Is he afraid I shall stand up and put the light on, thought Gordon, he's sitting closer to the switch than I am. And besides, I know just as well as he does how dangerous it would be to switch the light on now. We should give ourselves away immediately, because the house has been unoccupied for ages, they know that. Gordon leaned back, the back of the chair creaked faintly. He has no idea about my injury, that's just as well. Now that his fearful anticipation was receding, he clearly felt the pain in his thigh again. Damnation, fancy getting hit at the very last minute. Now, when it's all up anyway. The injury is going to hinder my escape. He stared in the direction in which he guessed Ham to be and he listened for the other's every movement. He felt the saliva, viscous and sticky in his mouth, and he was overcome by an agonizing desire for a cigarette. "Haven't you anything to smoke?" he asked.

"No, I've none left," came the answer out of the darkness. "Anyhow it's better not to strike a match here. They may be lying in wait outside already. They're lying in wait. . . "

Gordon interrupted him. It suddenly occurred to him that the Others might have followed Ham and so discovered the hideout. "What happened, did they follow you?" he asked hurriedly.

" . . .they're lying in wait everywhere tonight," Ham slowly and

273

emphatically completed his sentence. "I don't think anyone saw me; the streets are empty and deathly quiet. Before I turned off into Upper Street I was pulled up by a patrol. I showed my doctor's pass and told them I had to visit a very sick patient. They let me go unhindered." He stopped.

Gordon thought: Why did he come here? And then: It's a good thing he came here. He may help me to get away. He's intelligent and always finds a way out. And then he has that doctor's pass; that may save us. He asked: "Where are the rest?"

Ham let this question stand unanswered for a while in the room, growing larger and larger and more and more challenging, then he finally said in a low, rather resigned voice: "Dead, captured or fled. . . I don't know, I came alone."

Gordon didn't ask any more questions. At bottom he knew how everything had happened. When it was known the uprising had miscarried most of them went back to their families; the rest fled later, after the first shots were fired. We started too soon, thought Gordon. He involuntarily shrugged his shoulders, because once again a thought had forced its way into his mind that had already struck him while he was still alone in this room. He quickly thought of something else. We shall get out of here, he thought. Next time I shan't rely on reports, I shall check everything for myself. . . And out loud he said: "If only this night were past! Tomorrow by daylight we may be able to get out of here. Once we're in the Northern District we'll be all right."

"Do you really think, Gordon, that we . . . I mean, do you really believe we shall get away?" asked Ham shyly.

Gordon immediately heard the uncertainty in Ham's voice, the slight vibration of the consonants, that betrayed doubt. He felt the old distrust of Ham rising up in him again. He's giving up. He's a coward. I shouldn't have put so much confidence in him. All trace of fear left him. He felt a weaker man beside him and that gave him courage. He said more loudly than usual, almost triumphantly: "Once daylight comes, if they haven't caught us by then, because I assume they'll comb the whole district, we shall be able to get other clothes and slip through into the Northern District. We shall be safe there for the time being. From there we can get to the frontier somehow . . . "

"And what then?" asked Ham hurriedly, with a searching undertone. Gordon involuntarily tossed his head. "Then we shall be in safety. And then we shall start all over again from the beginning, we shall form new cells and" (he raised his voice to provoke the other, who was still his friend even if, as it now seemed to him, a cowardly friend) "perhaps we shall succeed next time. . . " Gordon stopped, he listened for the reply, but from the opposite corner there came nothing but regular breathing. And after a while, very low, but clearly accentuated: "We're lost, we'd better give up. . . "

Gordon sat there and didn't know what to say. He pretended not to have understood, although he could distinctly feel his heart beating more violently. "Do you want to surrender?" The hint of a threat, which he wanted to ring through his words, turned into a hoarse hiss.

"I'm not surrendering, but I think it's senseless." The last word remained for a long time in the room, and it seemed to Gordon as though it was multiplied a hundredfold; he wanted to say something, really only to destroy the silence that was once again crawling towards him, paralyzing him, he was about to begin when Ham continued in a very resolute tone: "During the last few hours, when I had to hide from my pursuers in a stinking vegetable cellar, I thought a great deal, perhaps too much for a man of my stamp, but I had time and you know, when you're waiting for them to come and get you and send you where you can never think again, you suddenly have damn good thoughts. And all at once it became clear to me that we were bound to lose and will be bound to lose again. We're asking too much. We're running against a door that is locked from inside, and however hard we push it scarcely rocks on its hinges. But with time its lock will get looser, and gradually, bit by bit, it will open, and then we shall be able to go through this door to the inside. It may take longer, but it will be less bloody. And I can't stand the sight of blood any more, believe me, Gordon, when I saw them dying today—someone fired from a roof—I had suddenly had enough, and at bottom I wished they would hit me too. . . I know, you will be staring across at me now indignant and dismayed, I'm sure you think I'm a traitor, a renegade, a windbag. No, my dear Gordon" (Ham's voice grew bitter) "you can't deal with me as easily as that. I shan't betray anyone, not anyone; nothing will change between us—only I'm not taking part any more. I can't bear to see anyone else die in the street, I don't want them to perish senselessly, you see, that's it, at least I think that's it; and even if people preach to me that they're dying for freedom and for the future and all the rest of it, I don't want to see anyone else lying in the street with a hole in his head."

Ham's voice became urgent, almost imploring. It dawned on him that he had been speaking for rather a long time, but he wanted to rid himself of everything that had accumulated inside him. "Now you think I'm getting sentimental and soft-hearted about the body of a dead child" (and Gordon really did think so), "but I'm not a coward, I only want this business to come to a stop. . . ." Ham suddenly became a bit uncertain, he felt the cold sweat under his shirt. He scratched the left side of his chest and this gesture brought back to his consciousness the fact that he was still there and that he had a right to speak like this, because he didn't want to sacrifice his own life senselessly either.

Gordon had listened to Ham's words in silence. He thrust his right hand into his jacket pocket. It was bound to happen. I always sensed it. And yet at the time they had all been for Ham. They valued his intelligence, his eloquence, his uncritical enthusiasm. He had gained great sympathy among the younger ones. And then finally I chose him as my closest collaborator, as my friend. I didn't want to be pushed aside one day. What did they care for all my experience, my perseverance, my tough resistance, my craft and cunning, my unshakable faith? Ham was a newcomer, but he had made them promises, he didn't only attack the methods of the Others, he also told them what it would be like when they were the *Others*. That was the trick with which Ham caught the people, because they didn't want only to have an enemy, but also a home, and by the time I realized that it was almost too late for me. The leaders wanted to remove me, to push me out, and then I started the uprising. If it had come off, the people at the top would have seen what they owed to me. How right I was then. Now I can see it again, and the others will notice it too: Ham is a coward, he fears for his life, he's afraid. . .

He thought this; but all he said after a while was: "Coward. . . " He said it in a low voice, almost gently, as though the other were no longer there, as though he were speaking of a dead man, who hadn't died a particularly meritorious death.

He didn't count on him any more either. When he thought that Ham might refuse to help him escape, that he might even frustrate his escape, he suddenly felt rage—but at the same time the helplessness of his situation. He hissed "Swine!" and felt Ham wince, felt him lean forward as though to spring. Gordon repeated once more in a low voice: "Swine!"

"And you're a murderer, Gordon! You sacrificed our people senselessly, or are you going to tell me you didn't know perfectly well it was too soon for the uprising? You started because you realized that your influence was declining, because more and more people spoke up in warning against this adventure, and naturally you didn't want to

276

wait until they outnumbered you. . . And we all saw through the whole thing too late." Ham's voice was growing more and more excited and loud. Gordon hissed: "You're a weakling, get out . . . you traitor . . ."

Ham felt these words stir up turmoil within him. If he says that once more I shall fire, he thought, and he whipped his hand out of his pocket. "You can swear at me, but that won't save a single one of those who died tonight or are now being tortured somewhere or other. At least I want to save those whom you are ready to sacrifice all over again in one or two years' time. . ."

Gordon remained quite calm. He hadn't overlooked Ham's violent movement, he had heard the rustle of his clothes. But he couldn't imagine what had happened. The darkness seemed to him to have grown darker still, now that he knew that an enemy had come in here to him. Ham has to be disposed of, he reflected coldly. A man who suddenly gets scruples and blathers sentimental rubbish, simply because he has seen a few dead bodies, will betray everything. . .

And suddenly he couldn't bear this smell of rotting fruit any longer, it made him feel sick and he thought he was going to suffocate. There was no room in his brain for anything but the one thought: Ham must be rendered harmless. Both were silent.

Time breathed inaudibly in and out. Time turned to stone. Time in its helplessness. And all around nothing but darkness, lurking and dangerous, impenetrable and like a thousand gun barrels. And in this fortress of darkness, which expanded the room into infinity, two men sitting facing one another four paces apart, both of them thinking: I must stop him! Perhaps there's no other way. Perhaps it is bound to happen like that.

Each one listened to the other's movements. Their sense organs were so intently focused on the sounds in the room, that they failed to hear the low creaking in the yard. Suddenly a voice roared outside, a searchlight blazed out, and a cold flood of light poured in through the window. Gordon and Ham, dazzled, had to shut their eyes, and when the night passed away from their eyes each discovered the other sitting in a chair, leaning forward from the waist, and each was holding a pistol in his hand, a black, dully gleaming army pistol—the barrel pointing at the other.

THE MAN WHO ATE HIMSELF

JAMES KIRKUP

He had fallen into the nervous habit of biting his lips — whether because of some strange embarrassment with himself, or because he wished to satisfy some spectacular inner need he could not have said. Anyhow, nobody asked him. Maybe, though everyone loved him to distraction, he felt deprived of love. Maybe — who can tell, at this late hour of the world? — maybe he loved himself so much he had to put all of himself into his own sweet mouth. "Hotlips", he would sigh all over the mirror, gazing at that charming, ravenous hole in an innocent face that was covered with eyebrows and eyelashes fluttering and shrinking as if innumerable eyes were concealed just below the surface of his looked-after skin. On his actual eyelids, as a matter of fact, he had tight-packed little multicoloured feathers. But that's another story altogether, and must wait for another day.

Mind you, he wasn't just some poor crazy mixed-up kid. He courted convention and accepted institutions in order, one dateless day, to be able to kick them in the arse when they least expected it. No, he was not such a fool as he looked, and he certainly looked one. He was simply the Great Fool, and if people thought him foolish, that was their own blind loss. So he would muse to himself, often, of an evening, toying with his chopped-nut granary-loaf sandwich and his glass of phantom milk.

Well, as I said, it all began with him biting his lips. His sharp little ice-white teeth would seize upon some shred of winter-hardened or kiss-blistered skin on his summery lips, and cautiously tear off a strip, like snake-skin or a fish-scale or the dog-ear of a piece of parchment. In fact, he pulled off so many shreds of faintly horny skin from his lips that he was able to make them up into lampshades tattooed with indelible pencil marks, the vestiges of creative hesitations.

At first, he would tear his lips very gently to shreds, stripping off layer after layer like wallpaper with precise and delicate teeth. Then one day he began to use the end of a dry cigarette to collect this precious dandruff from his lips, and he went too far.

But he felt his skin and his body were limitless, that they would go on providing him with their ghostly fodder for ever and a day.

Well, the day came, and there was no dry skin left, not a morsel. But he could not curb his inquisitive teeth, those voracious, perfect demons. When they saw they were not being adequately nourished, they threw themselves upon the quivering, naked, indecently wet lips, crimson with bashfulness, and tore them up with many an appreciative little noise like: "Snack-snack! Stockpot! Snicketty-snick! Snip-snap! Knick-knack! Get that!" Soon there were no lips left, anywhere, in his charming visage — only a double-row of bared teeth, bathed blushingly in blood and bits of nerve-endings.

Now they had tasted blood, the teeth were insatiable. They longed to eat up the tongue, but they wisely decided to bide their time, and make friends with it, for they knew that something so articulate could be extremely useful, at least for a while. Yes, they trained the tongue to grow long and rough and prehensile as a monkey's tail. Taught it to reach out like a hand that is all wrist and draw down into the mouth all the remaining head, all the remaining flesh on the head — such tasty tidbits as the richly dimpled cheeks, the cleft chin, the forehead lined like music paper, the crawling scalp, the thinker's nape, the dancer's nose, the clown's gobstopping eyes, and each crisp ear, red and dainty as gammon rashers.

The teeth ate them all with relish, hair and everything, including a heavy layer of pancake make-up, that tasted like damp whitewash. The tongue sucked the warm brains like mucus down through the nasal passages. And as a final delicacy, the teeth snapped off, with barely suppressed grunts of pure greed, the tongue at its tonsilled root — swallowed it in one gulp, like an enormous scarlet oyster.

The rest, of course, was dead easy. The man, fascinated, let his impulsive teeth roam along each arm, tearing the piano-practice muscles and browsing the downy flesh away, tattoos and all, like blood-buttered corn on sound, sun-ripened cobs, crunching up the hands' bright, bony fans and sucking at the blue wrist-veins as if they were merest straws. The teeth, wild with ganglia, slowly sucked out, too, the long whiteish worms of marrow from the salty bones, drank water from the knee caps, ravened the leg bones with their luscious calves and outrageous thighs, let loose the sweating deltas of the feet that were webbed with dust and dreams. It was "becoming a proper orgy", as conventional people always say.

By now, everything had disappeared into the mouth's vast maw except the trunk. The belly was grumbling. So the teeth, with a growl, went for each of the blood-bright nipples, badly mauling and savaging those tasty young buds. Like another oyster, steaming hot, the palpitating heart was gulped appreciatively down. The lungs were devoured in a frenzy, like giant tripes. Then came the teeth's long love affair with the stomach, with thirty-five long, thrilling feet of bowels and guts and irridescent intestines! What gluttonous slobberings and foragings in the vivid breadbasket of our hero's inner man!

But now he was really his own inner man, and he kept eating himself up over and over again, a ceaseless rumination and regurgitation, a perpetual chewing of his own bloody cud!

He cleaned out next, with deftly-picking teeth, the noble cage of the ribs, and let the teeth travel like mowing-machines or barbers' shears up the smooth and fruitful lawns of his back and loins. O! those tussocky buttocks! They were gnashed away in a flash, with a final, reluctant fart like a petulant thunderclap.

Now he is nothing more than a great clot, sprinkled with splintered bones, a clot in clot's clothing, a blot on the bloody landscape of disaster, leaving his trail of blood and lymph for the hounds to lick in the unsurprised street of furtive pillars and posts and letterboxes, in which he mails his blood, his lymphatic letter of disgust.

And here, in Kensington Gore, affronting the nursemaids wheeling perambulators slopping over with bloody babies, he essays the final, cryptic violence, the last easy stage towards a definition of vulture. "Be your own vampire!" he calls insidiously to the trollops of the Gore reading newspapers screaming LADIES! HAVE A GOOD BUST! And down on his non-existent knees and hands he performs a miracle of acrobatics, bringing his grovelling teeth down lower, lower . . . O, will he make it, the thing so many tried in vain to make? . . . down towards his tree of sex. Down! Nearer! Nearer! Near! He's got it! And with a defiant but triumphant SNAP! off comes the whole apparatus, a swift detumescence.

They buried him at the crossroads, what was left of him. A clear case of *auto-da-fé*. Suicide, they said, if ever there was one. A wise old woman read the future from his mangled guts, but she kept it to herself. And there he will lie, only a little longer, that monument to the doom of western man, who in his fear is about to bite his lips once too often.

tr. MICHAEL BULLOCK

PALE ANNA

HEINRICH BÖLL

I didn't get back from the war until 1950, and there wasn't a soul left in the town whom I knew. Fortunately my parents had left me money. I rented a room in the town and there I lay on the bed, smoking and waiting, not knowing what I was waiting for. I had no desire to go out to work. I gave my landlady money and she bought everything for me and cooked my meals. Everytime she brought coffee or a meal to my room, she stayed longer than I liked. Her son had been killed at a place called Kalinowka and after she had come in she would put the tray down on the table and come over to the dusky corner in which my bed stood. Here I used to doze away the hours and stub out my cigarettes on the wall, so that the wall behind my bed was covered in black patches. My landlady was pale and thin, and when her face hovered above my bed in the dusk I used to feel scared. At first I thought she was mad, because her eyes were very bright and big, and she asked me over and over again about her son. "Are you sure you didn't know him? The place was called Kalinowka — didn't you ever go there?"

But I had never heard of any place called Kalinowka and every time she asked I turned over towards the wall and said: "No, really not, I don't remember any such place."

My landlady wasn't mad, she was a very decent woman, and I felt sorry for her when she asked me these questions. She asked very often, several times a day, and when I went to see her in the kitchen I had to look at her son's photograph, a coloured photograph hanging over the sofa. He had been a laughing, fair-haired lad, and in the

281

coloured photograph he was wearing an infantry walking-out uniform.

"It was taken in the garrison town," said my landlady, "before they went to the front."

It showed his head and shoulders. He was wearing his steel helmet and the dummy of a ruined castle wreathed with artificial vines was clearly visible behind him.

"He was a conductor on the streetcars," said my landlady. "A hard-working lad." And then she always picked up the cardboard box full of photographs that stood on the sewing-table among patching-cloths and balls of thread. And she put a lot of photographs of her son into my hand: school photographs in which there was always someone sitting in the middle of the front row with a slate between his knees, and on the slate was written a VI, a VII and finally an VIII. In a separate packet, held together with a red elastic band, lay the Communion photographs: a smiling child in a black suit like a dinner jacket and holding a gigantic candle in his hand was standing in front of a transparency with a golden chalice painted on it. Then there were photographs showing him as an apprentice mechanic at a lathe, his face calm, his hands gripping a file.

"That wasn't the right job for him," said my landlady. "The work was too heavy." And she showed me the last picture taken of him before he became a soldier. He was in conductor's uniform standing beside a Number 9 streetcar at the terminus, where the line circles a round-about, and I recognized the lemonade kiosk at which I had so often bought cigarettes in the days before there was a war; I recognized the poplars that are still there today, I saw the villa with the gilt lions outside the door that are no longer there, and I remembered the girl about whom I had often thought during the war: she was a pretty girl, pale, with narrow eyes, and she always used to get into the streetcar at the terminus of the No. 9 line.

I always looked for a very long time at the photograph showing my landlady's son at the No. 9 terminus, and I thought of a great many things: of the girl and of the soap factory in which I had been working at that time, I heard the screeching of the streetcar, I saw the red lemonade I used to drink in the summer at the kiosk, green cigarette advertisements and again the girl.

"Perhaps you did know him," said my landlady.

I shook my head and put the photograph back in the box. It was a glossy print and still looked new, although it was already eight years old.

"No, no," I said, "I don't know Kalinowka either — really not."

I often had to go and see her in the kitchen and she often came to my room, and all day long I kept thinking about what I wanted to forget — the war — and I tapped the ash from my cigarette under my bed and stubbed out the glowing tip on the wall.

Sometimes, when I was lying there in the evening, I heard a girl's footsteps in the next room, or I heard the Yugoslav who lived in the room next to the kitchen, heard him cursing as he looked for the light-switch before going into his room.

It was only after I had been living there for three weeks, when I was holding the photograph in my hand for about the fiftieth time, that I saw that the streetcar in front of which he was standing laughing with his money-bag slung over his shoulder wasn't empty. For the first time I looked at the photograph attentively and saw that a smiling girl had been caught by the snapshot inside the streetcar. It was the pretty girl of whom I had so often thought during the war. The landlady came up to me, looked closely into my face and said: "Now you recognize him, don't you?" Then she came round behind me and looked at the picture over my shoulder, and the smell of fresh peas crept up my back from her tucked-up apron.

"No," I said, "but I recognize the girl."

"The girl?" she said. "That was his fiancée, but perhaps it's a good thing he never saw her again."

"Why?" I asked.

She didn't answer, she moved away from me, sat down on her chair by the window and started shelling peas again. Without looking at me, she said: "Did you know the girl?"

I held the photograph firmly in my hand, looked at my landlady and told her about the soap factory, about the No. 9 terminus and the pretty girl who always used to get in there.

"Nothing else?"

"No," I said, and she tipped the peas into a colander and turned on the tap, and all I could see was her thin back.

"When you see her again, you will understand why it's a good thing he never saw her again."

"See her again?" I said.

She dried her hands on her apron, came up to me and carefully took the photograph from my hand. Her face seemed to have become even smaller, her eyes were looking past me, but she quietly put her hand on my left arm. "Anna lives in the room next door. We always call her Pale Anna, because she has such a white face. Have you really not seen her yet?"

"No," I said, "I haven't seen her yet, although I've heard her a few times. What about her?"

283

"I don't like to tell you, but it's better you should know. Her face has been completely ruined, it's covered in scars. She was flung into a shop window by a blast. You won't recognize her."

That evening I waited for a long time until I heard footsteps on the landing, but the first time I was mistaken: it was the lanky Yugoslav, who looked at me in astonishment when I suddenly rushed out onto the landing. I said "Good evening" awkwardly and went back into my room.

I tried to imagine her face covered in scars, but I couldn't, and every time I saw it, it was a beautiful face even with scars. I thought of the soap factory, of my parents and of another girl with whom I had gone out a lot at that time. Her name was Elisabeth, but she got people to call her Mutz, and when I kissed her, she always laughed and I felt silly. I had written her postcards from the war zone, and she used to send me parcels of home-made cakes that were always reduced to crumbs by the time they reached me, she sent me cigarettes and newspapers and in one of her letters she wrote: "You will soon be victorious, and I'm so proud that you are there."

But I wasn't in the least proud to be there, and when I came home on leave I didn't write and tell her, but went out with the daughter of a tobacconist who lived in our house. I gave the tobacconist's daughter soap that I got from my firm, and she gave me cigarettes, and we went to the cinema together and dancing and once, when her parents were away, she took me up to her room, and I pushed her onto the couch in the darkness; but when I bent down over her she switched on the light and looked up at me craftily, and in the harsh light I saw Hitler hanging on the wall, a coloured photograph, and round Hitler, on the rose-pink wallpaper, men with hard faces had been hung in the shape of a heart, men wearing steel helmets, either postcards or pages from illustrated papers pinned up with thumb tacks. I left the girl lying on the couch, lit a cigarette and left. Later both girls wrote cards to me at the front saying I had behaved badly, but I didn't answer them. . .

I waited a long time for Anna, smoking a great many cigarettes in the darkness and thinking of many things, and when the key was slipped into the keyhole I was too scared to get up and look into her face. I heard her open the door and walk up and down in her room humming softly, and later I got up and stood on the landing. Very suddenly it went quiet in her room, she wasn't walking up and down any more, nor was she singing, and I was afraid to knock. I heard the lanky Yugoslav walking to and fro in his room muttering softly, I heard the water simmering in my landlady's kitchen. But in Anna's room it was quiet and through the open door of mine I saw the black patches from all the cigarettes I had stubbed out on the wallpaper.

The lanky Yugoslav had lain down on his bed, I couldn't hear his footsteps any more, I only heard him muttering, and the kettle in my landlady's kitchen wasn't boiling any more, and I heard the tinny rattle as the landlady put the lid on her coffee pot. In Anna's room it was still quiet, and it occurred to me that later she would tell me everything she had thought while I was standing outside her door, and later she did tell me everything.

I stared at a picture hanging by the door frame: a silvery shimmering lake from which a water-sprite with wet blond hair was rising to smile at a peasant boy who was standing hidden among very green bushes. I could half see the water-sprite's left breast, and her neck was very white and a trifle too long.

I don't know when, but later I laid my hand on the latch, and even before I pressed down the latch and slowly pushed the door open, I knew that I had won Anna: her face was covered all over with little scars that had a bluish shimmer, the smell of mushrooms frying in the pan came from her room, and I pushed the door right open, put my hand on Anna's shoulder and tried to smile.

Translator GREGORY RABASSA

SEVEN SERPENTS AND SEVEN MOONS

DEMETRIO AGUILERA-MALTA

Selection from Chapter Three

Santorontón! He had come to Santorontón—how many, many years ago?—when the fingers on his hands were more than enough to count the houses there. He built the church with his own efforts. —Could that shed that laughed with cracks all over it be called a church? Only partly roofed at first? Where the congregation sat on the ground?—He drove in the stakes. He set up the roof beams. He tied boughs together to support the bijao leaves. Watching him struggle alone, a few Santorontonians offered to help him. They began working together on Sundays. And they ended up doing it every night. After work. That was how the bamboo walls were made. The rough wooden benches. That table that was transformed into an altar. In addition, from the first days on, he had to take trips to surrounding villages. The Bishop had warned him: "There aren't any priests there. You'll have to be a kind of missionary. If you can, build a church. If not, fulfill your sacred ministry by seeking out the faithful wherever they are." He was doing both. Building the church so that they could visit him later on. And seeking out the faithful "wherever they were." Wherever his small boat and his courage could take him. The Santorontonians advised him: "Don't go too far away from shore, Father. You might get caught in a treacherous wind. A hammerhead might attack you and break a hole in the canoe. Or a contrary tide might drag you away . . . who knows where? Don't go too far out." He paid no attention. He felt that his sacred function made him invulnerable. And if something unforeseen happened to him and he paid for his imprudence with his life, what more could he ask for? It would be a quick step toward God. That was why on days when the Sun squeezed him like a mango. Or on dark nights when the cold was a set of teeth in his bones, he was never absent from where he was needed. It was to all that that he owed what was doubtless his most miraculous adventure. It happened one night when they came to get him for a stranger. He thought that perhaps it was the case of a premature voyager to the Land of the Bald. Four men came to get him. Four. Four evil-looking men. Four oarsmen in a lighter. Their speech was somewhat strange. They wanted him to come with them at once. Four. They said they had no time to lose. Four.

The Santorontonians were against it.

"Corvinas don't chase after harpoons, Father."

"Why don't they bring the one taking his last breath here to him?"

"You don't gather unknown eggs, Father. They might be snake eggs."

"Did you see their faces?"

"Aha! And their eyes."

"That's it. Their eyes are like dry blowfish."

"They talk with cemetery voices."

"And they have a smell about them. The smell of death."

"Maybe they've got some connection with the Taily One."

"Don't mention him. Just mentioning him brings bad luck."

"Really and truly, Father. It would be best if you didn't go."

"It's best not to look for wrinkles on a shark."

The Priest calmed them down. What could happen to him? Would they beat him? Would they kill him? Would they throw him overboard?. . . They wouldn't dare mistreat a defenseless priest. Besides, there was no reason to prejudge things. The ones who did have good reasons to persuade them, on the other hand, were the strangers. When he said that he looked significantly at the weapons they carried: long daggers and double-barreled shotguns. He finally convinced his new counselors. He went off with the other men. They didn't exchange a single word during the whole trip. Not among themselves. Not with him. They rowed ceaselessly in a rhythmic way. They made the boat go very fast. After about three hours they drew alongside a sailing ship. It was an eerie ship. With three masts. Huge in size. They climbed up on deck along a rope ladder. His attention was drawn to the number of cannons and armed men. Most of all because it seemed to have been drawn out of another world. Another age. Could it be a warship? Or was it perhaps the ship of the pirate Ogazno who was sailing along the coast in those days?—Those days or a hundred years before? Had the Santorontonians told him? Or was it an old tale he had heard from his grandparents?—It was the pirate Ogazno's ship. They took him into the latter's presence at once. He was lying in a wide bunk. Half-dressed. When he heard the footsteps he raised his head. He opened one eye. Not the other. It was closed forever.

"Come closer!"

Cándido obeyed.

"Are you the priest?"

"Yes, sir."

He raised his voice in a menacing way.

"You must say: 'Yes, Captain.' I am Captain Tiburcio Ogazno!"

"Yes, Captain."

"Did you know that?"

"No, Captain."

"Well, you know it now."

"Yes, Captain."

He stood looking at him for a long time. He took out his good eye. He brought it close to Cándido's face, studying him minutely. Then he put it back into the empty socket.

"You're young for a priest. You're not tricking me, are you? You're not the sexton?"

"I'm the priest."

One of the men who had brought him intervened.

"He's the Priest, Captain."

The latter's face grew ironic.

"Do you have any idea as to why you're here?"

"To help someone die a. . . "

Ogazno interrupted him with a loud laugh.

"Oh, you dummy of a priest!"

He turned to his men.

"Didn't you tell him anything?"

288

They answered in a chorus:

"No, Captain!"

He faced the priest.

"Mr. Dummy: you're not about to help anyone die a proper death here. The ones who were supposed to die are already good and dead. Do you hear me?"

"Yes, Captain!"

He laughed again.

"You can't tell, maybe we're the ones who are going to help you die a proper death."

He got goose pimples. He controlled himself. He lowered his eyes.

"The Lord's will be done."

"Lord? I'm the only lord here."

And to his men:

"Get everything ready! We'll soon see how this priest behaves! All hands on deck, right now!"

He got up with difficulty. He had bandages all over. He began taking wobbly steps. Cándido went over, attempting to help. He was refused.

"Leave me be! That's all I need! A priest to keep me on my feet! I can go by myself. Besides, I'm used to it. I've got more holes in me than a sieve. I always walk like this. It's an occupational hazard!"

Limping. Stumbling. Leaning against the walls and whatever he had at hand. He went forward. He left the cabin. He went up the steps. And he went on deck. The Priest went with him, not saying a word. On deck, the Captain made a sign. Obeying him, they brought a stool over to the rail. He sat down on it and waited. Almost immediately several men emerged from the hold carrying something. Cándido saw what it was at once. But he thought it was a hallucination. No. What he was seeing couldn't be. His own eyes were deceiving him no doubt. Or could it be that he was dreaming while he was awake? Because that something was a Cross with an almost life-size Christ. They carried it over and stood it up beside the Captain. The tall Priest could bear no more. He fell to his knees and kissed the feet of the Nazarene.

"Stop acting like a clown! Besides. . . the Christ is yours!"

He was paralyzed with emotion. He gained control of himself. He babbled:

"Mmmmiii...ne?"

"Yours!"

He stood up. He looked the image all over. Then he touched it in

several places. As if to convince himself that it was real. He repeated:
"Mine!"

"Now it's only proper for you to know how it came into our possession."

Almost as if walking in his sleep, he agreed:
"Yes, Captain."

"Some time back we attacked a town. To the South. Far away from here. When we got there most of the inhabitants had run off. It was all quite easy. All we had to do was go from house to house picking up everything we wanted. We saved the church for last. When we got there we went half crazy. There were a lot of gold items. Jewelry. But most of all, there was a chalice. What a chalice, Jesus! I'll bet that all they ever did there was work to pay off that chalice. We carried on board all we could. This Christ among other things. The Cook had taken a fancy to it. Or, rather, he planned to send it to his wife. Since he was the only cook we had, I had to humor him. Because as far as I'm concerned, I never take images! They take up too much room and they're hard to sell. Besides, they're not worth very much. But the cook died yesterday. And I don't know what to do with that thing. Do you really want it?"

"Yes! Of course! But. . . "

"But what?"

"What if its owners want it back?"

"Oh, God damn it! Do you want it or don't you?"

"Of course I want it. The only thing is. . . "

"So don't start begging! Now we're going to throw you overboard with it. If you get to shore it'll be because it's miraculous. And you'll deserve it. If not, give my regards to the sharks!"

Without another word he raised his arm. Lowered it. And the Crucified One and the Priest were immediately thrown into the sea. They still hadn't touched the surface of the water when the mocking voice of the pirate could be heard.

"Bon voyage!"

Cándido saw the three-master—with its rusty cannons and time-gray sails—immediately disappear into the mist. He swam the short distance over to the Crucified One. He said reverently:

"Forgive them, Lord, they know not what they do!"

Christ raised his head! He looked at him somewhat sardonically.

"As far as I'm concerned, they're forgiven. And since we do know what we're doing, let's hurry up so we can get there soon. I'm made of wood and it's no good for me to get all water-logged."

"That's true."

"Get onto the Cross the way I'm going to!"

With an agile movement, the Son of Mary detached himself from the Wood. He hung over it. With hands and feet he began to move it. Cándido did the same as he. And in a short while the little improvised craft slipped rapidly over the waves. Behind it a strange cortege had formed: everything from crabs to sharks. From that moment on Jesus and Cándido were blood brothers. That is, perfect comrades. Sometimes the priest had his doubts. Didn't he carry the Nazarene inside of him? In order to see him might he not be drawing him out of his own eyes?

Translator CHRISTINE COTTON

Kamal Ibrahim

If you love the desert
Speak in the Word
Simplify life
Lower your hands into lakes of mist
Where the air condenses

If you love the desert
Eat your mouth a bit
Like me
You will be all body

Kamal Ibrahim

And I in ruins of Order
I piss blood in the face of each remorse

Kamal Ibrahim

Blood darkens the packaged fingers
Death pales and the corpse is late
The mouth spills out a scream
Into the ravaged glass
The earth gives way and the eye extends

Ronald Bonilla

THE LONE CHILDREN

They fell, tearing strips
off the deep.
The voices hunted a live echo in death.
They mulled over dark entrails.
Locked their fingers into the void,
grafted their selves to their roots
without finding a response.

In the mornings
the children grew like birds.
The voices blurred their absurd eternal games.
Cries they were, spiraling in space.

The adults, the men
went on falling, limitless.
They rolled and the void locked about their fingers.
The women too fell, unable to catch hold.

The children remained unhearing,
full of voices.
In and out the dead cities they ran.
They returned to the flowers
and caught their scent.
Returned to the night
and raised up the stars,
pinned like eyes to the void.

One wanted to call his mother
and they filled his eyes with sea.
One wanted to pray and with love they sealed his mouth.

One by one they were joining hands,
joining every pore, igniting them.
The universe was then
a long chain of small fingers,
indestructible.

Laureano Albán

HERE EVERYTHING

Everything watches us. Entrails watch the son
make his journey eternal. The sea
withdraws to the cape of deep fingers.
Everything will fit in the wound of the lips. In the
dead signal left by an arm.

In the midst of blood there are echoes of the new-born
reaching our palms. In the gaze
of everyone there is a village of children heading
for the light between their eyes. We hear rain fall
among arms. Everything is fixed within
the heart of man. Everything is sunken amidst
what is inexhaustible in us. The conclusion of the arm falls.
The sea falls through our veins, stirring us.

Excavating signals, everything watches us. The strength
of sap pours through our necks
when they are undone. The depth of night
pours through a kiss. And our impregnated entrails,
through the stars. And the sea extends outward in one's gaze,
for only there can it extend itself.

Everything watches us breathe. Speak.
Subdue the signal, so that it will kiss.
Create from the depths a lip among children.

Everything watches us from within.
From the slow kindling of the light in us.
From the weight of death that gathers in wounds.
From the blood that beats against the impassable depths.

And we go breaking every eye against a deeper eye.

Enclosing every hand in another that is deeper.
Moving every arm in another that is inexhaustible.
Subduing the light with lights already dead.

Everything watches us.
And the sea will never fill our tracks.

Samuel Hazo

THE DAY'S ROULETTE

To know my place . . .
                        That last
    impossibility.
                        What is my place
    if where I am is where
    I'm not?
                Forget cartography.
I dream myself through walls,
    walk Mars at will, shoot
    azimuths that arrow down
    the stars.
                My only maps
    are poems written as I
    go.
            Ferret the heart
    of thieves, and there I hide.
Along the flying carpet
    of a jet, I pass my face,
    my face, my face repeated
    down an aisle.
                        Before
    the blinkless peering of the blind,
    I have no eyes.
                        A town
    of starving, black Pinochios
    so limply shrinking into death
    can shrivel me to tears.
Without my choice, I'm cast
    from role to role and back
    to me.
            No acts, no scenes,
    no curtain.

Playing the day's
roulette as cad, king,
clown, cock-o'-the-walk,
I am a compass dropped,
the needle dancing north,
east, south, west,
then steadying, steadying.

Denise Levertov

FOR THE BLIND

Listen: the wind in new leaves
whispers, smoother than fingertips,
than floss smoothing through fingertips . . .

When the sighted
talk about *white* they may mean
silence of sullen cold, that winter
— no matter how warm your rooms —
waits with at the door.
(Though there's another whiteness,
more like the weightlessness of a flake of snow,
of a petal, a pine needle . . .)

When they say *black* they may mean the persistence
of cold wind hopelessly, angrily
tearing and tearing through leafless boughs.
(Though there's another blackness,
round and full as the notes of cello and drum . . .)

But this:
this lively, delicate shiver
that whispers itself
                    caressingly over our flesh
            when leaves are small and moist
            and winds are gentle,
is green. Light green. Not weightless,
light.

Juan Liscano

SILENCE

The full silence
speaks of some transparency
of clarity amid crystals
of marble dunes which crumble
of snowfalls that blend in the aristas
of river sources
it fills us
erases the tracks of the persecuted and the persecutors
it billows and disperses the words
enlivening the ember
of an eloquence that is nothing but sound.

———

Ephemeral season.
We embrace the joy
already overdue
and we gave in to drinking
in the shelter of time.

Thirst was the fountain.

———

From some threshold
barely crossed
she flings her arm against the wind
quiets her hair
smiles
she is detached and she smiles
as if appointed by the sun
concocted by sailors
brought by the last days of summer.
She offers backdoors
          apart
possibilities beyond
and gives answers
         gives answers.

Translator ROBERT LIMA

Mauricio Marquina

OBSCENITIES TO PERFORM AT HOME

once again today you haven't let me love you always the same
   silent negation I can acquire a mystical purr
   to place myself at your naked back doubling myself
      you haven't allowed and fear flies once more with the
      pathway knotted at the throat
and the subtlest way to look on you again day after day
   is upheld in the midst of a small murmur of hatred
   and it shouldn't be that way
         we should mutually tie together the laces
   of our shoes the pair that we bought having run around
the tired city and ended the watch simply kissing
   it seems to me then that your love crumbles in jealousy
   like a pale package of melted ulcers
you give me but rather a tepid gift of bitter
   fruit you give me rather the sadness of totally lacking
     love vivid sensation but you are crowned
   obscenely with prejudice mounted on ancient jewels
     of tenacious idols and a dark path from your eyes
   minute breasts memories disguised in courage and desire
     little pubis give me a solution for my world
   for our worlds counterfeit seminal give me
patience and valor to do ultraphilosophical things to take
   the measure of man give me a measure that lacks a
   stain of blood but I'm certain I'm firm
   that it doesn't exist that we can't sense the fetid odor of death
  of excrement of heroes chained and rotting away
       piece by piece
   I want to give you my interior world I want to make
    of our sexual act a kind of transplant a
    rain of sweat slowly hot
a destructive last judgment of your love which I hear at a
    distance put my head on your tiny guillotine
you who count lichen and algae among your family you who
   softly embrace like a nip on the ear
play a sonata on this single chord which resists the
   violence and the wiles of the world and let comrades
   go on dancing to their song of love between strikes.

Kaneko Mitsuharu

SEAL

I.

How foetid the breath
Steaming from his mouth—
His back wet and clammy like the edge of a grave-hole.
It all makes us feel sick with black despair.
O, what misery. . .

Its body's dead weight and languor, like a sandbag,
Gloomily elastic—glum rubber—
Self-admiring—banality incarnate—

Pockmarks—
Big balls—

"I was always trying to get away from the rest
As I was shoved around by crowds that
Made my nose blue with their stink.
The jostling town they are racing through like swarming clouds
Was for me as lonely as Alaska in a scratchy old movie."

II.

These—these vulgar crowds, as they are called—
These are the masses that drove Voltaire into exile
And thrust Hugo Grotius into prison.

From Batavia to Lisbon
These are the ones who dominate the dust and blather of the world.

Seal sneezing—seal spitting decayed shreds of fish
From yellowed teeth, from bristling whiskers—
Suppressing yawns—affected gestures—
These are the ones who congregate screaming
Traitor—you madman—

Pointing their fingers at breakers of convention.
They all seem to be each other's wives and husbands,
Each other's lovers and mistresses too.
Their sons take after them—even to the ill nature—
Dirty cyclings of blood.

Sometimes they form cliques
And these cliques link with other cliques
And their endless cliques and links create a wall of bodies
That seems to dam the tides.
Sunlight shot with sleet pouring over the withdrawing waves.
And always the wire nets imprisoning infinities of sky.

Today a wedding.
Yesterday a holiday—but all day long
In the slush they heard the ice-breaker
Breaking up the ice.

Bowing to each other all the time, rubbing themselves with fins,
Rolling their bodies like barrels,
Hustling and bustling meaninglessly, grubbily,
Wallowing in dirty sea-water foaming with their own piss,
Keeping each other warm by body contact,
Hating the cold, abandoning disintegrating groups,
They call to each other in feeble voices,
Longing for the sympathy of other eyes.

III.

O they—not one of them noticed that
The iceberg they are living on, darker than a midnight town,
Was starting to disintegrate and slide away into the abyss.

They go stumbling over the ice on fan-shaped, useless tails
Talking about literature and so on. . .

The sad evening shades into a hanging scroll
Where the sun declines like a great swollen chilblain!

Dragging their long shadows like zebra stripes on the snow,
The masses bow their heads all together in worship,
Bowing their heads as one, as far as the eye can reach.

But with an air of open contempt,
One alone
Is facing composedly in the opposite direction.

I am that one.
I am that seal who, disliking my fellow seals,
Can still be nothing but a seal among seals.

All I can do is
To turn my back on what the others bow to.

Emily Borenstein

CHANGE

I remember things before they happen
the way a blind woman feels things

all the hidden edges and ends of things
tearing loose from their moorings

carrying me along like a haunting *raga*
that will never leave you

We are like trains that go dark
moving quietly away to be yarded forever

This is the point of no return
the place we have come to

We enter it the way a river enters the sea
with the voice of a great rushing

I look at you receding and receding
like lost music

You wave your hand goodbye
until I am a speck on the horizon

Tomorrow another sun will come up
out of a river of song with no banks

Pedro de Oraa

AFFIRMATION OF THE WORD

The light from the window on the blank page
the extended hand overflows
spilling out serpentine phrases
that nest in the silence of the room,
    the house,
the silence of my flesh.

On the pure whiteness of the page
I see clouds, the blue night
    transparent in the day,
restless violet shadows, shades of gray,
the uncertain light that rejoices, becomes saddened,
according to the whims of the blue and the clouds.

The word is something more than signs inscribed
on the obedient page.
(When was the word oppressed, endlessly giving us
a horizon close to its world in repose?)

In the discordant light of another afternoon
I will seize this paper peopled with signs,
or this page still deserted by time
and the word will blossom
in the instant it was created: a night of cold stars,
a rainy day, the blue delirium of the sun,
a shadow with shades of gray,
and the silence, this silence
where the word lives,
is the silence of the room, the house,
and the silence of the world.

Translator: Sargon Boulus

Tawfiq Sayegh

NO, AND WHY

No, and Why

   for two eyes from Rome
their youthful years
stretched into generations
wounded, dragged
behind leaping horses,
buried in caves,
picked out to fill
lion bellies
or to hollow out
spines of soldiers—
   gazed out, sprang up

   for two eyes from Galilee
aged, two cemeteries
of radiance, gouged,
wallowed in mud, given
back, their tears the urine
of conquerors and heretics,
nailed, abandoned
to rot unburied—
   gazed out, sprang up

   in flight, fearful:
like a brother
who suddenly sees
in his young sister's glances
a horrible love forbidden
by earth and heaven—
and leaves home to wander
uncertain if it is lust
that keeps him running
or sheer terror

Dennis Scott

SOLUTION

Small fish throttle
home at low tide; above, the gull is falling
intently. Falls a long time. Cataracts
down the eye. The claw scars
white into the retina. The feet
are stiff, its head hurls out, the hectic air chills, freezes,
cracks. Flensed,
the eye spills.

Night.

But at the moment of its arrival, when
the slashed eye is widest
the fish swing under, slung deep by the tide,
the clashed air closes safely behind them.
Nothing. The bird shrugs up
out of the sea. Then over

the tide my hand across
the wheeling air across
time and salt and the dunes of sorrow, look—I stretch, I am
    reaching
out, I
wrench its wings into stillness
I blunt that mouth
the hard feet break like straw.
Slowly the eye heals. Weary of watching murder, it dissolves,
    it invents

dream

Sergio Mondragón

NOVEMBER

like the wave of autumn that levels the day
    with its tide of leaves
like the laugh of the sun falling powerfully and splitting in two
    just like a waterfall
that's how november came to my life commanding and chaotic
with its staring eye and its broken wing
with its snake in its hand and an eagle on its shoulder
with its pack of voracious dogs that talk all night

all my being filled with birds decked out in premonitions
the forest bent and moaned like a woman in labor
and by the east towards dawn we heard a prayer
of a single syllable, damp and heaving

(november in mourning reclines in the garden across the street
november crosses its legs as long as I spy on it
    from behind the shutters
november arrives inexorable as it had been expected
and eucalyptus and books of poems were good for nothing
my years like a train of old people weren't good for a thing

in a bend the sharp motionless eagle waits)

the wells in the patio have filled up with rats
the wounded leaves form heaps like tombs
the rivers fall asleep and at nightfall
there are cries of owls and eyes watching secretly
all is a sound of trees doing penance
trees that become alive to surprise me
    with metallic, miraculous words
while I standing on the bridge meditate about the water
and the moon goes on singing   pompous and libertine
over november that dozes
        folded in the attic

Sergio Mondragón

GURU

the lion's mane covers the sky's animal zoo.
its claws are exercising on my bleeding breast
its tail gently swings across my lashes

it's the lion that's there· every year
that's there every day

it's the lion of the tapestry in the temple
the white lion with its prophet's beard
and its tame eyes, its elastic muscles

it's the lion of Justice
the lion born in july but that reigns in august

it's the lion of the huge bursts of laughter
the lion only the just can look into the eye

the lion of the long and penetrating roar
whose echo resounds in all corners

the lion's mane falls upon my forehead and
nests in my brow:
                        my brow
which remains here pondering about the lion
of Justice.

Translators MARGUERITE DORIAN AND ELLIOTT URDANG

Ion Caraion

TOMORROW THE PAST COMES

No longer for me is there anything late. All is late.
The blood runs like a subway through capitals.
And the past   is   everywhere   like the blood.
                In the sunrise of the rivers red
with lightning   and groups   of centaurs
there was a kind of light—I don't know what kind of light that was.
                In the fog much becomes clear.

Ion Caraion

UNORNAMENTATION

No one discovers anything for you, alone
you discover the miracles you can believe in.
All other miracles have died a thousand times
in a thousand people
and no one wonders about them any longer
but to lie again and again.

This weariness was needed, needed
these solitudes to surround me,
to be without splendor, to heed
as before the symmetrical air—
. . . not to be able to tell anything.

To hear
the gunfire, the spoken sadness
of the city
twice ornamented in red.

With barrels
stained green by absence,
needed the wound, needed the wind

unlimited and chaste. And the tear
forbidding sleep.
Nothing but the shadow. Under butterflies
another sky deceives.

No one discovers anything for you, alone
you linger
in the verdigris of grass among skulls and crayfish.
A thousand birds walk without a magus—
and then it is silence, it is weariness,
always there is someone who won't be gone enough.

Ameen Alwan

A TARTNESS OF MY ANATOMY

ants

walk
up and down

the hollow
of my bones

looking

for honey
in a misplaced

joint

Ameen Alwan

BY THE SEA

He wants
to insinuate

his revelations

into the conch
of my ear.

I listen
with the placid

calcium
of myself

to the sea
in his voice.

My ear
shall never

smell
his breath.

John Biguenet

A SONG

The opening mouth,
a stone under water,
a skiff poised in the bruised stillness of oars.

The voice,
ice cracking in warm water,
the flutter of wings startled into flight.

The lyrics,
words trembling, boiling water,
a man in the distance walking on gravel.

The music,
to the eyes, falling water,
to the hands, a rope unraveling into strands.

The final chord,
a wall of water,
already dead, a man about to fall.

The silence after song,
the hard edge of water,
glaciers advancing on the cities.

ASPECTS OF THE KNIFE

The knife against his throat cautioned his irony.
No one doubted that a knife had done this.
Fumbling for a knife in the drawer, his hand deserted him.
The loneliness of the knife quivered in a tray across the room.
If you drink your water with a knife, don't talk.
The eye being slit saw merely an edge.
Nine fingers.

Ricardo Lindo

SINISTER ANTS

The sea came to eat from your hand in the tunnel of memory dismal greenish drops of reptile blood of rosebush blood the night full of tiny bright gadgets opened a brothel for the ants in the rosebeds of the palace all the roses died at dawn at dawn the kings crying ordered boundless funerals for the ghosts of the roses the sorcerers summoned them with signs and spells the kings attended.

The ghosts of the roses blamed the ants they said they had died of shame for the audacity of the ants in the kingdom war was declared the generals appeared with hives in the kitchen of the palace they had eaten all the sugar it was useless to send seven million and seven ants to the guillotine it was useless and useless the kings hung white sheets in the ballrooms of the palace they surrendered themselves surrendered the brothel for the ants it was a flourishing business the kings should support in front of their very noses never again did roses grow in the desolate gardens of the kingdom.

THE CITY AND THE STRIKING OF A MATCH

At one point of the desert there stands a city of mirrors. The mirrors are so small and are scattered in such a way, that by striking a single match, the entire city swells with light. The blackest night disappears from the power of a solitary match.

Entire caravans are blinded when coming upon the city in broad daylight. They walk without direction; the darker the inside, the more brilliant the expanse until devoured by the silent drift of sand.

This city is a story.

OUR LADY OF THE CLOCK

Our lady of the clock was left all alone in the castle.

She watched the distant sea coming and going, coming and going and thought of her husband. She remembered the time when he tenderly murmured in her ear: "Tick . . . tock . . .", or when he carefully set the pendulum in motion. Now he had died. Only action ruled by the meticulous power of habit continued to happen, and nothing new would ever happen again.

In the whole world, the corpses of her husband slowly moulded.

309

Harry Haskell and Gregory Brehm

For Octavio Paz

The Tides of Day and Night

Dawn ripens the fruit of eyes
    With the lips of dawn and midnight
    On each other
Two birds on a tree of clouds
    And a horse made of wind underwater
    You enter my life like a landscape
Of words and silence
    While the sun's moon's bell's sons sing
    Stones undress their centuries
Your shadow embraces light

          *   *   *   *

A river of fire undercover
    A child drinks the milk
    Of its Mother's eyes
An eclipse of your eyes in my blindness
    Two hands invent a body
    Your fingers
    Are ten eternities
While past present and pluperfect are one
    Two stars kiss the neck
    Of the sky

          *   *   *   *

Two birds embrace a dream
    And from the shadows of centuries
    Light sings of childhood and darkness
The shadows of silence
Light kisses the moon
    Look! A man in a trenchcoat
    Singing your name
One boat on two rivers
    And silence is rescued in laughter
Dawn awakens and pulls off

The blanket of night
　　You sang no one's name

　　　　*　*　*　*

Like a dream you awake in my arms
　　The seed of your voice opens
　　And plants itself in the wind
With the tapestry of misery
Sewn in your eyes
　　Politics is a dream without words
Echoes sing
　　As dawn kisses the breast
　　Of night

　　　　*　*　*　*

Open your eyes
　　Let stars sing
　　And birds shine in the sky
Open your mouth
　　Let your tongue
　　Lick the face
Of your dreams
　　Who invents the night?

Like the rhythm of blue
　　In the sky underwater
　　You surface
From the depth of a color
　　With crystalline rhythms
　　Of laughter and tears
Lost in search of each other

She flows like a river
　　To the shore of his dreams
　　Stars open their eyes
Stones bathe in the waters
　　Of their centuries
　　Two eyes open night
With a shadow of ice
　　For a reflection
　　I have tried to tell you
The story of a man and woman's life
　　Which melts in the earth and stars

　　　　*　*　*　*

311

The man who played piano
    Rio '66
      A woman in rags and tears
A woman
    Whose laughter was stolen
    By invention
Night Night Night

Each man becomes a mirror
    Of something he does not want to reflect
    Each woman looks into that mirror
And sees only her transparencies

And visions are born in a transparency
    Whose colors are clear
    Like the invisibility of a sigh
The light by our bodies shines

When dawn fully awakes
    And night takes off her clothes
    When two people make love
In a garden they invented
    Darkness will ripen
    And stars will smell
The pollen of earth

Each wave is a man
    The shore is a woman
Of whirlpool and foam

Stars join sky and become light
    Stones join fruit and become clouds
    Two mouths join
And the moon loses its shadow
    In the water

Each night is a man
    Noon is a dark woman
Who searches for day

Life remains an unspoken word
    You and I
    On the shoulders of night
Return our silence to the moon

*   *   *   *

From a river of dreams
    You awake
    You bring back
The trumpet of your dreams
    Note by note
    The rhythm of echoes and silence
Tide of equators
    The shores of your eyes
    Filled with foam
Unspoken
    The flower of a word
    Whose petals are vowels
Time erases the night

                *   *   *   *

The sky dissolves
    Into noon
    Stars shine like clouds
A piano with 88 silences
    Six strings of despair
    Unspoken rhapsodies
Memories of stars
    That shine like stones
    The silence of silence shines
Like your voice in the dark

                *   *   *   *

A song out of tune
    Love run away
    Caught in arms and eyes
The dark clouds of your eyes
    A silence that speaks
    Like a stone
Arrivals Departures
    When you love me
    You leave me
Your hands hoist their sails
    The wind of your dreams
    Arrives

Lucia Getsi

MOTHER

death was born with her

illumined her presence
like sunspots
filtered through shade trees

with each tilt of earth
spilled night
over all her bright princes

she hardly knew
when the sun went down

so quiet
her dreams chasing light
smearing the horizon red

LULLABY

a long sleep
to dream
I am dreaming

one rises
to hear clocks ticking

the other chants
clusters of words
spun in long images
of waking

José Emilio Pacheco

BOUNDS

Everything you've lost, they told me, is yours.
And not one memory remembered that it's a fact.
I was alive, I loved, I said some words
that the hours erased.
I felt a deep pity
for the years to come.
Everything you destroy, they told me, hurts you.
It traces a scare that forgetting does not wash away;
it is reborn daily within you,
it overflows
those walls of salt that can't conceal you.

Everything you've loved, they told me, has died.
And I'm not able to define it,
but something there is in time
that hoisted a sail forever.
There are faces I will never
again remember;
and there's perhaps a mirror, a street, a summer
that has obscured the echo of another useless shadow.

Everything you've believed in, they repeated, is false.
No god protects you,
only the wind gives you shelter.
And the wind, you surely realize,
is an unbounded hollowness,
the noise the world makes
when an instant dies.

Everything you've lost, they concluded, is yours.
It is your only property, your memory, your name.
You'll never have the day
that you rejected.
Time
has left you on the edge
of tonight
and maybe
a fugitive light
will annihilate the silence.

315

Günter Grass

PLACED AMID OLD MEN

How at ninety they lie
  and put off their dying
    till it's a legend.

Into the mottled hands
  of old men who rise early
    the world was laid.

Their many times folded power
  and the folds of old skin
    despise what is smooth.

Placed amid old men, we
  bite our nails till they're spare,
    we make no new growth.

Hard, wise and kind
  they last ascetically
    and soon will outlive us.

THE CAT

MARIO ARREGUI

tr. GEORGE MCWHIRTER

The line "I'm gonna cure you, Boss, 'cause I ain't baptized" was uniquely *hers*, and the most famous and desired from the negress, Asuncion, who was the quack (*conqueress*, primarily) in that lost, almost forgotten, little settlement. When her prediction was fulfilled, the negress accepted no gift or payment whatever, she simply passed on or issued the reminder for an order which no one failed to respect: the convalescent had to go, on foot, to the neighbouring village, hear mass and take communion. When—as seldom happened—her *science* misfired and the sick person died, the negress shut herself up in her shack and didn't reappear until long after the burial. From the chimney of the hovel—a center hole in the reed roof—a thick, black column of smoke emerged on those occasions. The smoke's distinctive and pungent odor spread the news to inhabitants in neighboring fields, to the hunters, renegades and badmen in the bush, that one of Asuncion's patients had died in the settlement.

The settlement craned up over the ridge and rolled downwards, scattering out as far as the river and the mountain. There, just about in the shadow of the first uncultivated trees, was Asuncion's shack. Bamboos and creepers hid it; strange plants, medicinal herbs and vegetables grew beside its blind walls of cane and mud; its door—a low, narrow opening blocked off by a hide. Frankly, it was more a mud hut than a shack, as if the negress, who had built it by herself, wished to commemorate the dwellings of her African forbears along with the color of her skin. The patches and the years went by, giving it all the while an even greater resemblance to the huge, circular huts of the jungle.

Asuncion was neither young nor old; she was of indeterminate age: marginal, static . . . although, no doubt, the river had swollen with the passage of many winters since the day when, aided by no one, a runaway slave gave birth to her on that very bank. She was tall and lean, strong boned, with a man's body, which, however, neither possessed nor showed a trace of anything masculine or virile. Her feet and hands—large, almost too large, with pink, even fingernails; a small, oval skull. Skin, extremely dark; the nose, short and flat; immense eyes glittering as though with nocturnal light . . . the facial features, smooth, sinuous. . . She had been young and beautiful, mistress of a pair of large, slippery hips, which were very neatly repressed by a short, cylindrical belt, and of high-peaked, belligerent breasts of black metal.

She had had men, both black and white, who arrived at the hut of cane and mud—surreptitiously, alone, intent—sometimes from a long way off, and with a certain lunar periodicalness like animals drawn secretly by the smell of a female in heat. Men who arrived on foot and departed without being seen by anyone, and others whose horses, tied out there in the vastness of the bush, whinneyed with hunger, impatience and thirst.

There was always someone around the settlement who would maintain that quite a few times there had been knife fights in the proximity of the hut; furthermore, it was rumoured that the occasional body—its insides ripped out so that it wouldn't float—had been tossed into the river.

Asuncion never had children; it's well known that she interned herself in the bush, and there—alone, of her own free will—she abandoned a blood stained foetus, and after bathing in the river, returned to the hut with the same prolix and rhythmic walk as before—steps which her fine, spindley thighs imprinted so neatly on her rough cotton skirt.

Around the settlement it was said that the negress had plundered about during the civil war battles; she had drunk human blood, they said, and on those bloody grazing grounds, satisfied the last erotic desires of the mortally wounded. Also it was said, in a whisper, that on moonlit nights she visited the graveyard.

The years tightened about Asuncion's bones, stripping away the flesh and sexuality without bringing her any nearer the opposite sex. Around the time when, in reality, our story begins, she was a human being, self-absorbed, changeless. She lived alone in her hut where no men came any more, and at times, if no patient had need of her, she would lose herself for days and nights in the depth of the bush. Her steps were rhythmic as ever, but now her walk was a sheathed glide, almost shadow-like. Her black impenetrable face changed only harboring a certain moving thing—still more inscrutable at the moment when confronted with the sick person, she didn't deliver that line of hers which all were waiting for; then she would turn on her heel and leave without a glance at anyone—and everyone knew that the time had come to bury all hope. . . One evening (an evening like many others when she returned from the bush loaded down with herbs and firewood), Asuncion, the negress, found a two or three day old kitten—a sorry looking tabby which the mother—a mangy, domestic cat—had lost or deserted during siesta time. The negress dropped her bundle, squatted down and stared at it with an absorbed and continuous interest in her huge eyes; then she picked it up and continued on her way. The few people who saw her couldn't hold back their astonishment because she had always lived as if animals didn't exist.

From that evening the rearing of that kitten was the strange mission which channelled her life. With it in her arms, she set out at night for the fields. Damp with dew, huge wild cows watched her approach; she talked to them and the cows mooed fearfully, but didn't run away; the negress milked them, the milk fell on the pasture and the kitten drank. In the early morning Asuncion made her way to the slaughterhouse; in a hushed voice she asked for blood, the slaughterers allowed her to go ahead; she pushed an earthenware jar over the trough, spilled the steaming blood on the ground and the cat drank, and at times rolled in it.

In the bush and throughout the countryside, Asuncion hunted for mice, adders, armadillos, she dug owls out of their holes, she climbed trees after fledgling doves.

The cat grew, a cat like any other; only perhaps somewhat larger and fatter—a little fiercer in its look. It was a sad and ponderous animal, with watery green eyes in which metallic gleams shook like tangles. Always it padded behind the negress taking no notice of females in heat. Asuncion continued to feed it with great care, and in a manner which grew progressively more strange. Although she no longer raided the huge wild cows in the night, she attended the slaughterhouse more often; now she not only asked for blood, but she waited as well until the beasts were disembowelled in order to extract a piece of meat, some secret intestine, an innard which she hid from the slaughterers' eyes. She also brewed mysterious concoctions in her hut, and the smoke which emerged from the chimney smelt of unknown odors.

The cat went on growling; growling and contorting, as if a monstrosity were struggling inside it. Little by little its coat grew tiger-like; the entire body at times resembled that of a dwarfed and deformed tiger.

Uneasily, the inhabitants of the settlement followed the transformation which her *science* had wrought on the animal. Absorbed in her work, she became day by day more evasive, more savage. She used to lose herself for days on end in the heart of the bush, just like before, but now she returned, weary, the huge cat exhausted in her arms. During that time her clothes consisted only of rags which covered her dry, doubly darkened skin; she had taken to adorning herself with the teeth and bones of small animals. When she talked (when she found herself obliged to talk), her voice had the dumb ring of alien metal like a counterfeit coin. Making her put in an appearance at the sick bed was increasingly difficult. Each time, the cat showed itself to be more encumbered by something powerful—as if closer to exploding. A kind of fever took possession of it at times, generally at high noon. At times it thrashed about meowing, tumbling over and biting itself as if its skin were oppressing it. On other occasions it fell into a prolonged fit from which it would start, suddenly, with a convulsive shudder and two or three hoarse screeches, which appeared to be in answer to calls that it alone could hear. During the night and evening its howls reached a very high pitch, and they wavered there, dragging themselves out in rasping, spluttering roars. Often it made pointless leaps, and sniffed and bit at the wind which came from the North, clawing at the air, taking to its heels in flights, which it would immediately break off to return slowly, and with a subdued air, pleading, submissive to the negress's side. Each time it was less of a cat and more a small tiger; ferociousness and sadness fused in its eye.

The disappearance of the negress had lasted a long time, too long. No one had seen her in the bush, the shack's chimney wasn't emitting its usual column of smoke, the cat's meaulling no longer rent the air. One noon several men approached the hut of cane and mud. They shouted: silence; only the whispering of the wind among the bamboos. Two of them went forward; an unmistakable smell made them look from one to the other. They pulled back the hide which blocked off the entrance that was the door. An axe blade of light cut straight down from the center hole in the reed roof. The man saw dry blood, a scrap of meat, scattered bones. In the shadow of a corner, almost phosphorescent: the enormous cat; more precisely, the dwarfed, monstrous tiger —the killer—innocently gnawing on the black witch's skull.

Translator JOHN GETSI

OLD LOVE

ILSE AICHINGER

Two little, partially gray people worked their way tiredly up the street. In front of them the sun accented the sand, behind them the wind blew into the sailcloth. From time to time they stood still, faced one another and each observed the other cautiously and in detail. There was no familiarity in their gazes, no commitment, and they seemed indifferent to what flowed out of the park over gullies. "All that is western trash," the man said once, but he lisped badly and it just as easily could have been called something else. The woman nodded and pulled the loosely knit shawl tighter about her neck. "Wasn't a young man there," she said, "who wanted to visit us? They have put him behind glass." "And when?" "As far as I know, yesterday." "Crystals and their formation," replied the man concerned, "in this country one serves nothing else." To their left a church square appeared, and he had to hold onto his hat. "And what becomes of it?" asked the woman. Her voice was soft and clear, even though her accent was slightly foreign. "When I wish to have someone over for coffee, for example, after a joust, I expect him to come." "Naturally," said the man. "Covered with red dust perhaps," she continued more excited now and had to sneeze, "but I expect him to come. What do you think?" "That such expectations are natural," he replied. Children ran past with caps of blue, red and green, carrying something slung over their shoulders on nooses, ice skates, or maybe smaller boots also, hunting weapons, two each and many carried four. "Young grown-ups," said the man, "future whalers who won't visit us either." Again they stood still and examined each other briefly. "Where did you awaken?" he asked. "I was wrapped in yellowed sailcloth, lay under an icy breeze, the end, that was all." "And I awoke with the rams at the zoo entrance." "The old stories are of no further help to anyone. There are many who were

321

wrapped in nothing more than heavy packing paper." "I know," said the man, "these things I know." "When I think of my old school notebook," said the woman, "my script so fine and how they bent over me and cried 'Good, Muriel, good!' And then you fall asleep and find yourself again with people fishing at the river or in depot corridors." "So it is," he said, "whether you want to or not, there's more than enough of it." "Yes," she replied shyly. And added, fighting for breath in a gust of wind: "Besides, the whole thing has taken place in no more than half a day. Not even half a day. Too short a time to find conviction." "Conviction?" "I mean to revolt against the government and all that. Where your friend Morton now sits." "Not anymore." "Not anymore? But then it's too late!" "You wanted to see the boy," he said and without looking up he helped her over the curb. "You see him with us." "See him with us," he repeated, "and because of that we are on our way. Hat closets, cloakrooms, winter curtains and trays. Therein lies our present interest. In the appropriate reception. We want to pass over the avoidable associations, we want to come upon his whereabouts easily." "You say that lightly." "I mean," he continued patiently, "without garrulousness and vain repetitions, which previously we have been able to avoid." "Yes, do you think so?" she replied, uncertain.

They stopped in front of a window. This window did not resemble a display window, but instead looked the way shop windows usually look when they have been converted into ground-floor flats: no window bars, the single panes laboriously and badly cleaned so that one noticed traces of chamois on them. And the bright stringy curtains, whose stitch design gave a shredded effect, were not behind the panes but rather drawn together behind the somewhat too deep embrasure. Yes, it was a former display window and in turn could have been just a former window and who knows how often it had changed from one to the other without success. Still, the windowsill was lengthened artfully up to the inner recess and was covered with velvet. Yellowish leaf-plants in clay pots were placed left and right along the walls, but in the middle, illuminated by nothing but the weak morning sun, stood old furniture in miniature: a kitchen cabinet, a desk, a spinet, even washboards and tub, three ornate chairs around an oval table, an armchair, an optical illusion (as fake paintings are sometimes called) upon which the fortress of Finstermünz was depicted, and half covered by a black cloth, a Recamière and a rocking chair. One of the lower left drawers of the desk was open, a fountain pen lying across it. "Here," cried the woman, "here it is, it must have been here!" "Where we did not receive him?" "Where he did not enter." "It is in fact number seventy-eight," said the man, who surveyed the old narrow housedoor near the window, "seventy-four, seventy-six, seventy-eight." "Let's assume he might have been riding a horse," she said, "he couldn't have gotten through the door." "Had you started to write a letter?" he asked cautiously and pointed to the fountain pen caught in the half-open desk drawer. "I had always begun to write letters," she replied irritated, "except on a few Wednesdays in early autumn, four or five, you can count them on your fingers!" "And then the wash, your old weakness." "That proves nothing," she retorted as tears mounted in her eyes. The man had gone to the house gate and tried the latch, but the gate was locked. He pressed the only half-rusted bell button in the wall, but nothing stirred. "Everything's closed," he said, "and I am convinced: we should never have begun with the ship painting, and generally speaking, with all such undertakings, pen refillings, spinet lessons, and so forth." "Spinet lessons," she cried stricken, "the four schoolgirls and one of them. . . ." "Then they might have had no reason, nothing with which to reproach us," he said quickly, "and we might be able to complain like all the others, like the rest of humanity, my friend Morton," he again attempted to ring, "my friend Morton, for example. . . ." "Let him go," she said, "leave your friend Morton out of this once and for all. From now on everything without him." She pressed her forehead against the glass. "How wasted and ruined everything looks here. Not a place a person could depart from, in any case not like this. No, not like this!" She was still near tears. "When a place looks like this, one can't do anything but stay." She stamped her foot. "Stay, stay! Between washboards and waterspots, too." "I believe someone is coming now," said the man. "And these yellow flowers . . ." The door opened quickly and a large, fairly powerful woman looked out. She wore a kitchen apron, a white scarf, and horn-rimmed glasses, her short gray hair tangled about her head. "I think we know each other," the man said decisively. "Wasn't your maiden name Strauss? My wife on the other hand is close to the house where Eduard was born . . . could you have learned anything concerning his fate?" "Not a word," said the woman at the door. "To speak plainly, our concern is not with my wife's relatives," the man said quickly when she sought to close the door again. "Well, then?" She glanced behind her into the hall as if someone stood there and then turned once again toward the street. "But rather with a young man on a horse," said the man hastily, "born in Erfurt, headstrong, uninspired, and lovable. Imagine, he once said he would visit us and he came, too. He charged in as if between stone statues and took an interest in everything. But when he wished to come the second time, and that's just it—should have come," he interrupted himself with a glance toward his companion, "should have

323

come, then he didn't come again. We had arranged everything, we sat there and waited. I still had the possibility of devoting myself to my two major interests, but her? To be brief: do you know anything? We hear they put him behind glass, but we can't believe it. He always had so much open air about him, sand on his heels." "I would have associated him sooner with crises of the sea," he added after a shorter pause, "but by no means with crises of the street. No, by no means." "You are shameless," the woman at the door said in her tremulous voice, while over her left shoulder emerged the head of a horse which she stroked softly. "I think you go too far." "I hope so," answered the man, "that seldom lay in the realm of my possibilities. Isn't that true, Belle?" He turned again to his now silent companion. "And whoever reads the newspapers comes upon the most curious notions. For example, I can tell you quite plainly that you kept monkeys and peewits in the window. And that it was still in the recent past. Obviously, before you ever wore your apron. And your hair was prettier then, too!" "To be sure, a great many never got in," he continued quickly, "for you already valued leafplants at that time. And the poor animals suffered from isolation, didn't you think, Belle?" She nodded. "How are you coming along with our furniture? Have you gotten the dust out? I don't mean the gray, which is from us, that went easily no doubt. But the red, which our young rider let fly from the washboards. And even when he didn't come. How did you fare in this direction? Did you find a tool, and which one, or did you have to use muscle? The powers of the imagination should rise for both of them. I heard about a brush, for example, a kind of sweeping brush . . . ." "Stop!" said the woman at the door. "Merely because it interests me," said the man. "I was always afflicted with all sorts of interests, as opposed to Belle," he turned aside smiling, "to whom areas of interest always remained foreign. Yes, I would almost say that as soon as something became interesting, she lost sight of it, even in our happiest time. That provides one with much quiet, the opportunity, which otherwise might have eluded one, to busy oneself with household belongings. To think of the dust, I might have never thought of the dust otherwise." "You don't say," retorted the woman at the door and vainly attempted to push the horse back into the hall. "Also, I might never have had the opportunity to visit my female cousins," explained the man, "of whom only two were dim-wits!" "*Voyager*," Belle said suddenly and she succeeded for the first time in looking away from the plants and furniture. The horse drew breath. "Certainly two different kinds of dim-wits," he muttered, "astoundingly different." "*Voyager*," Belle said once again. "I warn you," said the woman at the door as the horse pushed past her into the street. She clutched its neck in a clumsy and somewhat rough embrace. "I would gladly tell you what you stand to lose!" "No need," replied the man and tugged on his hat. "These matters have already been made known to us at various times in other quarters." "Yes, they are known to us!" cried Belle. "Perhaps not well enough," replied the woman gasping. "We should be the judges of that," said the man, "Belle and I . . . ." "Come inside!" cried the woman and propped herself more forcefully against the horse. "We have both grown up in regions whose names promised too much." "Tell me about it when we are inside. We can examine everything by turns!" "Impossible," said the man. "There comes Henni," cried Belle and pulled timidly at his sleeve, "I lent my fur coat to her!" She pointed, without turning around, to the window whose pane mirrored a plump beggar girl across the street. It appeared as though she shuffled along between the spinet and kitchen wood. "The green fur, you know, the one I told you about. But she didn't know what it was for. My good Henni, I had lost sight of her. I was also angry with her then." The horse shook its mane and stood suddenly in the street. "My god, how many kinds of chance there are," said Belle happily. "And always when you least expect it." The horse went up to her and smelled her hat. "Yes, it is still the same one," said Belle, "believe it or not, I have changed only the scarf." "Henni, look at this," she called and looked over her shoulder. The beggar girl stopped short, overjoyed she put her hand above her eyes and hurriedly attempted to cross the street. "Are we ready now?" said the man calmly. "Only a moment," replied Belle. The beggar girl started to wave excitedly. "Hey, you two," she called, "who would have thought it? When we still sharpened pens, Belle, my dear one!" Belle laughed. "Are you leaving the nest?" "This time voluntarily," responded the man and helped Henni onto the sidewalk, "the spinet, pages of memories, the sweet muse!" "Then you can take me along for a stretch," said Henni, who was a little winded, "the area hereabouts is grazed out." The horse pawed. "Up to the third corner, that will do," she said, while he helped her and Belle to mount. He nodded and swung himself up between the two. "And what should one hold onto?" The horse fell in step. It had left the sidewalk and strove toward the center of the street. "We travelers," murmured Belle. "You will have to take the responsibility," called the woman in the door. She made a motion as if to enter the street, but remained standing on the threshold in her white apron. "You will see where this leads you. And your young hero, your horseman?" "The poor thing," said Belle into the winter sun which appeared before them in the sky. The horse had attained the summit of the street, it fell into a trot.

Pär Lagerkvist

WITH OLD EYES I LOOK BACK

With old eyes I look back.
All is so long ago.
A stony road
with weary oxen homesick at even-tide,
a wagon, an old cart-track, the farm's grey gable
with a light in one of the windows.
The marshy meadows beside the little river,
with mist over darkened water—

Why do I remember this? What has it to do with me?
My life was spent far away
in another world or as if in another world.
And now all is soon over
and does not matter.
Where man is born,
where his life begins,
only to end before the gates of death,
what does that matter?

A stony road,
a wagon, an old cart-track—

*

My soul is full of the evening's desolation
and of the light of the old cowhouse-lantern
when it is carried around the stalls
where the cattle are soundly asleep.
Afterwards it is carried up to the house
and its beams flicker over the garden path which is no more,
and the steps are heard of someone long since dead.
All is so long ago.

My soul is full of the evening's desolation
and the beams of the old cowhouse-lantern
on the garden path up to their grey farm
which is no more.

My soul? What has my soul to do with that? With marshes beside
        a little river,
a misty evening, the beams of a cowhouse-lantern—

My soul has been chosen to search far away
for hidden things, to wander under stars.

A stony road, a wagon, an old cart-track—

*

With hands folded they listen to words,
incomprehensibly big words for the human soul,
with folded hands at a worn table
where supper has just been cleared away and an old book
brought out in silence, heavenly silence.
A star from a far off land stands over the turf roof of the farm,
the house of the dead
in the late Fall evening.
Someone enters with heavy tread,
setting the cowhouse-lantern down at the door,
enters into the starlight.
Now none are missing
But all are dead.

*

They also lived in the light of a star
when their heavy working day was over.
Together they sat in the quiet light
of a lonely star, not the light of all stars,
a single star—not the star of all men.

Together. . .
At a worn table.
With large tired working hands.

Why do I remember this? What have I to do with it?

Burn alone, my soul, with your dark flame!—

A stranger am I, was a stranger born.
A stranger even in the autumn of my life.
With old eyes I look back.

Where do we come from? What is our soul?
A mist over darkened water, the beam of a cowhouse-lantern,
of a star?

With my hand over my old eyes,
which were once those of a child—

. . . the house of the dead
in the late autumn evening.

Someone enters with heavy tread
setting the cowhouse-lantern down at the door,
enters into the starlight.
Now none are missing. . .

Why do I remember this?

Translators SAMUEL HAZO
AND MIRENE GHOSSEIN

Andrée Chedid

WHO REMAINS STANDING?

First,
erase your name,
unravel your years,
destroy your surroundings,
uproot what you seem,

and who remains standing?

Then,
rewrite your name,
restore your age,
rebuild your house,
pursue your path,

and then,

endlessly,
start over, all over again.

THE NAKED FACE

Faces of the counted years,
but still of such enigmas,

faces without rumors,
faces in expectancy,
faces in constant birth,
faces of so many cells,

faces that are you as you are
and already are not.

Never shall pulses stop
beneath your surfaces,
nor shall my thirst to understand you cease,

you,
one face beneath them all,
naked.

329

Tess Gallagher

SKIN GRAFT

With your one good hand
you find the word "feathers."
You're looking for a witness.
The lost hand stares like a turtle
baked alive in its plaster shell.
How you care for it, like a child,
held just below the breasts, or
cradled now in the lap of your gown.

On the white table an orange
would take you by the teeth.
I peel it, as though to be so able
were a way of listening to the wife
between us. Haven't we seen her children
ablaze like a fence built again
and again around the house
of your rescue? Ashes
have warned: the hand is a torch, the mind
as easily cut off
as an ear.

Even a mouth
will heal; repeat the doors
you could not please, the matches
they took from you. Repeat
the tongues nesting in the heat. Say
escape is no scar, no matter
how the skin crawls back.

Roberto Fernández Iglesias

In some far-off place
as happens
in every story
worthy
  of
    the telling
they have erected
a monument
        to memory
and they build it
with fragile stone
to be able to destroy it
          each
          day

Roberto Fernández Iglesias

You saw her growing
and she was always growing
It seems that when
her growing stopped
you stopped seeing

Diane Wakoski

STILLIFE: MICHAEL, SILVER FLUTE

AND VIOLETS   *for M.R.*

as if I could remember you still for a moment,
always moving,
like a fountain that passes and repasses
the same water,
keeping sparkling and pursed
against the metal lips
which shoot and crackle it

And violets coming
into the room where you are standing,
tho that gesture for you takes up many
square feet of space
held in the hand of a girl
who was herself fragrant and intense,
violet against the wet woody ground, was violet
against brown damp trunks

And you reading poems by a man
who probably broke his neck against the green scummed water
in a deep well,
        Green,
        I want you green,
        Green wind,
        Green branches. . .

      *   *   *

There is a small nut of life in me
that is never touched
by life around me.
I am myself moved, in retrospect,
by how little I had, and how not understanding
the extreme poverty of my life
left me innocent
of the worst thing poverty does to people
                            bitterness.
      *   *   *

Well, my friend,
you did not have your music lessons
when you were young.
And I had mine, though at a price.
And neither of us
is a musician today, tho we have each spent
a decade of time practicing our hands against our ears
and understand measured cadences better than most other speakers
can.
And neither of us can give up poetry or music
as emblems.
You carry your silver flute everywhere,
and a small wooden one in a case by your side.
And I my mythical piano
which makes my shoulders rounder each year.
Weight
of the past.
Who is the girl holding the bunch of violets?
For she was only an emblem
when my hands were still bloody from the keys.

Blanca Varela

tr. DONALD A. YATES

THE THINGS I SAY ARE TRUE

A star crashes in a small plaza and a bird loses its eyes
and falls. Gathered around it, men weep and see the new
season arrive. The river flows and sweeps along in its cold,
confused arms the dark material accumulated by years and
years behind the windows.

A horse dies and his soul flies to heaven smiling with
its big wooden teeth stained by the dew. Later, amidst
the angels, he will sprout black, silky wings for scaring flies.

All is perfect. Being shut up in a small hotel room,
being injured, cast aside and impotent, while outside
the rain falls softly, unexpectedly.

What is it that is coming, that leaps from above and bathes
the leaves with blood and fills the streets with gilded rubbish?

I know I am sick with a heavy illness, filled with a bitter
water, with an inclement fever that whistles and frightens
all who hear it. My friends have left me, my parrot now is
dead, and I cannot prevent people or animals from fleeing
the terrible black radiance my steps leave in the streets.
I must have lunch alone forever. Terrible.

KINGS AND DESPERATE MEN

RONALD TOBIAS

Hyacinthe of Mariscotti. 1585-1640. Tert. V., O.F.M. R.M.,
January 30. Beatified in 1726; canonized in 1807.

At dreen tide, lobstermen wandered out onto the mud flats of the Fundy to look for their lost moorings. Around them, the hulls of their weatherbeaten boats rested in the mud like nesting hens, while deeper in the reach, herring seiners sulked at anchor. The village of Viterbo was buried between the solemn desolation of the wintered sea and the bleak, flat barrens which isolated it at the end of a neck of land thirty miles from the nearest town. In summer a few people dared out to harvest peat and low bush blueberries on the heath or trawled for scallops and shrimp in the bay, but in winter the town was paralyzed in the same depression as the season itself.

Hyacinthe lived in Viterbo cloistered in a gray clapboard house at the edge of the barrens near where the St. Croix bled into the mouth of the Fundy. She had been born in the same house in the dead of winter the year the bay froze over and locked everything in ice. It was the year desperate men set fire to their boats and the year, it seemed, that barren women conceived.

Hyacinthe's mother had resented the pregnancy and blamed her husband for it, just as she had blamed him for her stillbirth fifteen years before. The *accoucheuse* had blamed the moon, but she had blamed him, a ghost of a man who hid behind the counters of his general store and dispensed creams and cottons and beans, a man too frightened to lead the cortège for his unconsecrated son and too weak to dig his unconsecrated grave.

When it became obvious that she was pregnant, Hyacinthe's father had asked her about it. We are being punished, she said coldly. Your sin is inside me.

For five months they sat in silence; she in the deacon's chair, smoking her pipe and staring at him, and he, across the room, watching her reflection on the glazed enamel of the wood stove. Together they sat in their house empty of dreams. He had long ago taken to the sea where he begged the songs of Sirens that never came, and she, after the death of her stillborn son, watched his twisted body rise in smoke from the bowl of her pipe and evanesce, like her life, into nothing.

She expected her child to be born dead and seemed surprised when it wasn't, and while the *accoucheuse* held up the baby to the sun and hailed Mary, she cursed the girl and abandoned it to her husband, who, in despair, turned to Father Ferrier of Ste. Therése's.

Ferrier, a paladin of the cross and a man of countless spiritual anodynes, baptized the girl with the name Hyacinthe while her mother watched on faithlessly from the kitchen door. Ferrier purged the house with bitter smoke; he lit vigils, cut horseradish, and roamed the halls intoning chants and invoking Ste. Thérèse. She watched Ferrier throw holy water against the doors, where it ran to the floor like tears, against the sills and lintels, into Hyacinthe's cradle, but she stopped him as he stood poised over her bed.

I'm serving the Lord, Ferrier said angrily.

Well, she said checking his arm with a grip that made Ferrier's black eyes widen with surprise, don't serve Him to me.

Ferrier, enraged, retreated down the stairs, where he cruelly abused her husband for his unconfessed sins, and then disappeared out the door with his black manteau flapping behind him like a bat's wings.

*

In Viterbo, all men negotiated their death with the sea. But Ferrier tried to insinuate himself into their arguments by tempting people with the comfort of God. He tried to usurp the authority the sea had over their lives with ceremony and promises for salvation for those who obeyed and damnation for those who scorned him.

Ferrier was an ambitious man, and he aggressively tried to bring

Hyacinthe's mother into the church. But she staunchly defended herself against him even though she left him to claim her husband and her daughter.

Unmoved by Ferrier's arrogance, she would sit by herself in the front room smoking her pipe and listening to Ferrier in the kitchen with her husband as he cursed their bed until Ferrier finally drove him out of it and up into the attic where he slept alone.

For years Hyacinthe was kept sheltered in the house where she knew only the estrangement of her mother and the land. Her father timidly brought her playthings: scallop shells, hundreds of them, which looked like the calcified wings of butterflies and frightened Hyacinthe when she saw them on the floor: fallen, brittle, unable ever to take flight. He also brought her Clabber Girl tins from the store and lined them up on her shelf in a chorus of little girls' faces. Ferrier brought her years of his insistent catechism.

*

Years later she became the only one left in the house. Her mother had fallen dead in the front room near the spot where Hyacinthe had been baptized, and her father, who suddenly saw the fear he had dreaded all his life materialize, had shut himself up in the store eating canned foodstuffs and talking to God. For days people in the street heard him running around in frantic circles like a dog chasing its tail, upsetting furniture and shouting heresies. Later, when Ferrier forced open the door to take him out, he found only empty cans and hundreds of scraps of paper with the words "chose jugée" pencilled furiously all over them.

After her mother's death and her father's disappearance, Hyacinthe stayed in the house with its torturous solitude of rooms and its faint odor of horseradish. She knew only the wheeze of water from the river as it rushed the chokestones to the north and the hollow whisk of wind from the flat barrens to the west. She rarely ventured out of the house, and except for the hunters who cupped their faces at her windows, and Ferrier, who kept visiting the house begging for a confession she could not offer, Hyacinthe sat alone, yielding only to the mensal flow of tides and blood.

Like her father, Hyacinthe was ghostly, and frail, as if she'd suffered a long fever. She was as tremulous as the kerosene flame that lit the house at night, and she moved from room to room like fox-fire; she was a timid spirit of light that faded to the point of exhaustion. Those who saw her said she looked like the pale reflection of one of the nameless virgin martyrs in the sacristy windows of Ste. Therése, but the coincidence wasn't that startling since both of them had nondescript faces; in fact, it was their lack of features that made them look alike.

Ferrier's insistent, yet tender entreaties for her sin became too passionate, and Hyacinthe allowed him to take her as a lover. He introduced her to sex as he introduced any sacrament: with the intimidation of his authority. Together they struggled in an awkward, angry passion on her bed where he tried to deliver her the reality of sin. But as defiant as Ferrier was, as a man and as a priest, he failed, and only made her aware of a distant resonance, a slight trèmor of something alien within her she had never known before. When Ferrier climbed on top of her, she felt neither pleasure nor pain, but she felt its stirring, like an eyeless reptile living in subterranean depths disturbed from its ageless sleep. It was apart from her; its skin grazed hers. When Ferrier made love to her, she could feel its drowsed head turn slowly.

In the dark by her bed, the gilt of Ferrier's breviary danced in the air like golden insects.

*

When Ferrier realized the hollowness of Hyacinthe's body and her apparent impermeability, he withdrew and made her repent with him. In one sense he was frightened of her because not even the corruption of her flesh seemed to leave a scar. As much as he assaulted her, she was indomitable; he believed his only heritage to her would be the vague string of Pater Nosters and Ave Marias they had canted while kneeling on the cold linoleum of her bedroom floor.

But Ferrier was wrong. One evening, when she followed him downstairs after he had left her in bed, she walked into the kitchen where he was eating a plateful of eggs. She looked at him, still unaware of her presence, and found him intolerable. She sensed a profound threat and ran back upstairs into her bedroom. Later, when Ferrier tried to return, she refused to open the door. The next day, when he tried to return to the house, she locked him out and hid in the widow's watch while Ferrier pleaded to be let in.

But Hyacinthe couldn't escape the smell of Ferrier's body which reminded her of the wet, decaying forest floor; she couldn't escape the haunting sound of his choked breath or the feel of his damp body smothering hers. She could no longer shut out the melancholic sough and moan of stale water beneath the poisoned soil of the barrens or ignore its unending lament. And worse, she feared the animus inside her, again silent, waiting.

*

Driven out of the house, Hyacinthe took a job shucking clams for a food processor and spent her working days laboring in a shed at the end of the co-op pier.

The dark, salt-soaked shed was cluttered with baskets of hissing clams and crates of shrimp shivering on ice. Broken gaffs and rakes rusted in a litter of traps and broken hods. Hyacinthe stood at pitted steel sinks all day as her knife learned to cut open clams and her amnesic fingers tore the gems of entrails from their hinges and let them slip into the trays. The clicking of her knife was a metronome that vainly marked time against the void; the psalmation of water against the pilings outside, and through the hoses and trays inside, was as deadening as the drone of the wind on the barrens. Days became weeks, perhaps months or years, and Hyacinthe again drowsed in the anaesthetic of time. Only the muffled clang of the harbor nuns warned her of another world.

*

Hyacinthe, expectant with a vague dream of violence, walked home along the edge of the reach. She winced at the sight of the waterlogged balks of traders that littered the graveyard of the coast. Straining her eyes towards the flat horizon, she saw blurry images of a hundred ships sailing a phantom sky, tacking away from her and fading into the air as windward currents carried their darkling reflections to shore and slammed them into the shoals.

Tide pools teased her with their memories of sunken ships and bloated men. She was drawn to their pain. Hyacinthe felt she had once known the sailors' deaths: she heard their swallowed screams lost in the water, and the soft pop of their lungs bursting in their chests; she saw their bloodied eyes stare longingly at the soft bed of the sea. They seemed part of a memory that was slowly returning, and part of a promise that would transcend the emptiness around her.

She dreamt of the Clabber Girl standing on a somnolent shore wrapped in a shroud of fog, a drowned sailor at her feet.

*

Somewhere along the endless, torpid procession of days, two seiners threw a live nurse shark onto the floor of the shed, and while the seiners laughed, the shark's body thrashed wildly across the floor towards her. The brutal grace of the shark's dance excited Hyacinthe: the desperate snap of jaws as it turned up its bottlenose to assault the formless air, the pinched flesh as it scraped the splintery floor, and the rubine gills that beat furiously as they choked in the empty sea of air. Hyacinthe's heart pounded wildly, and as she watched the shark convulse on the floor, the almost forgotten creature within her uncoiled and lifted its head to nose the wet darkness around it. Its cool skin nuzzled hers as if it wanted to feed.

Then, in a movement that she would dream of endlessly, one of the seiners bent over and slipped a knife into the shark's belly, quickly slitting the entire length of its body. Its insides spilled out onto the planking, and with them, three fetal sharks in a tangle of golden yolks that flared as brightly as the apricot sun of summer.

For Hyacinthe, the blur of the silvery knife across the shark's skin was

339

a comet's tail. She saw a bright crescent slash a spectral sky of faint stars and distant planets. A sudden tumescence aroused her, and while she watched the shark bask in the languid calm beyond pain, she wished for the same placid breath and communion of blood.

*

A gray rain fell like a great sorrow. The windows of the pier shed wept with runnels of tears. While Hyacinthe worked her knife into the clams, she stared at the fingerling sharks she kept in a bottle on a shelf above her sink. Weighted by their jaundiced yolk sacs, they balanced on their noses and stared down at Hyacinthe with their cottony eyes. Mute, expressionless, they circled the jar with the rhythm of the sea, turning slowly either to face Hyacinthe or the limit of the reach.

Their perfectly formed faces were blank—innocent of the fear or memory of their birth. But Hyacinthe remembered what they could not: the seiner's blade stabbing the shark's soft belly and entering the foetid darkness of her body, the silken tear of her flesh, and the nearly inaudible sigh. And deep inside, Hyacinthe could hear the wash of fetal blood and the calm, confident beat of their hearts until violent bursts of cold and light sheared the walls of their sanctum for a moment of flawless ecstasy. The memory repeated itself like the reflections in the facets of a perfect diamond. As she stood at her sink, Hyacinthe trembled with the vision of it.

The angry wash of rain against her window seemed to want to beat her. Outside, taut hawsers droned at the niggerheads while the sea tugged at the ancient joints of the pier until they groaned. Hyacinthe's past returned to her like flashing cards of doom: the Clabber Girl with her sleepless smile, the hundreds of shells littering her floor, Ferrier's pasty face. The shed trembled and swayed on its pilings. The sudden odor of horseradish frightened Hyacinthe. She flinched and tasted the bittersweet of panic. Wind squalled around her. She flinched again.

Her body shook. As her knife worked itself mechanically, the odor of horseradish got stronger. She was afraid to turn around to see who was standing behind her, and so she continued, half in nightmare and half in golden dream, while fatal insects burrowed beneath her skin and into her blood. Pain skittered down her spine, rebounding from her brain to her womb. Its echo silhouetted the embryonic form within her as it swelled in its silent incubation. The virulent life within her made Hyacinthe feel strong and alive, unafraid of pain.

The water and air around her seemed to adore her with their violence. Hyacinthe felt herself soar above the waves, and above the clouds, free from the ugly, sucking bogs and the daze of fog which had bound her so mercilessly to their tyranny. When she looked down into the trays and saw her hands covered with blood, and the clammer's knife ridged with the bright red ribbon of her innocence, she cried with soft tears while she repeated the soft litany of *chose jugée, chose jugée.*

340

Somewhere unwound in time, Hyacinthe lay on the altar of her bed and drew the knife across her arms until she perceived the form behind the camouflage; she saw the gaunt, dark shape of the incubus that lived within her as it uncurled its fiddlehead fingers to embrace the walls around it. Hyacinthe saw the transfiguration of the shark as she spanned death and birth in a single act. As she cut deeper, she knew her suffering perpetuated all life.

The pain became a silver monolith rising out of the darkness, brilliant with light and strength. It arose from the heart of the barrens, growing out of the cruel soil that destroyed even the most insistent seed. It towered above the spruce hummocks thrusting out into space as if to violate it. The greater the pain became, the greater she could sense its presence piercing the bleak, empty universe. The monolith was a knife that stabbed the darkness.

On the last night, the first night, her womb pushed out a bastard child of darkness. Through her wet eyes, Hyacinthe saw the pinprick glitter of lonely stars turn into a blazing galaxy filled with swirling nebulae and cascades of fire as they spilled through the rent sky. Dragons clawed the obsidian flesh of the universe; bulls mounted cows in frenzy; an eggshell swan glided towards Andromeda. The chaos of the heavens was wild with phantom life. From her bed, her child-beast rose, glancing her tired flesh before rising into the nexus of stars.

At dawn, as the last light faded, Hyacinthe saw the china blue of falling snow fill the air like the wings of thousands of soaring butterflies.

Anne Sexton

ROWING

A story, a story!
(Let it go. Let it come.)
I was stamped out like a Plymouth fender
into this world.
First came the crib
with its glacial bars.
Then dolls
and the devotion to their plastic mouths.
Then there was school,
the little straight rows of chairs,
blotting my name over and over,
but undersea all the time,
a stranger whose elbows wouldn't work.
Then there was life
with its cruel houses
and people who seldom touched —
though touch is all —
but I grew,
like a pig in a trenchcoat I grew,
and then there were many strange apparitions,
the nagging rain, the sun turning into poison
and all of that, saws working through my heart,
but I grew, I grew,
and God was there like an island I had not rowed to,
still ignorant of Him, my arms and my legs worked,
and I grew, I grew,
I wore rubies and bought tomatoes
and now, in my middle age,
about nineteen in the head I'd say,
I am rowing, I am rowing
though the oarlocks stick and are rusty
and the sea blinks and rolls

like a worried eyeball,
but I am rowing, I am rowing,
though the wind pushes me back
and I know that that island will not be perfect,
it will have the flaws of life,
the absurdities of the dinner table,
but there will be a door
and I will open it
and I will get rid of the rat inside of me,
the gnawing pestilential rat.
God will take it with his two hands
and embrace it.

As the African says:
This is my tale which I have told,
if it be sweet, if it be not sweet,
take somewhere else and let some return to me.
This story ends with me still rowing.

Anne Sexton

THE CHILDREN

The children are all crying in their pens
and the surf carries their cries away.
They are old men who have seen too much,
their mouths are full of dirty clothes,
the Tongues poverty, tears like pus.
The surf pushed their cries back.
Listen.
They are bewitched.
They are writing down their life
on the wings of an elf
who then dissolves.
They are writing down their life
on a century fallen to ruin.
They are writing down their life
on the bomb of an alien God.
I am too.

We must get help.
The children are dying in their pens.
Their bodies are crumbling.
Their tongues are twisted backwards.
There is a certain ritual to it.
There is a dance they do in their pens.
Their mouths are immense.
They are swallowing monster hearts.
So is my mouth.

Listen.
We must all stop dying in the little ways,
in the craters of hate,
in the potholes of indifference—
a murder in the temple.
The place I live in
is a kind of maze
and I keep seeking
the exit or the home.
Yet if I could listen
to the bulldog courage of those children
and turn inward into the plague of my soul
with more eyes than the stars
I could melt the darkness—
as suddenly as that time
when an awful headache goes away
or someone puts out the fire—
and stop the darkness and its amputations
and find the real McCoy
in the private holiness
of my hands.

Richard Eberhart

CUTTING BACK

To cut the act of vegetation back from the summer house
Is an act of life to control the sprawl of nature.
One would get a better view of things farther off.
It depends upon the energy of the intellect.

If not cut back the sprawling nature of nature
Will occlude the view. It will drive us inward
Where nature is a memory of an outer adventure.
We will then have to have our own reality.

I cut back the small trees and let in the light.
I gave the older, tall exemplars more chance to breathe.
I consider this a commentary of existence,
It gives a closer look into a deeper mystery.

The deeper mystery is that of seeing clearer.
But if we have cut back nature to our own order
What is it that we see in the haze over the horizon?
It is ourselves we see, always ourselves that we see.

HALF WAY MEASURE

Friend, we meet on the street, you with the loss of one eye.
This word I write is the weapon of defense I have
Against destructive time. Poems aspire to super sight.
I touch your shoulder, feel thoughtful, do not know what to say.

You have had one eye taken away, science took it,
Prolonging your life. You speak with cheer in faith.
To malignant tumor you have a benign Christian faith.
I leave you like a savage in a wilderness.

Bartolo Cattafi

CLOTH

A color fades
and goes
another comes
the old cómes back
re-dyed
the flowings and returns
comings and goings
the shuttle of weft
of warp
the cloth that wraps you round
then it rains
it shrinks on you.

LIKE A BLADE

Like a blade of cold clarity
you enter the pages of a book
thick with deeds and days
you order events and words
implement that stops the flight the fever
the gallop the dust-cloud
eyes restless you lead back to yourself
still river inflexible mirror.

Translators MICHAEL IMPEY
AND BRIAN SWANN

Nina Cassian

QUARREL WITH CHAOS

My visitors are:
a man cut off at the waist,
a continuous lady
and their slab-like daughter,
a professor who teaches cheese,
a murderer with a cold, a swarm
of unmarried ants,
a mustached tree,
a young stork,
a child with a cardboard leg
and three ignorant of the laws of motion.

Last of all, the evening dog
appears
who barks loudly at them
and sees them off the premises.

KNOWLEDGE

I've stitched my dress with continents,
bound the equator round my waist.
I waltz to a steady rhythm, bending slightly.

I can't stop my arms
plunging into galaxies,
gloved to elbows in adhesive gold;
I carry on my arms a star's vaccine.

With such greedy sight
my eyelids flutter in the breeze
like a strange enthusiastic plant.

No one fears me
except Error,
who is everywhere.

Philippe Denis

Translator: Mark Irwin

Moored to your blood,
the hollow
left by your sleep,
now breathes
for you—

(wind between the last stars
flows

rooster
croaks
sputter in the paddock—

before roads begin
to swell
—like the veins
of your wrists.

Philippe Denis

To live as to breathe,
to advance
towards one's life—

what rejoins us
issues from the day
like the wind,

blinds
our breathing.

Alfredo de Palchi

Ashamed of myself? of this three-
dimensional life that shuttles me from chair
to wheel & return   completing its absurdity
day after day   each shorter
as I curse it & darker
in the slow work of demolition
                              —beyond all this
there's no shaft of light but a groove
that wandering men cannot break:
it's my luck to resist these vague
faces
      —there's no way out

I'm a chain of insidious origins
orders   mechanisms   fantasies
already charged with extinction
gruel of mud, tedious hush
laid on the coals of the still living—
I / witness of each morning's crescendo /
am nothing at evening but the simple
shock of two extremes

Alfredo de Palchi

Existence
            —solitary habit—
but who, who is alive . . .
it's like this pinched creature of a
tree, butted into city dust,
existing
            not living

Ivan V. Lalić

tr. CHARLES SIMIC

VOICES OF THE DEAD

I

Voices of the dead. They are not dead. Who hears
The dead? Rain on the bronze gates of the morning.
The freshness of wild morning guarding doves
In the cobwebs of roses. I was that emptiness between them.

I was on a bank of a river lost for days, hours.
It doesn't matter. In time beyond this time.
And the river is wide. River from the blood of ancestors.
How to swim up its stream? Who has reached its mouth?

O dead ones, by this river I found a roofless house.
House left in a hurry. And a thin thread of smoke
Woven into mist that grows thicker and thicker.

House uncompleted. Then Winter began.
A window frightened by the strength of a storm woke me up.
Voices of the dead. They are not dead. Who hears them?

II

In the night distant fire blazes. Then another.
Butterflies of flame settle the rim of the night.
Third fire. Soon, a clear line of fire
Completed. Ring of sleep. Nobody gets through.

Chestnuts shake off their leaves in fear.
Men say: Autumn. Melisa, it is a camp
Of a great dead army, settled on a distant hill.
Alone, breathless and troubled, I listen for the bugle.

Instead of ringing brass, I hear early snows
Falling in empty woods. The fires remain.
When the earth evens a wrinkle on her forehead

350

Entire towns collapse. The fires remain.
Ring around sleep. Has anyone heard the bugle?
Bugle beyond silence and the silence stronger.

III

Voices of the dead remain. Distant voices. Who hears
The dead? Perhaps, the color of old gold
And the foam of dark sea. Perhaps, like a storm
Lacking space. Perhaps, hushed after an illness.

Unknown, it doesn't matter. Perhaps, soiled by war,
Dust. Or with a quiet noise like a sea-shell
Placed against the ear in a burning summer-afternoon.
It doesn't matter. Voices beyond this game. Kindred words.

The buzzing of the spindle in the fairy lullaby
From a pure age. Dream disguised into an event.
Voices of the dead. Still they are not dead.

I lie in the night. Awake. Quiet. They are quieter.
I fall asleep and dream of drums. Ancient drums.
Great dark drums broken and left in the rain.

Jabra Ibrahim Jabra

FROM POETRY SEQUENCE

2

Masks collapsed, and
over splinters of rock
lips and breasts suddenly
were ripe to be plucked
as if a fugitive
from blaze had found
naked, a runaway woman
in a cave of blue rocks
where waves whisper
of the beautiful body
exposed out of boredom.

My whims are carved in stone—
inside caves, and in houses
white under the sun
of July and August.
Scattered over the slopes,
a handful of my years
and my voice crying
when ghosts roam about

to plant their lips
in my flesh: *rejoice!*
we shall cure the world
of its pestilence

3

Let others have
an arid hand.
The road I have taken
to reach my goal
high-headed, like an arrow
from a dexterous bow,—
is luminous with light.
Not your lips
nor some other's hiding

in the dimness
of a garden, are
my goal. My hand
is like the sower's
in September
my land expansive to no end
even though masked snipers
crouch among branches
hiding behind
every stone

Translator TALAT SAIT HALMAN

Edip Cansever

EYES

It seems nothing can provoke
Our inner silence
No sound no word nothing
The eyes bring out the eyes!

Nothing else but this unites us
A leaf touching another leaf
So close and so docile
The hands bring out the hands!

In our age love is an opposition
Let us unite to cast two single shadows. . .

Translator: Robin Fulton

Werner Aspenström

THE CAVE

No, not back to the countryside,
to the sleepy animals.
Not in the city either,
among the photographers reproducing each other.
To build himself a new habitat
(where)
of a new materia!
(which)
an igloo of air?
The thought of the impossible takes root in him,
hollows him out,
till he himself is a cave,
a man without images, without faith.

Translator CARL HERMEY

Tahar Ben Jelloun

I write to erase my face. I write to state the difference. That difference which joins me to those who are not me, that throng which obsesses and betrays me. I write not *for* but *in* and *with* them. I throw myself into the cortege of their alienation. I assault the screen of their solitude. A sharpened word. The void and a fragment of life gathered bit by bit.

I am first united to those who read me, perhaps, or those who will read me, by that which separates me from them. Through words and language I achieve distinction and identity. I communicate by exploiting this difference to the limits of perception. I perceive it and live it as a laceration progresses in a body or mind, as the local and general anesthesia of a crowd is administered every day.

I yield to the trembling ambiguity of words, naked in their limits, and I confront whatever remains. Very little. Only words remain, bound and consummated.

I am what I lack. This absence determines my direction, my itinerary, my objective. I create what is not in me. I proclaim. Words. I remove the veil. Words. In a text, a poem, I provide something of my difference, and I cut a slice of my inadequacy to complete—in a purely illusory way—the need of another.

And I state the limits.

My weakness disappears. I recover it sometimes in a glance, a gesture of a man or woman who does not know me, and cannot do otherwise, for recognition is not possible in the realm of writing. Yet the poem bursts forth and overflows in these same men and women. I define this absence and await implicit recognition to know myself I must record difference even if it forces me into the form of writing.

I frame gestures in furious memory, and I begin to strip away. I open the page of my weaknesses, my inadequacies, and my distance.

I uncover shame.

tr. Kimon Friar

Yánnis Rítsos

DANGER OUTSTRIPPED

Every so often a star or a voice
falls to such great depth that he holds himself
by the balcony railing or by a hand
(if a hand can be found) for fear of sinking into himself.

His most trusted hand is his other hand,
but thus his hands enclose him within a circle.
He cannot endure this. Then he stretches out his hands
as though to embrace someone, or in a balancing position.

And thus, like a tightrope walker, looking straight before him,
he holds himself upright above his own depth.

tr. John Constantine Stathatos

Yánnis Rítsos

THE COLOURED BEADS

The white horse closed up in the paddock; the stones around
seem lit up by its whiteness. A string of coloured beads
winds round its narrow forehead. Of course, the horse
would never think of beads as warding off the evil eye. The others
concern themselves over the saddle, not the whiteness.
And maybe in turn it accepts this spangled mark of bondage,
not to frighten the children bringing in its hay at dusk.
Later, the children stood for a while by its side
watching the beads which glimmered as it fed. But in that case,
whose and for whom after all the submission?

Translator TAMAR KANDO

MEMENTO PUTREFIERI

JACQUES HAMELINK

For the first time in at least half a year Evarist thought about the Colossus, and while he thought about her, shuffling aimlessly but rapidly along, he got the urge to visit the corpse garden where, in good time, they had planted her in the ground with noses pinched tight, when the white fruit juice already ran along all the openings and she swelled up in an unprecedented, no longer human offence, flouting all order and propriety, a silent explosion-like ripening into an infernal mirth.

Without choosing any particular route, guided by an uncanny and completely new sense of direction, he cheerfully shambled along the streets whose pavement was enameled, baked by sunlight, swinging his arms and muttering.

Around him the day was under way in a continuing detonation. Clouds of dust quivered in the sun. Blood-red geraniums clashed in front of the windows of the dwellings, geraniums that had lost the chance for development they had pursued since prehistoric times, that were doomed to dwarfing. Heaps of the most disparate objects lay flung together in shop windows and department stores, nonetheless still attempting to suggest a certain orderliness. Hordes of traffic lights let Evarist pass unhindered, continually leaping from red to bottle-green in the nick of time. Cars transformed into gleaming many-colored marbles rattled and clattered through all the grooves of the stone city, never touching, for they were held on a visible string from the control tower room of a small boy. Stuck fast to their saddles, screaming heatedly, cyclists in flight flogged their mounts with their feet and lay their flapping sail-ears. The sputtering of scooters made all the glassware jingle fiercely. Policemen, scarecrows, stood at all the important intersections easing the enormous muddle and helping it start again with wooden gestures.

All over the sidewalks dogs were busy sniffing each other; in passing, pedestrians separated them, with snarls and kicks, before they could come together. The clanking of the bunches of keys and coins which filled the pockets of the knights of respectability was deafening. The whole city stank of gas, suntan oil, garbage, baby soap and detergents. The men all swathed in dull black or mouse grey costumes which contrasted sickly with the egg yellow light in which they were shown.

Nevertheless the women, Evarist ascertained, possessed a more developed, less sepulchral taste. They wore transparent garments, reminiscent of flower petals, which contained all the colors of the rainbow and left large portions of their necks, breasts, backs and thighs uncovered in a refreshing manner. Embraced by a sort of flower-like rapture they paraded down the streets quasi-attentively looking in windows and moving their conversing lips, but actually only paying attention to themselves, to the surfaces of the shop windows which they used exclusively as mirrors, to their unceasing sampling of their inhaled fragrance, to their red lips softly closing over each other, to the form and movement of their awning eyelids, soft visors behind which they only seemingly attended to their surroundings, almost constantly keeping their eyes turned into the infra-red depths of their own unthinking and therefore mysterious beings.

A chaste enraptured lover, Evarist almost drifted past them, refreshing himself in the lavender fragrances, in the dozens of perfumes with which they had besprayed and besprinkled the secret hollows of their bodies, almost fanatically in love with them all, sensing them all to be sisters, addressing them in his mind with merry roguish speeches and declarations of devotion, completely disinterested and without intentions clouded by, for example, egotism.

He realized that the women lived closer to the truth and in narrower contact with it than the men of the city. Not one of them, as he observed, would have stopped repeatedly and resentfully thrown a stone at a boxer overcome by the mating urge and chased the animal to flight. The women themselves were mild-tempered animals adorned with flowers who had nothing evil in mind, concealed no hidden designs. The only danger they were vulnerable to and which threatened them was their susceptibility to being influenced, a susceptibility which, as he noted more than once during his intractable walk, the gloomily clad men used. By nature the women were yielding, the men demanding, full of power lust.

From the way he saw a young half-naked woman, made up as a flower fairy, become intoxicated and dissolve into a mist of flower-sweet willessness under the harsh chopping chatter of an emaciated umbrellaed hypocrite, he realized what a risk the women ran despite their natural lead.

He who wants to found a kingdom must begin by winning the women over to his ideas, the saying went. The whole world stood open to him who had the women in the palm of his hand, doors swung open which had previously been hermetically locked.

I must bear this in mind, thought Evarist. Perhaps some day he would need the women's help in attaining a goal whose general outlines weren't even clear to him yet.

On the edge of the city, where the dust was thinner and the sunlight even stronger, he stood still before the mighty, rust-gnawed railing of a stone-built trellis straddled by a metal banner. Its curling letters proclaimed the motto

MEMENTO PUTREFIERI

Behind it lay the corpse garden, swathed in honey and balsam fragrances, where groups of laborers were busy raising colossal sunken flagstones and laying them again. To Evarist's delight there weren't any other strollers to be seen. Aside from the noises, the calm laughter of the workers and the misfiring of their instruments on the stones, it was quiet, and there was even a light breeze blowing through the richly leaved oiled trees which were so plentiful. Butterflies skipped from flower to flower, bees buzzed and burrowed in their appetizing obliging calyxes.

Evarist passed a gilt sundial and noticed that some twenty yards away a group of workmen were resting for a moment from their labors, which appeared to be quite hard, on a deep hole. They had stuck their spades in the ground and, with a pitcher in their hands and a rolled cigarette in the corners of their mouths, they sat quietly and neutrally regarding him. He walked towards them and, at a warning shout from one of the men, abruptly came to a halt.

"Hey there!" called the man, a young fellow with blond sideburns and sky-blue eyes, "get the hell outa here, you!"

Suddenly Evarist saw that both he and some of the other men had rubber gloves on that reached to their elbows and wore hip boots full of yellow earth and blackish sediment.

"The public actually ain't allowed in here," another, older man, apparently the foreman, called out obligingly enough, "we're diggin' somethin' up. Rules say we oughta do it with a strong fence round the whole thing. But we're in a rush. It happens sometimes and then we gotta hurry up, with no messin' around."

"Hurry, in what way?" said Evarist, trying to peer into the hole. The men began to laugh in a circumspect way and beamingly winked at each other. One of them held his nose between his thumb and index finger and bared his wide white teeth.

"Yeah, well look," said the foreman, standing up and walking over to Evarist, "you people ain't got the haziest notion. You bring your corpse to the garden or you go there yourself and so far as you're concerned that's that. But not for us. Sometimes that's only the beginning for us. You get all sortsa tomfoolery with the corpses once they're under the ground. Sometimes they'll simply be damned if they'll lie still. They don't set no store by the resurrection of their flesh, so to speak. Course we prefer it when they lie still. Respectable corpses do, too. But fortunately there's unrespectable rascals too, otherwise we might as well go into the buildin' business. Go laze about on the roof. Anyhow fewer and fewer folks come to the garden every week."

"And the unrespectable corpses?" said Evarist in some suspense.

"Well, they more or less just go their own way a bit," answered the foreman, "I normally don't talk none about it to visitors. You're an exception and not some young brat who'll joke around about it. 'Cause it's nothin' to laugh at, though you'll understand it happens to us occasionally. After all, it's our profession and we have fun with it, we laugh ourselves stupid often enough about all the unrespectable stinkers. They play the silliest tricks. Especially lately, now it's gettin' on to summer, more than one of 'ems had a gas bag. These guys've nearly always croaked from some nasty sinful disease or other. They simply rise up out of the pit like dough. Sometimes there's no stoppin' it. Weighing 'em down with stone only works once. And the family don't always like the idea. Tombstones cost big money nowadays. That's well known, they know it. They flatly refuse to dig into their pockets for their corpse. And they're right, what's the use of a stinker like that anyway except as dung for the garden? Whatta they care? Besides, sometimes there ain't even time to let the family know. One day you tuck the bastard nicely in, the next he's already kicked himself free and in the evening you gotta pick the worms outa your hair. In a case like that there's only one thing to do and that's haul the crap out and dig a deeper hole. That's what we're doin' now, for example. If you wanna. I guess you can have a peek. Here."

He turned around and walked over to a metal vehicle a few yards away from the hole which resembled a dumping cart.

"I'd advise you to hold your nose or hold your handkerchief in front of it," said the foreman, "if you ain't used to it you'll think you're gonna be knocked out flat by the stink. And it's poisonous too, for that matter. If you got a cut somewhere and some of that junk gets on it, you're a goner if you don't run straight to a doctor."

White slips of skeleton parts or roots stuck out here and there from the dung or mud-like substance lying in the overflowing dumping cart. It all seemed to have been ladled out of a cesspool stagnating in its frothy pulp. Tiny crystal-clear gas bells floated all over the surface of the jelly, linking up to form coils and continually bubbling to the surface like small burps.

"A well-known criminal lawyer," declared the foreman, "we hadn't even got him under before he began to disputate."

He spoke the last words loudly, half turning towards his fellow workers who immediately burst out laughing.

"The old shrews fly off the handle too," continued the foreman, while Evarist's eyes probed the pit which was at least three yards deep, "they've usually got some rotten disease or other, in their stomachs if possible. While they were alive the whole mess there was already festering and molding from tumors. When one like that comes along we say to each other, he could become a stinker, there's somethin' fishy about this paunch. And that's how it always turns out."

The young man with the sideburns joined them. He looked at Evarist with a glance of half-recognition and then hesitantly said:

"Haven't I seen you before here, some time ago, a half year ago or so?"

"That's right, I buried my wife then," said Evarist.

He had taken out his handkerchief and smothered his rising fit of laughter in it.

"You don't come here too often otherwise," said the young man somewhat scornfully, "seems to me this is the first time since the burial."

"Yes, I had a lot to do, business and such," said Evarist, who had himself entirely in hand now and skillfully squelched the quiet gasps that welled up in his breast.

"That's how it goes," said the foreman agreeably, "when you grow older and ain't so steady on your legs no more. And what difference does it make. You come here anyhow eventually I say, one way

361

or another. In the end you get afraid of the pit and you think, well, why not have a look now, how do they work that exactly. Can't do no harm. It does more for the peace of the soul than rushin' through little prayers and scheming with the pastor and his cronies."

"That wife of yours," said the young man, "she was really something. I remember her perfectly. The way she carried on!"

"The stuff was already running out when she'd just died," said Evarist, "she swelled up idiotically. They had to enlarge the coffin right away."

He spoke with a certain sensuality which seemed to please the two workers.

"I remember her perfectly," said the young man again, "do you, Magus? You remember, don't you? The suds were bursting between the planks before she even went under. What a woman, brrr!"

"That wasn't a woman, that was an invalid colossus," said Evarist slowly, "she could hardly walk while she was alive. She sat behind the window peering at the street all day long. She hated flowers like the plague. She almost never spoke. Sometimes she moved her hands a little. That was all."

Perhaps aroused by his confabulators, he found he had to force himself to hold back the wild curses and allegations which wanted to spurt from his lips.

"Tuttuttut," said the foreman, "you shouldn't talk about a stiff like that if you ain't a corpse gardener. That ain't good style."

"Still seems to me he's dead right," said the young man, confusedly eyeing Evarist with a sort of awe and horror.

"But you still remember how she shoved the whole damn mess to the top. We spent at least a day and a night on it and when she finally lay in a new bed it still wasn't over."

"Now you mention it, yeah," said the foreman, "I do recollect it now. That was a filthy skunk. Worst stinker we've had here in years. A real swamp of a hag. So. And you're her widower?"

He looked Evarist over from top to toe, appraisingly, but didn't seem to find a single encouraging sign of the past year or so on him.

"Oh well," he said good-naturedly, "they got their good sides too. All the mess they make is good for the garden, like I already said. Just look—the trees you see here are the highest and healthiest in the whole neighborhood. That's the work of the stinkers. An ordinary corpse keeps the grass fit, but a stinker has more up his shirtsleeves, I always say. He can keep up an entire forest all by himself. I'm dead set against cremation, if only because of the stinkers. Stick a stinker in a bare patch of ground and within a year you got flowers and bushes by the barrel. Their sap is the best fertilizer there is. Just look around—ever seen such trees? That's the work of the unrespectable corpses from beginning to end, the dung-whores, so to speak, you can take it from me."

He glanced at the reclining workers and in an apologetic tone said to Evarist:

"We gotta get to work again, the break's over, I won't keep you no more. Of course you want to go to your wife. See you, sooner or later."

He winked at the laughing men as they stood up, threw their butts in the pit and picked up their tools.

"It's that way, if I'm not mistaken," the young man called after Evarist, making a vague gesture that took in half the garden.

Thanking them for their information with a wave, Evarist withdrew, leisurely inspecting the tree trunks which were indeed abnormally massive and had root talons sticking out here and there high above the ground, the luscious tall grass and the hard, strong shrub bushes which flourished on all sides.

He found the mound of earth the Colossus' remains lay under without much difficulty and stretched out with a feeling of contentment on the high layer of sod which had covered the mound, under a gigantic and yet seemingly very young elm, in the rustling foliage. From its depths a bird repeatedly struck his clear tuning fork.

IN THE BEGINNING

HUMBERTO COSTANTINI

tr. Norman Thomas di Giovanni

This is the story of a great slaughter. When the hunters of horses came out of the east in whooping bands, when the handsome men arrived from over the plains and the mountains, bringing death and annihilation to the last of the earth's ancient men.

This is the story of a great slaughter. Of how that great bloodshed spread its black wing over the whole of Europe, and awakened with its death cry even the least cleft of the rock.

Of how the silent beings who squatted about their fires, the shambling Neanderthal men, woke up one morning and their hearts were filled with wonder before the blossoms of the wild apple. Because spring, at that moment, had taken possession of the land.

A light mist slowly stretching itself rose from the ends of the earth, and vast herds of bearded ponies grazed in peace on the neighboring plain. And the horse had no fear of the stooped head of the cave dwellers.

This is the story of a great slaughter. When the bearded ponies suddenly snuffed the air and smelled fear. And this fear, twitching through their muscles, started them running in terror toward the west.

And the men asked themselves to what such frenzied galloping was owed, such a shaking and tossing of manes. For they had not yet heard the war cry of the hunters from the east.

But the cry materialized. On the crown of a hill, an immense circle of dancers and a great display of colors and feathers. And also of spears and arrows. And again the hearts of the hairy Neanderthal men were filled with wonder, as when they beheld the wild apple tree in flower.

And the singing and the feathers and the rhythmic movements of the dancers drew them with an irresistible force. In wary groups they moved closer and closer, and they felt ashamed of their own thickset hairy bodies. Wanting to approach the beautiful newcomers to make them gifts of mushrooms and fleshy roots.

But the dancers ignored their dark beseeching gaze. The newcomers went on in their play until the sun stood directly overhead in the sky.

This is the story of a great slaughter. When the graceful Cro-Magnons ended their singing and the rhythmic swaying of their bodies painted in three colors and loosed themselves upon the hairy onlookers.

And the spear whistled in the air. And the ax struck out at the squat heads. And death came suddenly, unbidden, decked in feathers, howling, and daubed as for an orgy.

And only those who fled to the mountain saved their lives. For the rest remained behind, their blood soaked up by the earth that the tide of spring had kissed.

And this was the beginning of the great slaughter. One after another came the conquering hordes, all skilled warriors and agile dancers. And all of them hunters of the wild horse and the reindeer. And hunters also, all of them, of the stolid inhabitants of cliff and rock.

And the cave dwellers could not grasp how those beautiful heads harbored so much hate. Those graceful bodies such fierceness.

And that great slaughter lasted many hundreds of years. For the Neanderthal men lived over a great extent of the land. Their eyes, for century upon century, the only eyes to have lifted, questioning the stars.

And that great slaughter lasted many hundreds of years. And the rock dwellers became skillful in the handling of the new weapons. And in place after place the smoke of rebellion often rose up over the land.

But the Cro-Magnon men were bent upon death and annihilation because the presence of the shambling hairy creatures was loathsome to their hearts.

And because the sheltering caves were coveted by them. More even than the flesh of wild horses or the secret sources of red pigment with which they beautified their dead.

And it came to pass that after many centuries none of the race of ancient dwellers were left on the face of the earth. All of them had perished at the hands of the lordly hunters from the east.

The race of hunters multiplied and increased over the whole extent of Europe. And on the rock walls in the caves their beautiful animal drawings looked down in splendor.

This is the story of the last Neanderthal man. One who lived in the region of the French Dordogne.

This is the story of the last Neanderthal man, and his name was called Grug.

And Grug's age was thirty-six years. Thirty-six were the years of his life when the men from the east became complete masters of the land. And when by blade and by blow they finished off all the old dwellers.

This is the story of the last ancient man on earth. When he abandoned his squatting place and fled to the mountain with the rest of his family group.

And the group was small. Five only were those who followed his steps. All the others had perished. Their blood-tattered corpses strewn over the ground.

And before this, for five years' time, Grug had reigned among his people. His voice was heard on both banks of the river.

Because Grug knew the language of the winds. He knew what dangers lurked in each rustling of the leaves.

And because upon the death of the Old Man, he, the eldest, had led his tribe far from the hunters of the east into the valley of the Garonne, where the land was favorable.

And for five years the tribe had remained there. Little more than a few bright points of light disturbing the night.

The water's gladness flowing between the stones. Lichens, snails, and small reptiles in abundance.

Circles of men and women squatting around fires. Their whelps tumbling in play at the river's edge. An appearance of peace.

Until death suddenly caught up with them in the valley of the Garonne.

The untiring hunters sought the river valley. They raised their song in the region of the last Neanderthal men.

They appeared from the end of the valley. Feathers, arrows, and shouts, spreading fear over the land.

Like fire which in its passage destroys all the trees of the forest. Such was their appetite for death.

The tribe wailed under their shafts. The women growled with grief for their brood struck down by the arrows.

The men scattered. Their clumsy bodies scurrying. Fleet arrows tumbled them in the middle of their flight. The arrows caught them at the mouths of their caves.

Death came to and fro through the valley of the Garonne. It strode the air. It quickened the legs of the rangy hunters of horses.

They killed in the valley and under the rock ledges. They killed alongside the river and in the deep shadow of the caves.

And Grug howled in the midst of his people. By his shouts he attempted to lead the escape. Claiming of the mountain its distant refuge.

But fear turned the men deaf to Grug. Mad scurrying in the valley cut off by death's agile steps.

This is the story of the last ancient man on earth. When he uttered loud cries among his people and he signaled the way to the distant cliffs.

And when five of his family group heeded his call and bound their lives to him. They gathered their fears around the eldest, who was leading them to the mountain.

Two of his women with their whelps. All the others had perished. Their blood-tattered corpses strewn over the ground.

And first it was a creeping of bodies through thickets. The thorns pained in the flesh.

They questioned the rock. In each movement of their bellies they sought its response.

And then a great silence. A concealment of life among the lower life that droned on the mountainside.

And then they called on the night. They gathered it round them for the protection of their bodies.

And with the night they started out on their march. The moon showed their shadows shambling across a clearing among the thickets.

They crept up the slope. They hushed the fear of the whelps.

They wrested shelter from the mountain. A place to hide their weariness. To conceal their bodies from the hunters.

A spot for their thirst beside the soft patter of water flowing between the stones.

And then again they called on silence. Days and nights squatting in a crevice of the mountain.

Days and nights the voice of the slaughter howling in their ears. Expecting death in each rustling of leaves.

Three days and three nights awaiting some sign in the wheeling of birds. Cowering at the faroff rumble of hooves. Heeding the earth's hidden voice.

Until on the fourth day the war cry of the hunters of the east reached their mountain cranny. (The women clutched the whelps and their flesh shook as with cold.)

And they were able to make out the great display of colors. The circle of dancers, a shifting flower down in the valley.

And then the five increased the silence. They sank their heartbeats in the rock. A nameless waiting beside the trickle of water.

Night after night the wind brought the smell of death. A smell that grated the teeth and made the hair of the flesh stand up.

And endlessly the trickle of water questioned the heavens. Slipping silently over a glimmer of mosses.

But then hunger came to keep them company. Torsos daubed with color prowled about. A sudden startling noise over the stones.

This is the story of Grug and of the five who fled with him to the mountain. And they were the only survivors of the old Neanderthal race.

Of how all at once at the beginning of the sixth day Grug shattered the mountain silence.

And how all at once beside the trickle of water a thin line of red appeared. Over the glimmering mosses, the glimmer of blood.

Because at the beginning of the sixth day, Grug raised his slow hairy frame.

And the women wondered at seeing him stand there. And the whelps did not grasp it because he no longer concealed his hulking frame from the hunters.

The stone ax obeyed Grug's bidding. With blind fury it obeyed the command of his hands.

Five well-aimed blows and little more than a few whimpers. Little more than some eyes questioning Grug's wet black eyes.

Little more than a thin line of red beside the trickle of water. A new glimmer of blood over the glimmering mosses.

But the hunters responded to the muffled call of the blows. Packs of rangy Cro-Magnons leaping over the stones.

While a hefty male stood over them, higher up the ledge, observing. A magnificent specimen for their hunter's appetite.

But as they reached him their free and easy bearing was blunted. Standing on the rock a terrible stare awaited them. The bloody ax between his hands.

And all of them saw—because this was what they had always

heard—that the inferior race was not a race of warriors. All these loathsome hairy beings were tame and cowardly.

And then Grug let out his fighting cry. A howl that seemed to come out of the mountain itself.

And a first corpse fell in blood under his hand. And another's neck went down in the path of Grug's demolishing stone.

Like a bison that turns enraged upon its pursuers, so Grug flailed out in the midst of his earthly enemies.

But the clash did not last long. Two more Cro-Magnons fell under the blows of Grug's ax.

(Five were the blows that awakened the mountain cranny. Little more than a thin line of red beside the trickle of water.)

But the clash did not last long. For the hunters came in great numbers to vanquish that enraged Neanderthal specimen.

A bone point in his back. But the stone kept obeying his hand.

A bone point in the hip and the groin. But in each of its blows his hand was still a bearer of death.

An arrow-riddled bison whose last onslaught implants fear and makes the hunters cower in fright.

A bone point piercing his belly. And then the edge of a huge stone bringing him the night.

And the night was a heavy sleep that enclosed him. A memory of faraway bonfires in the valley of the Garonne.

And sweetly the earth called him back.

This is the story of the last Neanderthal man. When he went out to his meeting with death next to a trickle of water.

This is the story of the last of the earth's ancient men. Of those whom the bearded ponies did not fear. Hundreds of centuries asking the only questions of the stars.

This is the story of Grug. How he died at the hands of the tall hunters from the east. The plumed dancers who embellished the walls of the caves.

And who asked new questions of the stars.

Pablo Neruda

Translator BEN BELITT

AMORES : MATILDE

I. *The Lovers of Capri*

The island hoards at its center the spirit of lovers, like a coin
scoured by wind and time's passing, to its integral burnish,
intact and uncouth as an almond, cut into the sapphire's patina;
there the invisible tower of our love trembled up through the smoke's
scintillation, a blank comet steadied its tail in the zodiac, like
    a netful of fish
in the sky: because the eyes of the lovers of Capri were closed, a bolt
    had pinned down the ocean's whistling periphery,
all fear fled away, tracking blood in the wake
of the menace, a sudden harpoon in the side of the seabeast of chaos;
and at last, in ambrosial salt, the figurehead rose from the wave, a
swimmer of nakedness, rapt in its masculine cyclone, and wreathed.

II. *Description of Capri*

The vine in the rock, fissures cut into musk, the walls laced with
    the web of the
climber, the plinths in the stone and the flowers: the whole
island waits like the frets of a zither in the sonorous altitudes,
light moving wire over wire, improvising through daylight and distance
the sound of its voice, the alphabet colors of daylight
from whose fragrant enclaves dawn lifts itself skyward
and flies, dropping dew on a world and opening the eyes of all Europe.

III. *The Ships*

All ends in the sack of the ship, like a marketplace: onions and coal,
alcohol, paraffin, carrots, potatoes, oranges, meatchops and oil:
the ship is an aimless disorder, a shakedown for whatever
tumbles into its hold: the hale and mellifluous, the hand-to-mouth
    gambler, storekeepers,
sometimes they stop to squint back at the custodial water
looking cheezy and blue and opaque with a menace of eyes:
a fear of the motionless bores through to the voyager's fantasy.
They would rather wear out their shoe-leather, whittle down their
    feet and their bones,
keep on the move in infinity's horror till nothing is left of it.

IV. *The Song*

The tower of bread, the device that the archway contrives out of altitude
with melody moving aloft in its avid fecundity,
the intransigent petals of song growing big in the rose
— your presence and absence, the whole weight of your hair,
the pure heats of your body like a pillar of grain in my bed,
the victorious skin that your springtime aligned at my side
while my heart beat below like a pulse in the stone of a wall,
wheaten and gold in the power of its contacts, your sunburst of hips,
and your voice flowing down in cascades of a vehement honey,
your mouth turned in love for the gradual pressure of kisses
— all seems to me now like the knot of the day and the night, cut
    through and showing
the door that unites and divides light and shade, ajar on its hinges,
and beyond it, in the spaces, a glimpse of that distant dominion
man seeks his whole lifetime, hacking away at the stone and the dark
    and the void.

V. *La Casa Chascona**

Boulder and nail, the plank and the tile are here joined: I have built
out of water that writes all things down in its cursive calligraphy
    La Casa Chascona;
I have planted the berry and blood of the thicket to keep watch
on this place till its stairways and walls know you by name, till
the flower crisping its petals, the vine, and the feathering tendrils,
the figleaf like a heraldry raised on the alien life of a clan
blossom like wings in the shadow that darkens your head:
the walls of victorious blue, the abstract onyx of earth —
your eyes and mine — here break on this rock and this timber
in the name of all places and time's fever and the peace we have won,
to preside on a house's successions in your person's transparency.

Your house and mine, your dream in my eyes, your blood on the paths
    of the body asleep
like a pigeon locked into its wings' immobility and its flying momentum;
time gathers your dream and mine in its cup
for a house barely born to the world from the vigil of hands.

---

*Neruda's house and estate in Isla Negra: "chasacona," a word special to Chile,
has the sense of "unkempt" or "dissheveled."

Night brings us at last to the ship we have fashioned together,
the repose of the sweet-smelling wood where a backwash
of wind and birds lost to us, lives again in the leaves,
the roots crop the succulent peace of the humus,
and the moon climbs the water to accomplish my slumber,

the meridional dove of the forests whose dominion
is heaven and air and the somnolent wind which commends
you, a dreamer asleep in the house and the work of your hands —
now so slight in your dream, in the seed of the humus's midnight,
yet multiplied there in the dark like a harvest of wheat.

Beloved and golden, earth gave you wheat's armor,
a color that ovens bake in the clay, with the sweets and enamels,
that singular skin neither black, white, red, green,
but hued like the sand, the bread-crust, the rain,
the sun and the wind and the cut in the virginal timber,
a flesh colored like bells, colored like savory grains,
yet shaped by a ship's keel and enclosed in a wave.

All that delicate light my soul gathered up from the stars,
the gifts of the dew and the night, are transformed into ashes by day:
I drink from a dead planet's cup amidst weeping and tears,
the tears of all men and their griefs: the prisoner's tears and the jailer's,
all hands lifted up to me, showing the sore's
suppuration, woe or entreaty or importunate hope:
no respite from heaven or earth —
one terror feeds on another and is changed in its turn.
There is only your clarity under the sun, day's figurehead,
the flowering branch of your kingdom in darkness,
      in the moon, in a dream,
at whose touch my blood comes alive and sings in the kingdoms of death.
The packed honeycomb, the radiant sweets of the consummate voyage,
my darling: here, after long roadways we have planted a tower
      in Valparaiso:
here at your feet I send down the force of my roots'
restoration: together we open the seaport, unconfined, together
we charge the Sebastiana to summon its navies
and display in the smoke of the port the rose's excitement,
the lanes carved in water for the movement of men and commodities.

Pink and blue, wormeaten and sour, swinging ajar on its filaments,
looped on its threads and its thorns and its matted entanglements,
triumphant and beggarly here, colored like bells or like honey,
vermillion and yellow and purple, violet and silver,
joyless or joyful, sealed or slashed open, like a melon,
here is the port and the doorway to Chile, the bright cloak of Valparaiso,
the sonorous stupor of rain on a saddle of hills like a sufferer's
burden, sun vying with shade in the loveliest eyes in the world.

For you, all the furors and joys of a seaport that grapples
the breakers' successions, drenched in the freeze of
        mid-ocean, acquainted
with peril: comely, that vessel's sobriety; comely, the months of the
        vesperal light of
antarctica, the ship roofed with amaranth, the hand's strength in our
        sails and our houses
and lives, each arrayed in the cloths of its status, pennants displayed,
intact in the pull of the vortices, earthquakes that
        open and shut their infernos,
hand clasping hand in the harbors; walls, people, and artifacts
joined in one body, atremble in muscle and bone, on a rattletrap planet.

Pablo Neruda

tr. BEN BELITT

I KNOW NOTHING AT ALL

In the perimeter and exactitude
of the inexact sciences, there you have me, my friends,
not knowing how to explain all those vocables
that move toward the sky, little by little,
to robuster existences.

We get nothing
by knocking the ostrich's head
and making our hole in the ground.
"Everyone knows that there's nothing to know."
"Don't rattle my brains with geometry."

This much is sure: an abstract uncertainty
comes and goes with each chaos, to turn
into order again;
and oddly enough, all
starts with a word,
new words that sit themselves down
at the table, alone, uninvited,
detestable words we toss off,
that rummage our clothes-closets,
get into our beds and our loves,
and stay on for good: till
the beginning begins once again with a word.

José Gorostiza

tr. LAURA VILLASEÑOR

FROM THE THWARTED POEM

Prelude

That word which never turns up
in your chanted language of questions,
the fainting one
that freezes in the air of your voice,
yes, like a breath of flutes
condensed against an atmosphere of glass
—look at it, touch it!
look at it now!—
in this bled mist of magnolias,
in this tiny flowering of vapor which
—the eye dying, darkened by light,
and the soft rustle of wings
anchored to sinister bolts—
an angel of sleep guards on the window.

What crystal walls, love, what walls!
to hold what silences of water?

That word, yes, the word
that curdles in the throat
like a cry of amber
—look at it, touch it!
look at it now!

Look how, night by night, decanted
through the filter of a harsh silence,
such long hushing left it naked,

harmful and unequivocal
—like the death in the heart of a clock,
like the clarity in a number—
to engender, inaudible,
this language of ours,
that opens at the sleepless touch
in sand, in the bird, in the cloud,
when, black with oracles,
the panorama of prophecy thunders.

What, if not that word,
could forge this prodigious universe
born like a hero in your mouth?
Look at it, touch it,
look at it now,
kindled in an echo of white lilies!
Does not here its anguish take on the innocence
of an empty rhetoric of vines?
Here, among lichens of the jeweler's art
that issue from tiniest channels,
did it not cast its white hoarfrost butterflies
to thrum the air?

Isn't it here, rather than in that faith
spending it into the clarity of destiny,
that a palm tree—escaped from
the stubborn dart of stature—
soars madly to explode
in its fiction of sky,
not a master in fireworks,
but in their sheer delights?

That word, yes, that word,
the fainting one
that smothers in the smoke of a shadow,
the one that turns warily—like a puff of wind—
on hinges of secret slime,
the one on which the voice's breeze splinters,
winded,
as if it rebounded
on an exquisite silver ulcer,

the one that bathes its acid vowels
in the foam of sacrificed doves,
the one that freezes into fever
when, bemused, it does not char
in the abrupt inclemency of a tear
—look at it, touch it!
look at it now!—
look at it, all word-bare,
voiceless, echoless, languageless,
exact,
look how it traces
amours of water on crystal walls!

tr. DORA M. PETTINELLA

Giuseppe Ungaretti

SILENCE

I know a city
that fills with sun every day
all things rapt in that moment

One night I went away

The cicadas' shrill drone lingered
in my heart

From the white
painted boat
I saw
my city disappear
leaving
for a moment
an embrace of lamps suspended
in murky air.

Giuseppe Ungaretti

THE SEASONS

1

O gay light colorings
Rising in consuming calm
Softening
The eager brilliance of a gentle
Carved star.
O newly budded breasts,
Already sighing
Full and trembling to furtive glances,
Often I
have spied on you.

Flowering rainbows
Over your winged road
Scanned the mystic dialogue.

Wind is transient
Deluded adolescence.

2

Now you are tamed and disturbed.

This exhausting summer hour
Is already dark and deep.

Already toward a luminous high
burial, we leap.

From the nocturnal meridian,
Alone now, weakly wavering,
Remembrances invoke:

I shall not plan your sorrows,
But on the high moonlit ditch
The shadow will waken.

And in declining dawn
The supernal violence
with its passion will crown
In calmness, reminiscent and tender,
The gentle rustling foliage
And in freshness gild
The tormented earth.

3

Then an ultimate blush
Crossed the brow of day.

A chorus faraway
Was heard.

In garrulous water
I saw reflections of a flock of doves
Blending to starry grayness.

That was the wildest hour.

4

Now even the dream is silent.

Naked is the ancient oak,
Though forever rooted to its boulder.

Vicente Huidobro

tr. RICHARD LEBOVITZ

ALTAZOR or

JOURNEY BY PARACHUTE

(fragments)

I

Altazor you will die. Your voice will evaporate and you'll be invisible
The Earth will continue whirling along its precise orbit
Afraid of slipping like the tight-rope walker upon the wire
Which binds glances of terror
Eye maddened you seek in vain
There is no way out and the wind displaces the planets
You think it doesn't matter to fall forever if one manages to escape
Don't you see you're falling already
Free your head of prejudice and morals
And if wishing to rise up you grasp nothing
Let yourself fall without stopping your fall without fear into the
                                        shadow's depth
Without fear into the enigma of yourself
Perhaps you will find a light without darkness
Lost in the fissures of the precipices

Fall
        Fall forever
Fall into the depth of infinity
Fall into the depth of time
Fall into the depth of yourself
Fall into the deepest depth you are able to fall
Fall without dizziness
Through all voids and all ages
Through all souls all longings and all ruins
Fall and kindle the stars and seas as you pass
Kindle the eyes that watch you and hearts that await you
Kindle the wind with your voice
The wind that gets entwined in your voice
And the night that is cold in its cavern of bones

380

Fall into childhood
Fall into old age
Fall into tears
Fall into laughter
Fall into music above the universe
Fall from your head into your feet
Fall from your feet into your head
Fall from the sea into the fountain
Fall into the ultimate abyss of silence
Like the ship that sinks extinguishing its lights

All has come to an end
The cannibal sea strikes the door of the merciless rocks
The dogs bark at the fading hours
And the sky listens to the footfall of the receding stars

II

I am here before you
In the name of an idiotic law proclaimed
For the preservation of the species
Foul law
Vile law ingrained in the ingenuous sexes
For this basic law pitfall of the ignorant
Man is torn apart
And broken into mortal howls through all the pores
        of his earth.
I am here among you
My anxieties fall from me into the void
My shrieks fall from me into nothingness
My damnations fall from me into chaos
Dog of the infinite trotting among dead stars
Dog licking stars and memories of stars
Dog licking tombs
I want eternity as a dove in my hands.

Everything must recede into death hide in death
I you he we you they
Yesterday today tomorrow

Feed in the jaws of insatiable oblivion
Feed for the eternal rumination of tireless chaos
Justice, what have you done to me Vicente Huidobro?
The grief falls from my tongue and my faded wings
Fall and my dead fingers one by one
What have you done to my voice laden with birds in the evening
The voice that's been paining me like blood
Give me infinity as a flower for my hands

IV

    I am every man
Man wounded by nobody knows what
By a stray arrow from chaos
Measureless human clay
Indeed measureless and I proclaim it fearlessly
Measureless because I am neither bourgeois nor tired breed
Perhaps I am a barbarian
Barbarian free of routines and marked highways
I do not accept your seats of comfortable safety
I am the rebellious angel who fell one morning
Into your plantations of precepts
Poet
Anti-poet
Intellectual
Anti-intellectual
Metaphysical animal laden with anguish
Spontaneous forthright animal bleeding its problems
Solitary like a paradox
Deadly paradox
Flower of contradictions dancing a fox-trot

Upon the sepulchre of God
Upon good and evil
I am a breast that cries out and brain that bleeds
I am an earthquake
The seismographs signal my footsteps through the world

The wheels of the earth creak
and I am riding horseback into my death
I go fixed to my death like a bird to the sky
Like an arrow in the growing tree
Like the name on the letter I send
I go fixed to my death
I go through life fixed to my death
Supported upon the walking-stick of my bones

V

The sun rises in my right eye and sets in my left
In my childhood a childhood fervid as an alcohol
I sat in the roads of the night
Listening to the eloquence of the stars
And the oration of the tree
Now indifference snows in the afternoon of my soul
May the stars burst open into tiny fragments
May the moon split into a thousand mirrors
May the tree return to the nest of its seed
I alone wish to know why
Why
Why
I am rage and I scratch infinity with my claws
I howl and moan with miserable oceanic cries
The echo of my voice makes chaos rumble

I am measureless, cosmic
The stones plants mountains
Greet me The bees rats
Lions eagles
Stars twilights dawns
Rivers and forests ask me
Hello, how are you?
And while the stars and waves may have something to tell
It will be through my mouth that they speak to men
Fetch me an hour to live
Fetch me a love hooked by the ear
And throw it before my eyes to die

May I fall through the world at full speed
May I run through the universe at the speed of light
May I sink or rise up
Hurled without pity among planets and catastrophes
My Lord if you exist it's to me you owe your existence

Kill horrible doubt
And frightful lucidity
Man with eyes open in the night
To the end of time
Repulsive enigma of contagious instincts
Like the bells of exaltation
Bird-catcher of dead lights which move upon ghostly feet
With the indulgent feet of the brook
That the clouds carry off to another country

On the tapestry of the sky is played our destiny
There where the hours die
The ponderous procession of hours striking the world
There is played our soul
And the destiny that escapes every morning
Above the clouds with tearful eyes
The wound of ultimate beliefs bleeds
When the disconsolate rifle of human refuge
Takes down the birds from the sky
Look at yourself there fraternal animal naked of name
Near the watering place of your own limits
Below the kind dawn
That mends the fabric of the tides

Watch in the distance the chain of men approaching
Coming out the factory of similar longings
Eaten away by the same eternity
By the same hurricane of vagabond fascinations
Each one brings his shapeless speech
And timid feet to his own star
The machines advance in the night of the deadly diamond
The desert advances with its lifeless waves
The mountains pass the camels pass
Like the history of the ancient wars
There goes the chain of men among illusory fires
Toward the sepulchral eyelid

Alain Bosquet

EARTH WRITES THE EARTH
(Poems for a painter)

tr. WALLACE FOWLIE

I

Earth writes the earth.
The earth sings,
and it is for the moon,
and it is for the wind who does not know its course.
The earth is a hand
creating the earth.
The earth is a voice
speaking of the flower, the pebble, the furrow.
Earth writes man
and sings of the weight of time
and weeps over the forgotten season.
Earth is memory's memorial.

II

Under the stars the grain rises.
Under the grain the stars sleep.
Fruit and sun must be joined.
Night must be given to day
and day to night.
Why don't branches
have their roots
in sulking clouds?
To write of mystery
is to replace it with another mystery.
To paint nature
is to change its body.
Rain carries man away
as the brush carries the painter away.
The stars will spring up.

III

What hand cast out this landscape?
What woman's breast will take this sky?
The hill is human.
The horizon lives in the depths of the eye.
The sea would wish to be a knee.
A god has picked up the earth
as you pick grapes.
The sun gapes with joy.
The painter's hand itches:
he needs another planet,
he needs so many new sighs.

IV

A malicious spirit has carved
the kingdom into strips
as you butcher a deer in the woods.
It is true that each province
is game,
that each village is a pale insect.
Let us begin over:
a malicious spirit carved
the mountain for the painter.
It is true that each province
is a canvas
in honor of the painter who draws it.

V

Each time a firefly
becomes an island,
someone cries:
so that the tree
will agree to remain a tree;
so that the stone
will be willing to remain a stone.
It is not right that the one law
be that of metamorphosis.

What is real breathes,
what is true is sweet.
But one must dream
so that the true real
will at last become real.

VI

Unfinished,
like blood not daring to start on its course.
Unaccomplished,
like the body lost in the well of transparency.
Unspeakable,
like the word with blue feathers.
Unknown,
like that which moves between dawn and dawn.
Unlooked for,
like the sun hidden behind the sun.
Unimaginable,
like the face deep within the face.
Uncreated,
so that it will be created in pain
and in joy.
Endless, endless, endless.

VII

The plain is a mistake.
The sky is mad at being sky.
At times, space dreamed of suicide.
Ah! if the universe could be blotted out,
or become a more grown-up void!
The future like milk, turns sour,
and keeps on turning
until it begins vomiting.
Breathing becomes a torture.
Between ridicule and grinning
who can tell us
how many stars sleep in peace?

VIII

To place a crown.
To be many
at the edge of joy.
To teach madness
a better madness.
To provoke
those who are no longer provoked.
To be in agreement
within the maddest heartbreak.
To celebrate
when one sets free,
in order to set free
at the time of celebrating.

IX

My galaxy is dancing.
I offer it a youthful horizon.
I ask it to show a form.
It may prefer to sleep.
Why does it refuse a drink?
The skies are restless.
The lands are weary of racing.
I do not dream of bringing it down.
I allow it to slap all my islands.
It, poor galaxy,
prefers an exodus.
Tomorrow it will have its first face.

X

Law of the blemish.
Need of the line.
Necessity for the alphabet.
Desire for the pen.
Red, black, purple.
Word, word, word detesting the word.
Verb with eyelids.
Particles of conscience.
Shreds of reason.
The world is beautiful
if I agree to define it,
but I will die from doing that.

Translator: Sandra Smith

READING AND WRITING

DIETER WELLERSHOFF

Now that I am writing a new book I neglect my reading. I cannot muster any lasting interest for anything else. The books I open disintegrate into details and form new, transitory relationships with each other. Something different interests me in each one, single passages, scenes, dialogues or technical details like a change of perspective, a cut, a montage, an associative illusion, the peculiar interaction of perception and remembrance in a text, perhaps its form, the structure that organizes the material, but never the total work. I cannot let the book capture me, and perhaps it couldn't anyway, because I read against the order that the book wants to impose on me, leafing through, following my own inclinations, hunting for stimulation. More and more I gain the impression that the book I would like to read is exactly the book I am trying to write, which I see before me with varying degrees of clarity.

This seems to exclude a lot, but makes a variety of other phenomena interesting. My reactions are faster and more violent than usual, like a protective reflex against unwholesome food. Some books produce a faint

389

feeling of dissatisfaction, dull the senses, flatten the imagination. Be it those whose style presupposes and presents the world as a known entity, be it those that grant the reader an omniscient position, be it books with a low level of excitement, be it books with a decorative pattern, be it those that simulate subjectivity by bold stylization—the defence functions before I know it. Positive signals are just as spontaneous—a spurt of excitement, a moment of heightened, still undefined, expectation like in the movies, when it gets dark and the pictures begin; they are only separate images because I don't yet know their significance in the complete context. What is this? A world freed of all ordering principles. It promises that everything can assume new relationships.

"A train roars with a shrill whistle through his body . . . Rockets burst over oily lagoons . . . Gambling casinos expand to a labyrinth of dirty pictures . . . ceremonial gun salutes in the harbor . . . a scream reverberates through a white hospital corridor . . . down a broad, dusty, palm-lined street the whistle fades like a bullet in the desert . . ."

This is the kind of image sequence I experience while leafing through my reading. I don't know what it means, I only have the impression of a strong, expanding movement. As in an explosion, everything flies apart. Disparate incidents, but all motivated by the same impulse. It is the unity of the disparate which heightens the hallucinatory effect of individual images and strengthens at the same time the total impact created by their sequence as sound and motion. The text—it is only the beginning of the sequence—is supposed to be an imaginative correspondence to orgasm, a fantastic explosion of a sex-scene, that suddenly loses all individuality, bursts open time and space, and multiplies to the image of a thousand boys ejaculating simultaneously in different places. Then it passes over into a new sequence of tropical pictures. There is the black water of jungle lagoons, in which vicious fish grab for floating white sperm, howler monkeys hang in the branches, in slow brown rivers whole trees, full of bright-colored snakes, float by, a cobra rises up, spreads, and spits its white venom, "pearl and opal chips fall in a slow, silent rain through air clear as glycerine." And suddenly time jumps "like a broken typewriter" and the boys are old men, "young hips quivering and twitching in boy-spasms go slack and flabby, draped over an outhouse seat, a park bench, a stone wall in Spanish sunlight, a sagging furnished-room bed (outside red brick slums in clear winter sunlight) . . . twitching and shivering in dirty underwear . . . "

The text is a paragraph from *Naked Lunch,* by William Burroughs, a phantasmagorical prose in which everything is possible because the text has no subject that offers resistance. The ordering of his material is purely subjective, is perhaps directed by a goal calculated to shock and surprise, or a hallucination of the author, but I don't want to analyze that at all right now but rather expose myself to these flickering impulses, these sudden shifts of images. I read it as if going through a monstrous bazaar, excited by this confusion of stimulants, struck by details, but without stopping, without establishing any connection, any relationship. I can remain untouched by all of this. It is however the open, hallucinatory or kaleidoscopic structure of the text that intoxicates me to the heightened power of imagination: the prerequisite to writing.

Perhaps a variation in reading is already stimulating for that reason. One enters a different textual climate, and reacts to it with an inner adjustment, changes one's expectations, one's mood, the direction of one's attention. This is the suspense of the beginning, every time one opens a new book and tries to find out what kind of a text it is. Will it appeal to me, what does it expect from me, what mood must it create in me in order to be understood correctly? If one has no secondary interest in reading, such as a scholarly investigation, that determines one's point of view from a prior decision, then this very subjective choice takes place right at the beginning: now this is a book for me, that one is not.

In the novel *The Bell Jar* by the American author Sylvia Plath I come upon this sentence, that immediately compels me to read on: "Wrapping my black coat round me like my own sweet shadow, I unscrewed the bottle of pills and started taking them swiftly, between gulps of water, one by one by one."

What fascinates me in this sentence, which is part of a suicide scene, as I rapidly find confirmed in the context? At first I am put off by this mixture of sentiment and precision. A young girl sits in a niche in the wall of a furnace room, she has wrapped herself in her raincoat, and this superfluous preparation for dying is at the same time the most intimate detail—it shows the lonely, autistic tenderness of the incident, a childish need for protection and security, especially in this fatal moment. This wrapping herself up has no practical value, only emotion turned back into itself and embarrassing for any witness, an emotion without partner, narcissistic, that she yields to now by wrapping herself up in her coat as if in "her own sweet shadow." But at the same time she proceeds methodically, slowly and resolutely, she takes "one pill after the other between gulps of water." Apparently I have never really imagined it, or quite differently, more agitated, more hasty, more violent, and now, through my alienation, I understand it anew and am taken in by an immediate, unintellectualized insight; yes, that's how it is, that's it exactly, now I see it, and it is important to me. I have had an experience through the text.

Surprise and certainty come together in such existential experiences. Both are effects of a sudden correction in my concepts through the

391

appearance of unexpected characteristics of a situation or a process. New, more concrete pieces of information reveal my previous conceptions as simple schematic patterns, and thus destroy the illusion of familiarity with which the world usually surrounds me and behind which it is hidden from me. The human organism can differentiate 7 1/2 million color impressions; the English language, for example, contains nearly 4000 designations for colors, but only eight are commonly used. We thus apparently have a tendency to strongly reduce the diversity of the world, and to establish in its place a simple code by which we communicate. Not only the apparatus of observation functions this way, but also memory; it polishes experiences to schematic recollected images that contain just enough information so that one is quickly oriented in similar situations and can act accordingly. And indeed, it is only through this formation of schemata that actually similar experiences are created, that repetition is made possible, that a store of related recognitions and routine behavior is generated. This is all very practical, it guarantees security in behavior and protection against confusing impressions, but if this process continued undisturbed, we would find ourselves, in the end, in an unchanging, completely familiar world, to which we can always respond with the same answers and actions. A completely ritualized society would correspond to this, with petrified morals and immutable institutions. New experiences can only be expected from a crisis in the previous formation of patterns, or at least a correction. This is what I expect from reading, not the confirmation of already fixed ideas which the light novel offers its readers, but their transformation. Freed from practical goals, not obliged to succeed, I can venture into imaginary experimentation and every risk of irritation. Adventure and travel novels still clearly show this need for the unexpected and exotic, but extensively the world has been opened by travel and new techniques; only intensively is it unknown. The disappearance of reality even assumes the form of knowledge. It is the deception of the newspaper reader who thinks he knows the facts when he has read the war or police report; it is the deception of the intellectual who takes a concept, a symbol, a formula to the essence of the thing. This knowledge is suddenly revealed as a weakness of imagination by the individual perspicuity with which for instance Sylvia Plath describes a suicide attempt. You think you know such cases from the paper or from psychology textbooks, however it is only now that the process becomes an experience.

I want to bring up two further examples that occur to me, also representations of incidents that are in the newspapers every day. The first text, the novel *Sanctuary* by Faulkner, was even written on the basis of a newspaper account. Faulkner writes how the murderer Popeye abducts the college student Tessie in a truck, to take her to a bordello in Memphis.

On the way, he stops in a small town to get gas and a few sandwiches. When he returns, Tessie has disappeared. One would assume that she has fled. Instead, he finds her in the yard of the gas station hiding fearfully behind a barrel, because she saw an acquaintance from the college in the street and is afraid he will recognize her in her embarrassing situation. This is unexpected, but immediately understandable, and reveals the normal expectation, that Tessie would have fled or asked her acquaintance for help, to be an unindividualized generality. A person would act like this who could assess the situation correctly and still had control over himself, an abstract figure, a kind of textbook person who is not hindered by particular characteristics in being rational and efficient. But Tessie is confused. She has not yet fully grasped the situation, probably because it is so atrocious and nothing in her previous life has prepared her for it. When her acquaintance turns up now, she sees herself in her old social pattern, and her position is not perilous, but rather compromising. But she also indicates thereby that she already feels herself completely helpless; she has gotten into something totally different, from which there is no return for her into her old world. The instinctive impulse to escape is still planted in her, but with a change in direction; she flees from rescue; and in this violent, distorted reaction we see that she is after all in a panic appropriate to her situation.

Only an author who had put himself into the situation with a trancelike clairvoyance could write that. And it is so easy to detect those passages in his works when he was not in the situation. The text immediately becomes rhetorical and sentimental; one senses the attempt to bridge a weakness in imagination which becomes more visible through the attempt.

Another example. Posdnyshev in Tolstoy's *Kreuzer Sonata,* after he has stabbed his wife in a fit of rabid jealousy, goes into the next room, lays his loaded revolver on the table, picks up the sheath of his dagger, which fell behind the sofa when he took it from the wall, and sits at the table with a blank mind. The servant comes and brings his suitcase into the room, for Posdnyshev had previously returned from a trip that was like a gigantic overture to his homicide. He sends the servant to the police and lights a cigarette; he falls asleep smoking it. In a dream he sees that everything is all right between him and his wife, they have quarreled and made up again, but at the same time, although he sees a great continuing friendship between them, he still has the vague feeling that something is not quite right.

Here Tolstoy, like no other author to the same degree, makes every detail part of a chain of behavior observed in its minutest details: the diversion with the sheath of the dagger which must first be put back in its place, the next stage of self-protection with the subsequent blankness of mind and apathy, then further relief by objectivization of the situation and removal one stage further of the necessity for action by sending the servant for the police, thereupon a further drop in excitement by his attempt to smoke and being overcome by sleep, and in the dream the unconscious wish fulfillment, the horrible is cancelled out, down to a disturbing feeling, a little remnant of awareness, which however has been denied visualization by the dream's censorship. The totality of behavior is captured here, consciousness, subconsciousness, and the body are equally a part of the discussion between the individual and himself and his situation.

While I read this, I no longer notice how it is written, I am totally wrapped up in absorbing all the details, and only subsequently can I convince myself that there is really nothing decorative, no excess of formulation or mannerism in this text. The author must have been in a state of self-forgetful insight completely concerned with writing everything he saw, and indeed he suddenly knew everything there was to know about this person.

Those are high points. However, when I get into reading, even secondary details become fascinating. Someone says "the package with the water-soaked paper" or "the crunching snow, not very deep, already hard-packed" or "he put his hand, already stiff with cold, into his pocket"—sentence fragments from Robbe-Grillet's *Defeat at Reichenfels*—and immediately I see it before me, because, stimulated by the text, I create it myself, also as if in recognition, yes, I know that, I've seen that, but now it comes again, more consciously, more urgently, suddenly, perhaps by the isolation of details in the sequence of words, everything gains an intensified presence.

That is why I read. The same hunger for experience operates here as in writing. Earlier I said that in enthusiastic, fascinated reading lies a feeling of concurrence. I must supplement that with the observation that this concurrence, and the intensification of the sense of life that goes with it, are completely unaffected by the horrors that are presented. Death, misery, ugliness, can produce the same enthusiasm of recognition as the representation of a moment of joy. In contrast, any cliche, be it ever so humane, calls forth only aversion in me. A much more elementary need must be satisfied in reading than in writing, the wish for more life, for a broadening of existence, which would remain unsatisfied by establishing harmonies in which every movement would come to rest.

Vicente Aleixandre

FOR WHOM I WRITE

tr. BEN BELITT

I

For whom do I write? the historian asked, the reporter, or the merely inquisitive.

Not for the crackle of the jacketed gentleman, nor his choleric mustache, not for his lifted forefinger, admonishing us in the sad tides of music.

Still less for his carriage and its hidden señora (caught behind window-panes, like a cold coruscation, a flashing impertinence.)

I write, it may be, for those who never will read me. For the woman who strides up the streets, as if to open the doors of the morning.

Or the old guy asleep on the bench of the minuscule plaza, as the sunset takes him with love, circles him there, serenely unbinds him with lights.

For those who never will read me, who couldn't care less, yet care, none the less (not having known me.)

For the girl who flashed me a glance as she passed, my fellow-adventuress at large in the world.

For that hag who has seen all of life from her bench in the doorway— delivered up life after life with her wearying hands.

I write for the lover, whose anguish looked out of his eyes as he passed: for this one who heard him; for that one who never looked up as he passed; for that one who dropped in his tracks when he asked and nobody answered.

I write for them all. But above all, for those who never will read me. Singly, or crowded together. For the breasts, the mouths, the ears where, without once having heard me,

My word none the less lives.

II

Yet I write for the murderer, too. For the man who slammed his eyes tight, flung himself at a breast, ate death, sated his hunger, and rose up a madman.

For him who lashed out like a tower of resentment and toppled himself on the world.

For all dead women and children, and all death-rattled men.

For him who cautiously turned on the gas-jets, while a whole city perished, and awoke to a mountain of corpses.

For the innocent girl with the heart and the smile and a tender medallion, where an army of predators passed.

And the army of predators who spurred themselves to a gallop and were drowned in the waters.

And I write for those waters, for their infinite sea.

No, not for the infinite. For the sea in its finitude, with its half-human limits like a breast with its breathing.

(A boy enters it now, a boy bathes, and the sea, the heart of the sea, passes into his pulses.)

For that last look of all, the Apocalyptical Last, in whose breast somebody slept.

For we all sleep so. The murderer, the unjustly accused, the mentor, the emergent, the finished, the drenched and the dry-of-will, those covered with hair like a tower.

For the menaced, the menacer, the benign, the sad, the immaterial voice and the substantive world.

For you, the undeified man, who without caring to see them at all, are scanning these letters.

For you, for all who live on in your name, I write, I keep writing.

WE EAT SHADOW

The whole of you, unknowable power that never discloses itself.
Power that we sometimes invite with the thrust of our loving.
There, we come on a knot. We finger a body,
a spirit, we encircle it so, and we say: "Now I have you!" Morosely,
complacently, at leisure, we explore all the trials of the chance for
      whose sake we were warned.
Here is the head, here the breast, here the profile and flight,
the swift inundation, the escape, the ripe legs in their sweetness, that
      appear to flow out and still still eternally.
And we narrow our living tumescence a moment.
We acknowledge the truth in our arms, the desirable body,
      the overheard spirit,
the spirit so avidly coveted.

But where does it come from—love's power, the similitude given us here
      with a god's reciprocity,
A God who begrudges us nothing, sets no limits on loving, plucks us out,
      spirit and body, to solace us here in his name?
We stand with the crumb in our mouths and are quiet, like dogs,
      we go on,
we incarnate ourselves in the obdurate splendor, intent on our hunger,
we strain toward whatever is flung to us here by a hand.
But where does it come from, the singular hand that would offer
its great gifts of suavity, your infinite skin,
your singular truth, the caress that can quiet our breathing, that stays
      on, without end?

Half-dead, we look upward. Table-scraps,
bread-crusts, the whiplash, our rages, our living and dying:
you scatter them out to all sides, as if you would deal us your pity,
you fling us a shadow, while the glitter glows under our teeth,
an echo's resplendence, an echo's re-echo re-echoed: a splendor;
and we eat what is given.
We eat shadow, we gorge on the dream or the shadow, and are quiet.
We are struck with an awe: and we sing. Love is your name.

But later, the eyes, humid and huge, lift up. The hand
is no more. Not so much as a rustle
of cloth can be heard.
Only a great sound of weeping, or the silence's tension.
The silence that is all we can take with us
when, in the teeth of the vanishing shadow, now grown ravenous,
      we launch ourselves onward again.

Vicente Aleixandre

THEY WHO DANCE ARE CONSUMED

tr. BEN BELITT

The Dancer

All is too volatile here. The choices are hard. I don't know
which is more secretive, the dagger's point or the rose?
Something debauches the air. Is it silver? Or the aroma of
petals trampled under nude feet, that strikes at
the senses and incites and discovers them.
The enigmas gather power and break open,
and at last we see plainly: mountains like burial mounds
on the distant horizon; but the mystery stays.

The Stage Designer

Say that the scenery shakes in the flies, if you wish;
don't mince your words. Your foot in mid-air
imitates daybreak—but how shabbily!
The orchestra? Though the wood wishes sleep,
a sound breaks the silence, the lamp crackles more rosily now.
I sleep or I read, I wake or am silent.
Our science is only a kingdom where man wanders lost.
A forest, evoked at my bidding, brings
the onlookers verdure, but not life.
So I smile when the curtain is lifted
and the dancer ripples out like a tree: I conjure
his foot, his foot's ambiguity there, intense as a doubt.

The Dancer

I am what I am—a mere proposition
concrete in its colors, at best.
Not a concept. I dance and I dawdle: at times
I affirm myself with the arc of my body, while the air
intersects underneath, like a wish. But I feel nothing. No more
than the stone in the bridge feels
the water's velocity, or its calms: I dream
and my dream makes no sound.
My body waits like a crossbow where a pebble strains to be cast;
an arc whose arrow I am: a fugitive thought.

398

The Stage Designer

I am my own man. Nothing I did is believable, I ignore
what I posed and proposed: it was just an idea.
The background is just an idea, though the thought of it blazes.
I erected your name with colors and turns of my rage and credulity.
The canvas vermilions, the bristling yellows, the rose, the bared
foot and the body's whole rigor upraised in a dancer's extension,
the deceits and the draperies, all burn more candidly here.
Under the meshes, the physical cry of the rhythms:
I hold all the forms in my hand and I set them ablaze
for the world. All are consumed, and applaud.

The Dancer

The music sways forward. The sound of it ripples like sea-water,
as my body questions the world, dazzling and fearful.
I am the burst of primordial foam that broke from the wave,
the rainbow riding the crest, revealing your world.
Your name, or your history, a pillar of fire on your lips.
The strings sing away, the oboes complain
of some baffled beginning seen darkly, the flute's sound
is heard, like a delicate tongue in a flickering skin.

The Stage Designer

No, not sound, but my hands! Enough! The world is aroused.
Creation was never so simple. Chorus or shameless nostalgia,
all file soundlessly by, a procession of withering roses.
Do they dance or delude us? A wave of putrescent aromas
trembles and wavers as the lyres go silent.
Faces look up toward the burning juvenescence of man.
I present what I saw: the damnation, from beginning to end.
Black of the mourners, yellow-greens, the grayer conclusions,
like bodies asleep.
Lust's pandemonium burnt out in the shadow.
Or a pitiful waltz running down like a gradual sand.

The Dancer

It is done. I slept as I danced, O my dream!
All is light as a spirit that lips invoke in the sky.
I press on with my life, a rose I extend with my hand.
All is gold that I offer you now, a dagger's point or a death.

Vicente Aleixandre

POET

tr. BEN BELITT

For you, who know how stone sings,
whose delicate pupil interprets the mountain's weight for the eye's
    pleasure,
the forest's clamor that will some day drowse in our veins:

poet, for you, whose breathing intuits
the brutal assault of the bird in its heaven
in whose words wheel the powerful wings of the eagle, in sudden
    arousal,
like the fish's heat in the slime, quietly flashing.

hear this book I give to your hands
with a forest's gesture,
where dew glitters out, all at once, refreshing the rose,
or desire batters the world,
grief's eyelid
that shuts out the west and the sun, like a darkening tear;
where the great forehead's exhaustion
is kissed, feels a deliberate kiss, dumb
words with no light, that speak for the death of the world.

Poet: grief and love are your kingdom.
The flesh's mortality, assailed by the spirit,
burns in the night or ascends in the power of the noon,
enormous, prophetical, a tongue grazing the sky,
revealing the words that destroy us.

The heart's youth was never a shore
lashed by the sea and the foam's devastation—
love's tooth gnawing away at the world
or lowing away at the living.

No watchtower's beam, grown suddenly sinister,
lighting your forehead a moment, undefended,
wounding the eyes and kindling you there, scorching
space with your lifetime, the waste of your love.

No. The light of the world that
lives in the cinder,
unabated, a dust on your lips,
is you, poet: it was your hand I saw in the sky,
making night brilliant; not the moon.

A breast through which courses the repose of the sea,
a pulse in the heaven's immensity that breathes with well-being: its arms
open wide, touching, caressing,
exploring the uttermost verge of a world.

What then?

Poet: look past this book, whose pages would hold a whole sun-burst.
Look into the light, face to face, rest your head on this stone,
feel the west's benediction to the tips of your toes,
raise your hands, touch the moon softly,
till your hair fills the sky, leaving its wake in the stars.

Vicente Aleixandre

COME, COME ALWAYS

tr. ALAN BRILLIANT

Don't come close. Your forehead, your burning forehead,
    your inflamed forehead,
the traces of some kisses,
this radiance that even the day feels if you are near,
this contagious radiance that settles in my hands,
this luminous river in which I plunge my arms,
I almost don't dare drink in it, fearing to the end
    a hard life of splendor.

I don't want you to live in me the way light lives,
with this isolation of star one with its own light,
to whom love is denied throughout
the hard and blue space that separates and doesn't unite,
where each inaccessible splendor
is a solitude that, gem-bearing, dispatches its sorrow.

A lonely flicker in world without love.
Life is a vivid crust,
a dried-up motionless skin
where man finds no relief,
as much as he applies his dream against an extinguished meteor.

But don't *you* get near me. Your beaming forehead,
    incendiary coal that seduces me to my own consciousness,
flashing duel in which I immediately feel the temptation to die,
of burning my lips on your indelible rubbing
of feeling my flesh consumed by your scalding diamond.

Don't you get near me, because your kiss is prolonged
    like an impossible collision of the stars,
like space set ablaze suddenly,
fertile ether where worlds' destruction
is the last heart totally extinguished.

Come, come, come like the dark extinct coal
 that imprisons death;
come like blind night that brings me a vision of you;
come like two lips branded with red,
through this long line that forges metals.

Come, come my love; come, sealed forehead,
 roundness nearly rolling
that glows like an orbit that comes to die in my arms;
come like two eyes or two profound solitudes,
two imperious summonses from an unknown depth.

Come, come, death, love; come quickly, I destroy you;
come, I wish to kill or love or die or give you everything;
come, rolling like a fickle stone
confounded like a moon that desires my rays!

Vicente Aleixandre

MY VOICE

tr. WILLIS BARNSTONE

I was born one summer night
between two pauses. Speak to me: I hear you.
I was born. If you could see what agony
is in the easy moon.
I was born. Your name was the joy;
under a radiance a hope, a bird.
To arrive, arrive. The sea was a pulsing heart,
hollow in a hand, a warm metal.
Then, at last, lights can be—caresses, flesh,
 horizon—
that is, meaningless words
turning like ears, snails,
like an open lobe dawning
(listen, listen) amid the trampled light.

tr. Louis M. Bourne

Vicente Aleixandre

IDEA

There's a tremor of water in the brow.
And it starts emerging, exact,
The clean image, thought,
Floating hull, boat.
Ideas above in a flock,
All white. But below, intact,
The secret ship surges,
From a submarine depth
Invention launched, grace.

For a moment it holds
Its rocking poise
On the smooth fullness of a wave.
It joins the threads of winds
To its pointed mast,
And snatches them
With a violent stroke, towards the sea,
Fired with progress,
Knowledge and victory.

To the external limit—speech—,
Knife that frees it
From its watery entrails,
And tears it from the total seascape,
Behind and deep.

Vicente Aleixandre

FIRE

tr. MURIEL RUKEYSER

The fire entire withholds
passion. Light alone!
Look—it leaps up pure
to lick at heaven,
while all the wings
fly through. It won't burn!
And man? Never. This fire
is still
free of you, man.
Light, innocent light.
And you, human:
better never be born.

Vicente Aleixandre

ADOLESCENCE

tr. DONALD A. YATES

Were you to come and go gently
from another road
to another road. To see you
and once more not see you.
To pass over a bridge to another bridge.
—The brief foot,
the gay, defeated light.

  I would be boy looking
downstream at the current,
and in the mirror your passage,
flowing, vanishing from sight.

INDEX TO ANTHOLOGY

WRITERS INDEX

MUNDUS ARTIUM COMPREHENSIVE INDEX, VOL. I–XI

WRITERS

NAME

VOL/ISSUE

Abbott, Lee K. Jr.	VIII.2
Acosta, Oscar	VIII.1
Adler, Carol	VII.2
Adnan, Etel	X.1
Adonis (Ali Ahmed Said)	I.2;III.2;IV.2
	VI.1;X.1
Aguilera-Malta, Demetrio	IX.1
Aichinger, Ilse	I.1;VII.2
Akiman, Nazmi	IX.1
Akin, Gülten	IX.1
Aktan, Feriha	IX.1
Albán, Laureano	VIII.1
Al-Bayyati, Abd Al-Wahab	X.1
Alberti, Rafael	II.2
Alcála, Guido Rodriguez	IX.2
Aleixandre, Vicente	II.3;V.1/2
Al-Haidari, Buland	X.1;XI.1
Al-Haj, Unsi	X.1
Aliferis, Eudoxia	XI.1
Al-Khal, Yusuf	X.1
Alkan, Erdögan	IX.1
Al-Mughut, Muhammad	X.1
Al-Mala'ika, Nazik	VII.2
Alonso, Damaso	V.1/2
Al-Qasim, Sameeh	X.1
Al-Sabour, Salah Abd	X.1
Al-Sayyab, Badr Shakir	IX.1;X.1
Alwan, Ameen	IX.1
Alyn, Marc	I.2;IV.1
Alzola, Concha	VIII.2
Amprimoz, Alexandre	IX.1
Andersen, Benny	V.1/2;VIII.2
Andrade, Jorge Carrera	V.3
Andresen, Sophia De Mello Breyner	VII.2;XI.1
Antillón, Ana	VIII.1
Antonych, Bohdan	VIII.2

TRANSLATORS

NAME	LANGUAGES	VOL/ISSUE
Ackerman, Duane	Portuguese	V.3
Akiman, Nazmi	Turkish	IX.1
Alldridge, James	German	I.1
Allen, Roger	Arabic	X.1
Auden, W. H.	Swedish	VI.1
Banani, Amin	Persian	VII.2;IX.2
Barnes, Jim	German	VIII.2
Barnstone, Willis	French, Spanish	I.2;II.2;II.3;III.1
	Romanian	V.3;VI.2;IX.2
Batki, John	Hungarian	IV.1
Beekman, E. M.	Dutch	I.3;II.2
Beissel, Henry	German	II.1;II.2;IV.3
Belitt, Ben	Spanish	I.1;I.3;II.2;II.3
		III.2;V.1/2;VI.2
Bennani, B.M.	Arabic	VII.2
Bester, M.	Polish	VIII.2
Blackburn, Paul	Spanish	III.1
Bly, Robert	Swedish	VI.1
Boullata, Issa J.	Arabic	IX.1
Boulus, Sargon	Arabic	X.1
Bourne, Louis M.	Spanish	V.1/2
Boychuck, Bohdan	Ukranian	VIII.2
Bradford, Lisa	Spanish	VII.2;VIII.1
Brandt, Mieke	Dutch	IV.3
Brilliant, Alan	Spanish	II.3
Brof, Janet	Spanish	XI.1
Brogan, Geoffrey	German	I.1;II.1
Brower, Gary	Spanish	VII.1
Bullock, Michael	German, Polish	I.1;I.2;I.3;II.3
		III.2;V.3
Busza, Andrzej	Polish	III.2
Christensen, Nadia	Danish	VII.2;VIII.2
Colbin, Annemarie	Spanish	I.2
Costa-Picazo, Roland	Spanish	IV.3
Cotton, Christine	French, Spanish	IV.1;VII.1;VII.2
		VIII.1

Cran, Patricia Davidson	Spanish	III.3
Dalton, Eric	French	IX.1
Dalven, Rae	Greek	IV.2
Davison, Ned	Spanish	II.1
deJagers, Marjolijn	Dutch	VII.2;IX.1
De Rosa, Elaine	French	XI.1
Di Giovanni, Norman Thomas	Spanish	III.3;IV.2;VII.2
Doezema, Herman P.	Spanish	VI.2
Dorian, Marguerite	Romanian	VII.2;VIII.2
Duggan, Lilvia	Spanish	IX.2
Dukas, Vytas	Russian	II.2;IV.1;VII.2
Durán, Manuel	Spanish	III.1
Durán, Gloria	Spanish	III.1
Edkins, Anthony	Spanish	III.1
Emblen, D. L.	Swedish	VI.1
Evans, George	Spanish	VIII.1
Evin, Ahmet Ö.	Turkish	IX.1
Exner, Richard	German	XI.1
Farzan, Massud	Persian	V.1/2
Feldman, Ruth	Spanish, Italian	VII.1;VIII.1
Fersch, Peter Paul	German	II.2;III.2
Ford, R.A.D.	Croatian	IV.2
Fowlie, Wallace	French	I.2;II.1
Fox, Siv Cedering	Swedish	VI.1
Francis, H.E.	Spanish	III.3;VI.1;VI.2;VIII.2;IX.2
Freeman, Christine	Spanish	VIII.1;IX.2
Friar, Kimon	Greek	IV.1;VII.2
Fulton, Robin	Swedish	VI.1;IX.2
Gardiner, Elaine	French	VII.1;VII.2
Gardner, Donald	Spanish	III.3
Gavronsky, Serge	French	VII.1
Getsi, John	French, German	VII.1;VII.2
Getsi, Lucia	Spanish, French German	V.3;VI.2;VII.1;VII.2
Ghossein, Mirene	Arabic, French	VI.1;VII.2;X.1
Giacomelli, Eloah F.	Portuguese	V.1/2;VIII.2;XI.1
Gibbons, Reginald	Spanish	VIII.1;IX.1
Gillespie, Gerald	Spanish	IV.1
Gingerich, Alina	Spanish	XI.1
Gingerich, Willard	Spanish	XI.1
Gliese—Lee, Hanne	Danish	V.1/2
González, Eduardo	Spanish	III.1

Goumas, Yannis	Greek	V.3
Gray, Rockwell	Spanish	IX.1
Grolmes, Sam	Japanese	IV.2
Grol-Prokopczyk, Regina	Polish	VIII.1
Gross, Stuart	Spanish	VIII.2
Halman, Talat Sait	Turkish	IX.1
Hamburger, Michael	German	I.1
Haswell, Rich	Spanish	XI.1
Haskell, Harry	Spanish	VIII.1;VIII.2;IX.1
Haydar, Adnan	Arabic	X.1
Hazo, Samuel	Arabic, French	I.2;III.2;IV.2;VI.1 VII.2;X.1
Heaton, David	French	V.1/2
Hermans, Theo	Dutch	VIII.2
Hermey, Carl	French	VII.1
Hesse, Eva	German	I.2
Hoeksema, Thomas	Spanish	III.1;III.3;VI.2 VII.2;VIII.1
Hoffman, Daniel	Spanish	VI.2
Holkeboer, Robert	French	IV.1
Hollis, Ena	Spanish	III.1
Hunt, Julie	Spanish	VIII.1;VIII.2
Impey, Michael	Romanian	VII.2
Irwin, Mark	French	XI.1
Jones, D. G.	French	IX.1
Kando, Tamar	Dutch	VIII.2
Karageorge, Yuri V.	Bulgarian	IX.2
Kessler, Jascha	Hungarian, Persian	VI.2;VII.2;IX.2
Kirkup, James	Japanese	VII.2;IX.1
Kyle, Carol	Spanish	VIII.1
Lanser, Susan	French	VII.1
Lazar, Jože	Slovenian	IV.1
Lebovitz, Richard	Spanish	III.1
Legassick, Trevor J.	Arabic	X.1
Leggett, Lee	French	VII.1;IX.2
Lemaster, J. R.	French	XI.1
Levine, Suzanne Jill	Spanish	III.3
Levitin, Alexis	Portuguese	VIII.2;IX.1;XI.1
Lima, Robert	Spanish	VIII.1
Lipsky, John M.	Spanish	IX.2
Longland, Jean R.	Portuguese	VII.2
McBride, Ann	Spanish	VI.2

McBride, Mary	Spanish	VI.2
McWhirter, George	Spanish	III.1;III.3;VIII.1;IX.1
Marx, Leonie A.	Danish	VIII.2
Mayewski, Pawel	Polish	II.2
Mead, Matthew	German	II.2
Mead, Ruth	German	II.2
Mehrotra, Arvind Krishna	Serbian, Indian	V.3;VIII.1
Mihailovich, Vasa D.	Serbian, Croatian	IV.2;IV.3;VII.2
Miura, Fumiko	Japanese	IX.1
Moncy, Agnes	Spanish	II.3
Mondragón, Sergio	Spanish	III.1
Moran, Ronald	Serbian, Croatian	IV.2;IV.3
Morris, Tudor	German	VII.2
Nemet-Nejat, Murat	Turkish	IX.1
Nicholson, Ana Maria	Spanish	I.3
Nims, John Frederick	Spanish	I.1
Nieschmidt, Hans-Werner	German	IV.1;IV.3
Nybakken, R.	French	II.1
Oliphant, Dave	Spanish	VIII.1
Pardo, Mateo	Spanish	IX.1
Patnaik, Deba P.	Indian	IX.2
Peden, Margaret Sayers	Spanish	III.3;V.1/2
		VIII.1
Perdreau, Connie	French	VII.1
Pettinella, Dora M.	Italian, Spanish	I.1;I.3;II.1;III.2
		IV.2;V.1/2;V.3
Previtali-Morrow, Giovanni	Italian	I.3
Rabassa, Gregory	Portuguese, Spanish	III.3;VI.1;IX.1
Raizis, M. Byron	Greek	VIII.1
Raiziss, Sonia	Italian	IX.1
Randall, Elinor	Spanish	III.1;VI.2
Richardson, Charles P.	German	I.3
Robbins, Martin	Spanish	IX.2
Rodeiro, Joyce Ann	Spanish	VIII.1
Rudman, Mark	Ukrainian	VIII.2
Rudolf, Anthony	French	I.1
Rukeyser, Muriel	Spanish	II.3
Ryding, W. W.	French	I.2
Salinger, Herman	German	VI.1
Salomon, I.L.	Italian	I.3;IV.2
Sandstroem, Yvonne L.	Swedish	VI.1
Saradhi, K.P.	Indian	IV.2

Savage, Meredyth	Spanish	VI.2
Savory, Teo	French	II.1
Sawa, Yuki	Japanese	II.2
Schulte, Rainer	Spanish, French	III.1;VI.2;VII.1
Schwartz, Stephan	Spanish	III.1
Sedrika-Levis, Ilze	Latvian	VIII.2
Seidler, Ingo	German	I.3
Serna-Maytorena, M.A.	Spanish	III.3;VI.2
Shiffert, Edith	Japanese	II.2
Simic, Charles	Serbian	IV.3
Sjöberg, Leif	Swedish	VI.1
Smith, Sandra	Spanish, German	I.3;III.1;VIII.1
		VIII.2;IX.2
Stankiewicz, Marketa Goetz	Czech	V.1/2
Stark, F.	Turkish	IX.1
Stathatos, John Constantine	Greek	IV.1;V.1/2
Sternberg, Ricardo Da Silveira Lobo	Portuguese	V.3
Stevens, Peter	French	IV.1
Suarez, Nicomedes	Spanish	VIII.1
Swann, Brian	Spanish, Romanian	VII.1;VII.2
	Italian, Turkish	VIII.1;IX.1
Tamminga, Frederick	Dutch	I.3
Tarn, Nathaniel	Spanish	III.1
Ten Harmsel, Larry	Dutch	IV.1
Thompson, Don	Spanish	IV.3
Tokunaga, Shozo	Japanese	VII.2
Tomlins, Juan	Portuguese	III.3
Tomlins, Jack E.	Portuguese	III.2
Troupe, Quincy	Spanish	III.1
Tsumura, Yumiko	Japanese	IV.2
Urdang, Elliott	Romanian	VII.2;VIII.2
Vasils, Theodora	Greek	VIII.1
Villaseñor, Laura	Spanish	V.3
Walsh, Donald	Spanish	VIII.1
Weinberger, Eliot	Spanish	III.1
Weinstock, Paulette	French	IX.2
Welsh, David	Polish	VIII.2
Williams, Celia	Serbian	IV.3
Winn, Thomas	French	VII.1
Wright, Charles David	Serbian	IV.3
Wynand, Derk	French, German	II.2;III.2
Yates, Donald A.	Spanish	II.3;III.1
Zdanys, Jonas	Lithuanian	IX.1

ESSAYISTS

NAME	ESSAY TITLE	VOL/ISSUE
Adonis (Ali Ahmed Said)	"The Poem We Breathe"	IV.2
Alyn, Marc	"What Is Poetry?"	II.1
Apollonio, Umbro	"Art and Organic Reality"	I.3
Appleton, Jon H.	"The Electric Music of Tonga: The Use of Non-Western Music by Western Composers"	VII.1
Atiya, A. S.	"Contributions of the Arabs to Western Culture"	X.1
Austin, Larry	"New Romanticism: An Emerging Aesthetic for Electronic Music (Parts I & II)	VI.1;VI.2
Barnitz, Jaqueline	"The Persistence of Humanism in Latin American Art"	III.1
Battló, José	"An Introduction to New Spanish Poetry"	II.2
Belitt, Ben	"The Mourning Neruda"	I.1
Benamou, Michel	"The Structures of Wallace Stevens' Imagination"	I.1
Bosquet, Alain	"Current Approximations"	I.2
Boullata, Kamal	"Modern Arab Art: The Quest and the Ordeal"	X.1
Breton, Jean	"Colors in the Rainbow of New French-Language Poetry"	VII.1
Deeb, Kamal Abu	"The Perplexity of the All-Knowing: A Study of Adonis"	X.1
Dorian, Marguerite	"A Portrait of Ion Caraion"	VIII.2
Durán, Manuel	"Jaime Sabines and Marco Antonio de Oca: A Study in Contrast"	III.2
El Calamawy, Sahair	"The Impact of Tradition on Modern Arabic Literature"	X.1
Feldman, Morton	"Between Categories"	VI.1
Getsi, Lucia	"Inventing Us: The Open Word"	VII.2
Ghossein, Mirene	"Introduction: Adonis (Ali Ahmed Said)"	III.2
Gullón, Ricardo	"Miró and His Painting"	II.3

ARTISTS

NAME	VOL/ISSUE
'Abbud, Shafiq	X.1
Abularach, Rodolfo	III.3;VIII.1
Aeppli, Eva	VII.2
Aitken, Alexander B.	IV.1
Al, Abdul	X.1
Al-Akhras, Gayyath	X.1
Al-'Azzawi, Dia'	X.1
Al-Basha, Amin	X.1
Alberti, Rafael	II.2;II.3
Alechinsky, Pierre	VII.1
Al-Mursi, 'Abd Al-Wahab	X.1
Al-Qadi, Munira	X.1
Al Rahhal, Khalid	X.1
Al-Rawi, Nuri	X.1
Al Salahi, Ibrahim	X.1
Al Wahab, Ahmad Abd	X.1
Antes, Horst	VI.2
Antuñez, Nemesco	III.1
Arman, Fernandes	V.3
Arna'ut, 'Abd Al Qader	X.1
Ayaso, Manuel	VII.1
Bacon, Francis	II.1
Bauermeister, Mary	V.1/2
Boghossian, Skunder	IX.2
Borda, Arturo	III.3
Botero, Fernando	III.1;III.3;VI.2
Boullata, Kamal	X.1
Capozzoli, Glauco	IX.2
Caride, Miguel	III.1
Castillo, Jorge	V.3
Chavez, Gerardo	VIII.1
Clary, Morse	IV.3;V.1/2
Coronel, Rafael	III.3;VIII.1
Correal, Edgar	IX.2
Cortina A., Amalia	IV.3
Cuevas, José Luis	III.3;VI.2
Cusumano, Stefano	VIII.2
Dado	VI.1